St. Louis Community College

Forest Park
Florissant Valley
Meramec

Instructional Resources
St. Louis, Missouri

A FINE SILVER THREAD

A Fine
Silver Thread

ESSAYS ON AMERICAN
WRITING AND CRITICISM

James W. Tuttleton

CHICAGO   IVAN R. DEE   1998

Publication of this book has been aided by a grant from the Abraham and Rebecca Stein Publication Fund of New York University, Department of English.

Library of Congress Cataloging-in-Publication Data:
Tuttleton, James W.
    A fine silver thread : essays on American writing and criticism /
James W. Tuttleton
        p.   cm.
    Includes index.
    ISBN 1-56663-181-5 (acid-free paper)
    1. American fiction—History and criticism. 2. American fiction—History and criticism—Theory, etc. 3. Criticism—United States. 4. Ideology in literature. 5. Aesthetics, Modern. I. Title.
PS371.T88 1998
813.009—dc21   97-17241

THIS BOOK IS
FOR
NORA BELLE TUTTLETON
A LIFETIME TRAVELING COMPANION

Preface

⁂ *A Fine Silver Thread* is the delicate cord upon which are strung a great many reflections on art and ideology in American fiction. Whether each (or any) is in itself a pearl I shall leave to the reader to decide. (I have in my own mind's eye, as the aptest figure for these critical diversions, one of those wild necklaces of varicolored amber, shell, or stone.) In any case, at a time when the idea of literature has been dissolved by our academic critics into mere "discourse," a great many readers do not seem to be able to make a distinction between art and ideology. This book is about the difference between the two and about the ways in which ideology has not merely entered the work of some of our best writers but even grossly disfigured it. A secondary consideration is the way in which one or another ideology has dominated literary criticism, of late, and transformed even our best works of art into objects of shame.

Shame is the grand touchstone of our time. Every "minority" group in America today, no matter how loosely or arbitrarily organized, seems to be in the business of assigning blame. *We, the powerless, are being unfairly treated. The "dominant culture," "the hegemonic power," is to blame. Shame! Shame!* Insensitivity has been ratcheted up to the level of one of the Seven Deadly Sins. To offend, even if through honest criticism, is not permitted. We live in an age of wounded sensibilities. Women are wounded, blacks are wounded, Native Americans, homosexuals, immigrants, and the welfare class are wounded, among others. In savoring minority wounds, the Benjaminian complaint, if I may paraphrase it, seems to have caught on like candied Crackerjacks: there is no distinguished literary work that is not also a monument to barbarism, in that it was purchased through the pain of the dispossessed, the disfranchised, and the wounded.

I confess to little patience with the shame-mongering that permeates literary discussion today, particularly since the monuments of culture that really matter are in fact testaments of transcendence over the barbaric. Most of this palaver reflects what the Marxists used to call "false consciousness" (before they lost all consciousness whatsoever) and is merely a stratagem to make the "hegemonic power" (whatever that may be) feel guilty. Our self-indulgent reveling in shame is as factitious as the eighteenth-century cultivation of "sensibility" or the Victorian orgies of "pathos."

Of the two terms in my equation, ideology has always been more important to Americans than art. The aesthetic, or at least the idea of it, had a difficult time establishing itself in America. The reason will be familiar to any student of colonial literatures. To be a colonial means to have a dependency on the court and capital of another nation claiming to be the mother country. Most early American colonials were a simple farming people intent on building houses, founding families, establishing the church of Christ in the New World, and laying in the crops. If the horses had to be shod, the cows milked, the hogs slopped—daily, repeatedly—who had time for literary diversion? Thus, reading matter—except for the Bible, the sermon, and the almanac—was hardly a primary consideration at the end of the day. This was the hard case even though many of the first New England immigrants were literate or even university educated.

Making a work of art in early America did not fare much better than the "literary appreciation" of it. The Renaissance rhetorics might aphorize about *ars longa*, but producing anything merely belletristic ran afoul of the Puritan passion for unvarnished didacticism in the service of truth. It is this passion, in one form or another, that animates most American writing between 1607 and 1820. There was a cost to pay for our strenuous devotion to truth. The Puritan origin of America deprived us for a long time of a theater like that of Shakespeare and Jonson, Middleton and Marlowe. The American stage, in fact, was never properly launched and never properly evolved. The number of important plays that have been written and produced in America can be counted on the fingers of one hand. Lyric poetry and the epic form, practiced so well in London, did not, at first, fare well on these American shores either. Furthermore, at the precise moment that America came into being as a colonial dependency there had erupted an English Puritan aversion to fiction so stern as to equate it with telling lies, mere feigning, the absolute work of the devil. American colonials fell into line. Wherever conscience appeals only to truth; wherever moral strenuosity denounces beauty as such; wherever eloquence is condemned as a snare, and rhetorical ornamentation and verbal play are reviled as merely seductive or frivolous, and only plain-speaking truth that ministers to the soul's welfare is permitted;—there good men may arise but literature is not likely to flourish. Such an ascendant ideology, no matter how godly, seems invariably at odds with literary greatness.

Henry James, as my epigraph suggests, set great store by what he called "the imaginative faculty under cultivation." It is this that makes for a distinguished literature. If my first instance of it is Washington Irving's *The Sketch Book*, I do not mean to suggest that before 1820 there was no American literary art. Manifestly there was, and in William Bradford, Edward Taylor, Anne Bradstreet, Jonathan Edwards, and Nathaniel Ward (among some others), I find pages that I would not give up for all the exquisite lyrics or brilliant conceits of the cavalier or metaphysical poets or for the finer pages of Goldsmith, Fielding, and Smollett. (Fortunately, I do not have to.)

But it is useful to be reminded that, until about fifty years ago, Washington Irving (1783–1859), a relative latecomer, was regarded as the "Father of American Literature." He attained this reverential ascription precisely because his work was the first effectively to break free of the three coercive requirements of prose in the seventeenth and eighteenth centuries. The first of these was the demand of religious utility (manifest in the ecclesiastical annals, plantation histories, personal diaries, voluminous sermons, and biblical exegeses that set forth all of the *magnalia christi americana*). The second was the demand of practical utility. This demand is evident in the New World maps and advertisements of the natural wonders of the continent, in anthropological descriptions of the Native Americans, vivid accounts of geographical exploration, the agricultural manuals, newspapers, yearly almanacs, and so forth. And the third was the demand of American political orthodoxy. This grew apace after 1720, and by 1776 reached a revolutionary peak that was sustained through the War of 1812. This demand is obvious in the discourses—legal, political, and religious—that established the ground for separation from the monarchy and its class structure, from the politically established Church of England, and from the system of English finance and law, so laying the groundwork for an ideology of aggressive political and literary nationalism.

It is difficult for the writer to get into the right relationship to his ideological suppositions. Irving never completely solved the problem, as the Federalist slant of his satirical *A History of New York* (1807) makes plain. But his experience in writing that book taught him that positive reception by a wider audience of appreciative readers—indeed, especially a later audience—required matter and methods transcending the local or even the national politics and its discursive practices of the time. It was a lesson that took American writers two hundred years to learn; but it has it was never fully mastered, as a number of my essays try to show. Even so, in discussing *The Sketch Book* (1819–1820), I have tried to indicate Irving's evolving grasp of the filiations that link ideology to literature, and the relation of both to the fame that makes a writer still read long after his time.

Irving was the first American writer to be accepted abroad, his fame in England and on the Continent secured not only by *The Sketch Book* but also by *Bracebridge Hall, Tales of a Traveller, Grenada*, and *The Alhambra*. His acceptance abroad was purchased in the face of British hostility to American revolutionary intransigence—that is, achieved in the face of the starkest ideological opposition to the American origins of his fiction. How Irving achieved his success with British readers is a testament to the power of his imaginative invention coupled with a mastery of varied prose styles that still rival the mellifluous Addison and Steele. So polished were his sentences that the English decided he would have to be adopted, willy-nilly. The Englishwoman Mary Mitford Russell, in compiling a list of tales for *Stories of American Life by American Writers* (1830), omitted Irving because, as she casually remarked, "his writings are essentially European and must be content to take their station amongst the Spectators and Tatlers of the mother country."[1]

Most Americans will feel that English anti-Americanism is an ugly political sentiment. But American writers have been the victim of even more insidious ideologies. Indeed, they have been the spokesmen for them. Cooper never wrote a sentence worthy to be set alongside those of Addison, Steele, and Irving, and his fiction is the worse for it. But he did have an imaginative capacity superior to theirs in respect to the creation of gothic fictional effects and stirring dramatic adventure. The Leatherstocking tales are his best, substantially because Cooper reined in his perennial political animosities and gave expression to the epic possibilities of the westward march of civilization. However, my subject here is not the Leatherstocking tales but the lesser-known Littlepage trilogy. *Satanstoe* (1845), *The Chainbearer* (1845), and *The Redskins* (1846) are here adduced as instances of the ease with which a good fiction writer can fall prey to

---

1 Mary Mitford Russell, *Stories of American Life by American Writers*, 3 vols. (London: Colburn and Bentley, 1830), quoted in *Washington Irving: The Critical Reaction*, ed. James W. Tuttleton (New York: AMS Press, 1993), p. 3.

the distractions of a politics that disfigures nearly every page of the work: his preference for a social order commanded by a landed gentry and his hostility to the the leveling Yankees who wanted the old estates, established for the Dutch patroons by royal charter, broken up for the sake of the squatters and transients who had rented or invaded the properties.

So pervasive is ideological posturing in fiction that some writers take refuge in the imperatives of art alone. This seems to be the case with Poe, whose quest for Supernal Beauty is the subject of my essay below. Although he lived at a time when any number of political issues lay ready to hand—abolitionism, women's rights, the rent wars in New York, territorial expansionism inevitably leading to the Mexican-American War, and so on—Poe was one of the earliest and most ardent champions of a literature devoted substantially to aesthetic considerations. This was the case especially with poetry; fiction, he thought, could stand a dose of the didactic. But Poe is a striking instance of the continuing tension between the imperatives of beauty and the imperatives of politics in our fiction.

Thus the delicate balance between art and ideology is rarely managed by American writers. If Howells, Fitzgerald, Dos Passos, and Lewis caught "the Russian measles," as Charles Eliot Norton said of Howells, and if they devoted themselves to a Tolstoyan or a Leninist socialist ideology at odds with intrinsic American values, Irving, James, Wharton, and Auchincloss represent a kind of counter-tradition in which ideas are subordinate to their dramatic uses—at least most of the time. As my remarks on Mrs. Wharton's *The Fruit of the Tree* (1907) suggest, even she was not always immune to the seductive ambition to be sociologically up-to-date and politically relevant. In any case, I have noted below how the claims of Tolstoyan socialism, revolutionary Marxism, and Friedanian Feminism (as a Marxist derivative), among other ideologies (if they are not actually religions), periodically emerge as a deranging compulsion in the individual writer or as a distorting obsession in the literary criticism produced to interpret our writing. I hold no art-for-art's-sake view of literature, as will be evident to any attentive reader. Yet distortions of the kind that I allude to below cannot be passed over in silence.

It is commonly said that since most literary critics are liberals, if not leftists, much of our literary criticism is hostile to what I have called intrinsic American political values. There is thus a deep strain of anti-Americanism in our own criticism that goes back at least as far as the generation of Howells, Bellamy, London, and Upton Sinclair. This anti-Americanism has often been masked by its practitioners, who have called it a higher form of Americanism, or who have claimed to want a nobler America based on a redistribution of wealth, equal rights for oppressed minorities, a centralized bureaucracy for the production and distribution of goods and services, and so forth. This is, by now, old hat in the criticism—so much so that students of American literature regularly skip right over the leftist twaddle hoping to find something that might make for *literary* appreciation and understanding. This book is meant for them.

What seems to me novel, however, is the rise of an anti-Americanism in our recent fiction that rounds out a vicious circle. What Irving tried to overcome in his English critics—a virulent anti-American sentiment that made literature impossible to consider on its own terms—has now become the staple of much American fiction itself. I mean by this the tales of Coover, Vonnegut, Burroughs, Heller, Pynchon, *et al.* America, or "Amerika," as it has sometimes been spelled, has recently become the occasion for a plethora of paranoid conspiracy theories that would stupefy even a practicing psychoanalyst. In exploring these matters in "Tracking the American Novel into the Void," I have undertaken to chart the shift away from the novel of manners, with its emphasis on representative characters and action rendered with a premium on verisimilitude and elegance of style, toward modes of antirealism steeped in the bizarre, the grotesque, and the horrific, tending toward nihilism and the apocalyptic. As will be immediately apparent, I give short shrift to the studied misanthropy, misogyny, and nihilism of cultist and countercultural writers like Burroughs, Vonnegut, Hawkes, and Pynchon.

In presenting these essays, I see that a number of propositions herein advanced are grounded on some old verities that are now regularly denied in the academy and that will doubtless seem impossibly retro to those who think of themselves as the theoretical avant-garde. Nevertheless, it may be useful to bring these verities out into the open. This will be helpful to anyone who wants to know "where I am coming from," as the phrase vulgarly has it, especially since my critique of the academy is launched from within it. But an even more important use is this: there are a great many people out there who think more or less as I do, but who have been silenced by the critical terrorists who nowadays dominate literary studies. This came home to me during a recent oral defense of a doctoral dissertation at New York University. After a considerable amount of badgering by one of the deconstructionist avant-garde, the candidate, a young woman who had written a study of Willa Cather, blurted out: "I may be old-fashioned, but I still believe that some novels are better than others."

The examiners, I think, were shocked. I was electrified. Here was evidence that an education in graduate literary studies had not actually expunged common sense. This book is for that candidate and for others who think that discriminations of literary quality are not only possible but necessary.

A Fine Silver Thread is grounded, first, on my strong conviction of the existence of literature as a separate and higher form of writing discernible through comparison and discrimination and definable through an exercise of refined good taste. "Taste" is a dirty word nowadays, suggesting elitism and privilege, but I do not scruple to invoke it, as it conveys aesthetic judgment continuously clarified by a repeated reflective experience of works of art. Only those who do not have it deny that good taste exists or will assert that it is a mask for class, racist, or sexist prejudice. Of these there are many, of course, as the *MLA Directory* will show. But some novels, some stories, and some plays *are* better than others.

Second, I see that I have everywhere taken for granted the notion that literature is not reductive to mere ideology, propaganda, or protest writing. This view is sometimes denied by "activist" writers who, when the critical test is applied, are shown to be second-rate because they have subordinated the imperatives of art to ideological preachment. Their typical maneuver is to call *all* writing propaganda. An instance of this is the quarrel between Richard Wright and James Baldwin. Wright, like W. E. B. Du Bois, had insisted that *"All* literature is protest. You can't name a single novel that isn't protest," and he dismissed what he called "all that art for art's sake crap." Baldwin's rejoinder was that "all literature might be protest but all protest was not literature."[2] Baldwin has expressed my sense of it exactly. The relationship of politics to protest in fiction is so delicate a balance that most political novels are frankly third-rate or worse.[3]

The claim that art is not propaganda will also seem reactionary to the faculty-club Marxists in the MLA, who have transmogrified into ideology everything from the *Beatitudes* to *Beavis and Butt-head.* Since literature is readily contaminated by the coarse political motives of those who teach it nowadays, it is no wonder that the study of it has lost its interest for a great many students, the brightest of whom are departing in droves for any practical major. I hope they will continue to read on their own, as their combined judgment is

---

2 James Baldwin, *Nobody Knows My Name: More Notes of a Native Son* (New York: Dell, 1961), p. 157.

3 Even so, they are produced by the carload. See Joseph Blotner's fat volume, *The Modern American Political Novel, 1900–1960* (Austin: University of Texas Press, 1966).

likelier to have a more decisive effect on questions of literary merit than that of classroom ideologists.

No doubt I shall hear the rejoinder that all life is political, that literature is political, the personal is the political, and that *I* am political! This is the banal mantra of black studies, gay studies, feminism, and other contemporary "-isms" nowadays. It is a way of working *their* politics into every discussion. I am prepared to agree that I have convictions inseparable from my political views. I am a member of the Democratic Party, a Christian, a white (with a little Cherokee), a man, a sexagenarian, and so forth. What does any of this mean for *literary* criticism? Whatever it may mean, I do not hesitate on occasion to make my convictions clear. But if I do so, I do so because the overt political content of the novels and stories under discussion invites political analysis and evaluation. But the notion that everything we think and say or do is always political, well, that is the viewpoint of one who has dissolved the several departments of knowledge into a single subjective mirror. In sum, I am convinced that an obsession with ideology—whether in the artist or critic—tends quickly to date or invalidate the work at hand. Its true use, for the writer, ought to be as material reflecting the condition of the world, as reflecting the temper of the time or the passions of his characters—not, as is the case with Cooper, Fitzgerald, or Dos Passos, his own (transient) political predilections. In acknowledging that these premises will be widely regarded as retrogressive, I take consolation in noting that they may turn out to be premonitory of a cycle of return to an interest in literature as such.

J. W. T.

New York University
November 1997

Contents

A FINE SILVER THREAD

Style and Fame: Irving's The Sketch Book

We have it on the authority of the handbooks of literature that "the style is the man." This maxim, encoding a very old observation, grew out of the imprint the ancient scribe made, with his *stylus,* on a waxen tablet: one could distinguish the self-disciplined writer, as opposed to the slovenly or careless one, by the clarity and precision of his verbal inscription. By the Renaissance the maxim had come to express a class consideration: the writer's style, the level of his polish in performance, was an index to his social standing, to good breeding, class distinction, refinement of taste, and civility of manners. Later Buffon, in his *Natural History,* may have had something more phylogenetic in mind in saying *"le style est l'homme même."* But the maxim has persisted in pointing to the indivisibility of the man himself and the style by which he expresses that self.

But setting aside implications of social class, the problem with the axiom is this: which style is the man? There is no doubt that the experience of reading a large or representative sample of a writer's work suggests the character, personality, temperament, values, and literary idiosyncrasies of the writer—that is, those uniquely distinguishing qualities that we call the writer's signature. And some generalizations may safely be made about Washington Irving from an examination of his style: it is at once urbane, polished, marked by high civility, elegance, and grace. But it can also be witty, humorous, charged with pathos, marked by intense moral indignation, flippant, and filled with extravagance, exaggeration, and hyperbole. At times it is fittingly solemn, as in his biography of George Washington; at other times it may be judicial and objective, as in the history of Columbus; or it may be arch, as in the *Salmagundi* papers; or farcical, sexy, and occasionally obscene, as in the *Knickerbocker's History of New York,* where Irving descends into Dutch in order to get off some wonderful swearing by his ponderous and pipe-smoking burghers. There is thus a marvelous range of literary production in the *oeuvre* of Washington Irving. There is an Irving voice, but the differences amongst his works raise the question, "Which voice is Irving's?" Which style is the man? And how—in relation to the political ideologies then pressed upon him—did Irving evade the mediocrity that always attends the work of the propagandist?

The axiom, in Irving's case, needs to be altered: "The style is the mood of the man." If a study of his works—in the light of his biography—shows anything, it is that Irving was a writer of various and capricious moods, of shifting and transient emotions, of volatile and at times ungovernable feeling. And his various texts are partial reflections of changing emotional states, states wonderfully exploited as they are brought under the discipline of mind and craft. But creativity cannot be forced: sometimes Irving could not write at all. Other feelings, especially of discouragement, often subverted all literary production. And we are reminded that, in the preface to the revised edition of *The Sketch Book,* he quotes one of his own letters to Sir Walter Scott, who had offered him an editorial job, to this effect:

> My whole course of life . . . has been desultory, and I am unfitted for any periodically recurring task, or any stipulated labor of body or mind. I have no command of my talents, such as they are, and have to watch the varyings of my mind as I would those of a weather cock. Practice and training may bring me more into rule; but at present I am as useless for regular service as one of my own country Indians, or a Don Cossack.[1]

We may all take some consolation from the discovery that persons of great literary distinction, like Irving, are not able to produce on demand. But, as Coleridge observed, "as genius is not, so it cannot be lawless." The issue then is to discover the law, or rule, by which genius operates, to determine what accounts for the style, in its aversion to the ideological claims of the moment, that animates Irving's *The Sketch Book.*

In the case of this work, his most popular, we are confronted with

---

1 See Washington Irving, *The Sketch Book of Geoffrey Crayon, Gent.,* ed. Haskell Springer (Boston: Twayne, 1978), p. 5. All citations from this work are hereafter given as *SB,* in parentheses, in the text.

a book composed over many years, but chiefly between 1817 and 1820. In the final form in which he published it, the work is composed of thirty-three pieces, sometimes interlinked, together with a preface and the L'Envoy. It includes some fiction and nonfiction, supernatural tales and travel sketches, social history, antiquarian lore, ethnological comment on the American Indian, comparative social observation, and literary criticism. When he advertised the work for serial publication (it came out in 1819–1820 in individual paperbound numbers), Irving remarked that the author

> is unsettled in his abode, subject to interruptions, and has his share of cares and vicissitudes. He cannot therefore promise a regular plan, nor regular periods of publication. Should he be encouraged to proceed, much time may elapse between the appearance of his numbers; and their size must depend on the materials he has on hand. His writings will partake of the fluctuations of his own thoughts and feelings; sometimes treating of scenes before him; sometimes of others purely imaginary, and sometimes wandering back with his recollections to his native country (*SB*, 300).

How, then, may one speak of the relation of style to ideology in a book so miscellaneous in content, diverse in subject, with numbers composed at different times, in different places, by a man whose advertisement for the book promised only irregularity and interruptions, as dictated by the accidents of his travel and residence, and the vagaries of his whim and memory?

One concedes at the outset that the matter and style of *The Sketch Book* are various and that its politics are generally latent. But there are two considerations that make for the unity of the book, what indeed may be called the governing style of its narrative intelligence. The first of these is of course the putative author of the work. *The Sketch Book* is the production, as the title page indicates, of one Geoffrey Crayon, Gentleman. It ought not to be necessary to remark that Geoffrey Crayon is not Washington Irving. In electing to present this miscellany under the pen name of an invented character, Irving has dissociated himself, in some measure, from the personality, temperament, and character of his imagined persona. Crayon, Jonathan Oldstyle, Diedrich Knickerbocker, Fray Antonio Agapida are all fictive characters, invented personae, pen names Irving chose, but at the same time they are imagined individual authors who differ from one another as, indeed, the books they "compose" differ from one another. And since "Rip Van Winkle" and "The Legend of Sleepy Hollow" (which appear in *The Sketch Book*) are prefaced by or postscripted with Crayon's comments on the legends of the old historian Knickerbocker, we have one fictive character commenting on the political whimsies of another, a doubling of the dramatic irony of identity that is my point in these remarks.

But if one insists on the element of imaginative projection or literary play involved in the fictionalization of a narrator, yet at the same time Crayon is nevertheless one aspect of Irving's complex identity. He is that idle, drifting, spectatorial, dilettantish, curious, conservative, old-fashioned aspect of Irving's mind. The real Irving, as his biography makes plain, was also disciplined, self-controlled, in command of his talent, energetic in his private life, and overtly political in his public life. Tammany Hall wanted him for mayor of New York (a post he declined), but he did accept service as a secretary in the American legation in London in the 1830s and as ambassador to the court of Spain in the 1840s. The real Irving was quite productive—as the thirty volumes of his journals, notebooks, letters, histories, biographies, travel narratives, and short stories reveal. Hence the voice of *The Sketch Book* is principally that of a fictive persona, the irregular and inconsistent Geoffrey Crayon.

The other principle of stylistic unity, aside from narrative voice, derives from Crayon's varied subjects. And here there is perhaps less need to separate Irving from his persona. Despite the miscellaneousness of subjects in *The Sketch Book,* it seems to me that the thirty-odd pieces are unified by an often latent, frequently eruptive, and finally dominating theme that sets at naught all ideological posturing in literature: time, time's ruins, dilapidation, dust and decay, the mutability of all things, and oblivion. Irving's feelings about this subject give rise to the signal tone of the book, which is rue, melancholy, and anticipatory regret—yet all experienced, like the style of the graveyard poets, as an affect of pleasure.

An extraordinary number of variations is played on this theme of time's ruins, with modulations of the tone even into comedy and wit, so as to prevent pathos from degenerating into morbidity. Clearly there are too many essays and stories in this work to notice them all. I shall therefore skip over "The Wife," where the single man, like Crayon (or Irving), "is apt to run to waste and self-neglect; to fancy himself lonely and abandoned, and his heart to fall to ruin like some deserted mansion for want of an inhabitant" (*SB*, 23). I shall say little of the nostalgic "Rural Life in England," of "Rural Funerals," or of "London Antiques," this last presenting the old pensioners at the Charter House, "eighty broken down men who have seen better days" (*SB*, 195). I shall say nothing of "Little Britain," which "still bears traces of its former splendour" (*SB*, 197); or of "Traits of Indian Character" and "Philip of Pokanoket," which mourn the vanishing American Indian; or of "The Angler," with its elderly Piscator, out of Isaac Walton, seen in his small cottage "after being tempest tost through life, safely moored in a snug and quiet harbour in the evening of his days" (*SB*, 270). Instead, let me concentrate on a few of those stories and essays that deal in a more direct way with Irving's awareness of mutability, Time's ruins, decay and oblivion, in relation to literary fame and immortality, as attained through the triumphs of style. For as we engage with this theme, it is clear that Irving's, rather than Crayon's, is the voice we hear. Crayon, as conceived by Irving, could have cared little about the concern with immortality that his flesh-and-blood creator so movingly evinces.

Irving's self-consciousness as a writer is inseparable from his interest in the past. But that interest, it must be insisted, is not merely antiquarian: it is obsessively concerned with Irving's own death and his immortality as an author. So congenial, sunny, and optimistic is our general sense of Irving that we do not ordinarily associate him with such morbid thoughts. He is not one of those given, in Harry Levin's term, to the power of blackness, the dark consciousness of Melville, Poe, and Hawthorne. Yet *The Sketch Book*'s opening account of the voyage from America to England accents fear, anxiety, and estrangement; and it is well to remember that the young man who was sent from New York to London and Liverpool, to assist in managing a foundering family business, had his economic as well as his physical well-being to consider:

> But a wide sea voyage severs us at once.—It makes us conscious of being cast loose from the secure anchorage of settled life and set adrift upon a doubtful world. It interposes a gulph, not merely imaginary, but real, between us and our homes—a gulph subject to tempest and fear and uncertainty, rendering distance palpable and precarious (*SB*, 11).

The tone here—though atypical of *The Sketch Book*—is not different from that of Melville's *Moby-Dick,* particularly in the express fear of the watery world below, where, Irving writes, "the finny herds" "roam its fathomless valleys," where "shapeless monsters" lurk "among the very foundations of the earth," where abide those "wild phantasms that swell the tales of fisherman and sailors" (*SB*, 11–12). The dangers of the sea voyage to England, in 1815, were real enough, but they were felt by Irving with an acute intensity, and rendered here in a Gothic mode. When they encounter the barnacle-encrusted debris of a shipwreck, Irving meditates on the perished seamen:

> But where, thought I, is the crew!—Their struggle has been over —they have gone down amidst the roar of the tempest—their bones lie whitening among the caverns of the deep. Silence—oblivion, like the waves, have closed over them, and no one can tell the story of their end (*SB*, 13).

Telling the story, retrieving and perpetuating some vestige, through narrative, of a transient existence—this is the burden of many of the tales in *The Sketch Book*. But the burden, as Henry James was to say, is without any question greater for an American, for the American must deal, even if only by implication, with Europe. How could Irving deal with Europe, make a name for himself, attain a literary identity in the world of Scott, Byron, Southey, Shelley, Wordsworth, Coleridge, and Keats? For who, at that time, even deigned to read an American book?—as Sidney Smith had contemptuously asked. As he lands on the English coast, Irving remarks, like Melville's Ishmael, "I stepped upon the land of my forefathers—but felt that I was a stranger in the land" (*SB*, 15).

Emerson was to say that we had listened too long to the courtly muses of Europe, thus injecting into American literature and its criticism a political ideology of aggressive antimonarchical egalitarian nationalism. But Irving remarks in "English Writers on America" that despite hostile British criticism of American authors, we look to England "with a hallowed feeling of tenderness and veneration as the land of our forefathers—the august repository of the monuments and antiquities of our race—the birth place and mausoleum of the sages and heroes of our paternal history" (*SB*, 47). Irving is here trying to defuse a political passion aroused to the point of war not merely in 1776 but most recently in 1812, a mere seven years before. He wishes to replace the political assessment of writers with an assessment based on the principles of belletristic criticism. Still, we note that his remark on England indirectly accents the funerary, while he remarks that Americans "are a young people, a necessarily imitative one, and must take our examples and models, in a great degree, from the existing nations of Europe" (*SB*, 49). Irving has seen the future and it is American, but it is not a future separable from Europe. Any pride in American letters, then, is tempered by a piety for the British authors, making *The Sketch Book* a signal document in the early American writer's passionate pilgrimage abroad. This essay is essentially an appeal to his British audience of critics and readers, an appeal for fair consideration from a relatively unknown American writer, still insecure about his literary gifts. He asks to be judged as a writer alone, not as the tool of transient American party politics. How to make a name for himself as a writer in England, how to secure literary immortality, is a central problem for Irving at this stage of his developing career.

However great his aspiration to attain fame in England, however, Irving was troubled by the brevity of life itself and therefore by the transience of human reputation. In the piece called "Westminster Abbey," what strikes him most is not the seat of English Christendom or the noble architecture but the tombs of the once famous, now dead and unknown. What is Westminster Abbey, he asks, but a "vast assemblage of sepulchres,"

> a treasury of humiliation; a huge pile of reiterated homilies on the emptiness of renown, and the certainty of oblivion! It is, indeed, the empire of death; his great shadowy palace; where he sits in state, mocking at the reliques of human glory, and spreading dust and forgetfulness on the monuments of princes. How idle a boast after all, is the immortality of a name!

Then, altering the trope, he concludes: "Time is ever silently turning over his pages; we are too much engrossed by the story of the present to think of the characters and anecdotes that gave interest to the past; and each age is a volume thrown aside to be specially forgotten" (*SB*, 141–142). This recourse to the analogue of the book is not accidental, and the meditation on the vanity of fame is more than mere conventional moralizing drawn from Ecclesiastes. It is Irving's rationalization, his defense prepared in advance, should he not attain the fame in England he so assiduously sought.

Irving's essay "The Art of Book Making," set in the British Museum, meditates likewise on "the decay and oblivion into which ancient writers descend; they do not submit but to the great law of nature" (*SB*, 63). He also returns to this theme in "The Mutability of Literature," subtitled "A Colloquy in Westminster Abbey." There, in the Abbey library—a kind of "literary catacomb, where authors, like mummies, are piously entombed, and left to blacken and moulder in dusty oblivion" (*SB*, 101)—a dream vision occurs, a fantasy that has a significant bearing on Irving's sense of his literary future.

Crayon takes a little Renaissance quarto, loosens the clasps, and to his "utter astonishment, the little book gave two or three yawns, like one awakening from a deep sleep," and at length the little book begins to talk. The burden of the colloquy is the indignation and dismay of this "fluent conversable little tome" (*SB*, 101) that his distinguished forebears are no longer read. The motif is a literary *ubi sunt*. Where is "Robert Grosteste of Lincoln? No one could have toiled harder than he for immortality. He is said to have written nearly two hundred volumes. He built, as it were, a pyramid of books to perpetuate his name; but, alas! the pyramid has long since fallen." Who now reads or hears of Gyraldus Cambrensis? "What is quoted of Joseph of Exeter, styled the mirror of his age in classical composition?" (*SB*, 101–102). What of Henry of Huntingdon? John Wallis, the Franciscan? Of William of Malmsbury, of Simeon of Durham, of Benedict of Peterborough, of John Hanvill of St. Albans? etc., etc.

This honor role of now-forgotten authors is of course a protest at the neglect of writers who aspired to outlive their time, to transcend the transient ideologies of the moment so as to create an enduring literature. And the scope of Irving's allusions alone discloses that he has read extensively in six hundred years of English writing. Why these allusions? The answer seems to be that, for Irving, literature represents a means of transcendence over time. If everything else changes, dies, molders, turns to dust, he yet observes that

> the intercourse between the author and his fellow men is ever new, active, and immediate. He has lived for them more than for himself; he has sacrificed surrounding enjoyments, and shut himself up from the delights of social life, that he might more intimately commune with distant minds and distant ages. Well may the world cherish his renown; for it has been purchased not by deeds of violence and blood, but by the diligent dispensation of pleasure. Well may posterity be grateful to his memory; for he has left it an inheritance, not of empty names and sounding actions, but whole treasures of wisdom, bright gems of thought, and golden language (*SB*, 136).

But if the antiquarian volumes in the Abbey library suggest anything to Irving, it is the instability of the medium of literary art. Grosteste, Cambrensis, William of Malmsbury, and the others are largely forgotten because we can no longer read the Saxon, the Anglo-Saxon, or the medieval English dialects in which they wrote. Crayon speaks his author's mind in observing, to the talkative little book in his hand, that

> the purity and stability of language, too, on which you found your claims to perpetuity, have been the fallacious dependence of authors of every age, even back to the times of the worthy Robert of

Gloucester, who wrote his history in rhymes of mongrel Saxon. Even now, many talk of Spenser's "well of English undefiled," as if the language ever sprang from a well or fountain head, and was not rather a mere confluence of various tongues, perpetually subject to changes and intermixtures. It is this which has made English literature so extremely mutable, and the reputation built upon it so fleeting. Unless thought can be committed to something more permanent and unchangeable than a medium, even thought must share the fate of everything else, and fall into decay (*SB*, 103–104).

Yet ever the moralist, extracting wisdom from adversity, Irving remarks: "This should serve as a check upon the vanity and exultation of the most popular writer. He finds the language in which he has embarked his fame, gradually altering, and subject to the dilapidations of time and the caprice of fashion" (*SB*, 104). For Irving the problem is providential, in that the decay and disappearance of writers make room for new ones to spring up. But he clearly suffers a melancholy pang in the anticipation of his own literary demise—even before the race for authorial fame in England had fairly begun.

In essence, though, there is ground for Irving to hope, and a stimulus to literary enterprise is at hand. When the talkative little volume expresses astonishment and indignation that, amongst all his contemporaries, Shakespeare is still being read—that vagabond, that actor with little learning, and a deer poacher to boot—Irving remarks:

There arise authors now and then, who seem proof against the mutability of language, because they have rooted themselves in the unchanging principles of human nature. . . . Such is the case with Shakespeare, whom we behold defying the encroachments of time, retaining in modern use the language and literature of his day, and giving duration to many an indifferent author, merely from having flourished in his vicinity (*SB*, 106).

How to transcend time? Shakespeare offers the clue. He more than any other writer acclaimed in *The Sketch Book* is the key to Irving's not quite fully articulated struggle with the problem of how he could attain fame in England. It is therefore no accident that Irving recurs to Shakespeare again and again. In "The Boar's Head Tavern, East Cheap," he tracks Shakespeare back to the tavern where Prince Hal and Falstaff came dramatically to life in their madcap revelry. And in "Stratford on Avon," Irving visits the Red Horse, the bard's birthplace, the church where he is buried, even the park at the Lucy family estate, where Shakespeare was said to have committed the youthful offense of poaching.

These essays on Shakespeare and his world are not ordinary nineteenth-century bardolatry of the kind so much indulged in by hack travel writers of the time. They are imaginative journeys backward in time to get in touch with that transcendent imaginative presence whose dramatic language, grounded in the unchanging principles of human nature, still lives, braving Time. It is the greatest stimulus to Irving to imagine that Falstaff and Hal may never have really lived, may not have been modeled on real individuals at all, but are sheer inventions: "To few readers does it occur that these are all ideal creations of a poet's brain, and that, in sober truth, no such knot of merry roysters ever enlivened the dull neighbourhood of East Cheap" (*SB*, 92). But Shakespeare himself lives, in our experience of his plays, in the magic of his enduring language.

In order to get in touch with Shakespeare's imaginative power, Irving surrenders himself to a trance while wandering through the town of Avon, thinking of Shakespeare's plays:

> Under the wizard influence of Shakespeare I had been walking all day in a complete delusion. I had surveyed the landscape through the prism of poetry, which tinged every object with the hues of the rainbow. I had been surrounded with fancied beings; with mere airy nothings, conjured up by poetic power; yet which, to me, had all the charm of reality (*SB*, 223).

This is more than a comment on the power of mental associations, as reflected in the then-current metaphysic of the Scottish School of Common Sense. For it was Irving's wish to immerse himself in these sites associated with the playwright in order to tap that *genius loci*, that poetic power which animates Shakespeare's plays. The trance comes near to achieving a merger of his own identity with that of the bard of Avon. For he remarks, apropos of the charge against young Shakespeare of stealing deer, that it was

> one of those thoughtless exploits natural to his situation and turn of mind. Shakespeare, when young, had doubtless all the wildness and irregularity of an ardent, undisciplined, and undirected genius. The poetic temperament has naturally something in it of the vagabond. When left to itself it runs loosely and wildly, and delights in every thing eccentric and licentious. It is often a turn up of a die, in the gambling freaks of fate, whether a natural genius shall turn out a great rogue or a great poet; and had not Shakespeare's mind for-

tunately taken a literary bias, he might have as daringly transcended all civil, as he has all dramatic laws (*SB*, 215).

This is as much a fantasy of self-description as it is a comment on Shakespeare, seen through the prism of romantic notions of the artist (à la Byron or Schiller) as the alienated outlaw or even as a law unto himself.

How could Irving apprehend that poetic power of Shakespeare's and make it his own? How could he tap into that store of creative genius evident in the plays and poems? "Rip Van Winkle" and "The Legend of Sleepy Hollow," attain, it seems to me, something of that wizard influence over the reader that Irving ascribes to Shakespeare. What can be said about these short stories from the point of view of style and form?

First, the fact that Irving's best-known stories strike us as inescapably the literature of the Catskills, yet in fact derive from folk legends and myths, points to a universality transcending time and place that generations of readers, in many different countries and cultures, have found enchanting. Rip and his wife, Hendrick Hudson and his men, Ichabod Crane, Katrina Van Tassel, and Brom Bones —though airy nothings, though mere illusions conjured up by the poetic power of language and imagination—have, like Falstaff and Prince Hal, that charm of reality that signals great creative accomplishment. For they are instances of powerful particular characterizations, yet they are rooted, like Shakespeare's characters, in the unchanging principles of human nature. The lazy, irregular, vagabond Rip, the shrewish wife Dame Van Winkle, the avaricious schoolmaster Crane, the delicious morsel of a coquette Katrina, and the burly practical joker Brom—all of these are recognizable from the archetype, yet are wonderfully individualized. We must add to this the pleasure of reversal in the plot of both stories, for nothing offers greater delight than the spectacle of the overreacher brought down, like Ichabod, or the victim of a petticoat tyrant, like Rip, delivered from that body of affliction called Dame Van Winkle.

There is insufficient space here to discuss both of these marvelous stories, but in that adjective "marvelous" is to be found a source of the perennial appeal of *The Sketch Book*. One of Irving's contemporaries, young Thomas Wentworth Higginson, echoes in his college journal in the 1830s the complaint of other young romantics at the poverty, for American literature, caused by our lack of myth and legend. Reading "Undine" late at night, he remarks: "Just now I heard a noise outside the window and looked up in hopes it was

Kühleborn—oh, how dreadful it is to be in a land where there are no supernatural beings visible—not even any traditions of them."[2]

A literature based on myth and legend could not be created in the new Republic unless writers treated landscape and character in a new way. Both "Rip" and "The Legend" attain this metamorphosis. For Irving, the Catskills are not merely a mountainous region of New York State; the Hudson River, the Tappan Zee, Tarry Town, and Sleepy Hollow are not merely picturesque areas familiar to Irving. He has made them into alternate worlds, imaginary geographies, the *topoi* of the imagination. Both tales transport us into a world where the mysterious and supernatural are not only possible but are fully actualized before the reader's eyes. It is sometimes said that Crayon and Knickerbocker memorialize the lost world of Dutch antiquity. But the settings in the Catskills and Sleepy Hollow and the events that occur therein are not memorials: they constitute freshly re-imagined material intended to offer this new country a foundation of myth and legend, a past available to literature.

We know the bizarre game of ninepins that the dwarfs play in the mountains, to Rip's astonishment, before he passes out for two decades, perhaps from the Hollands gin, if not from a spell. The amphitheater in the mountain cleft, where that silent bowling yields to deafening thunder, is the scene of the absolute fantastic. As the locus of the surreal, this mountain playing field is the utter antithesis of ordinary village domesticity, with one's termagant wife, cumbersome children, ubiquitous dog, and nagging tasks. In "The Legend," where Ichabod is driven off by the headless horseman, Irving is also at great pains to describe Sleepy Hollow as the site of the supernatural:

> A drowsy, dreamy influence seems to hang over the land, and to pervade the very atmosphere. Some say that the place was bewitched by a high German doctor during the early days of the settlement; others, that an old Indian chief, the prophet or wizard of his tribe, held his powwows there before the country was discovered by Master Hendrick Hudson. Certain it is, the place still continues under the sway of some witching power, that holds a spell over the minds of the good people causing them to walk in a continual reverie. They are given to all kinds of marvellous beliefs; are subject to trances and visions, and frequently see strange sights and hear music and voices in the air (*SB*, 273).

---

2 Quoted in Mary Thacher Higginson, *Thomas Wentworth Higginson: The Story of His Life* (Boston: Houghton Mifflin, 1914), p. 45.

It is in this kind of world, as defined by imagination and faith, that a headless horseman, a Hessian trooper, could very well rout Ichabod Crane by flinging his head after the hysterical schoolmaster, as he flees astride the galloping nag called Gunpowder. But it should be remarked that this invented world had nothing to do with the actual Tappan Zee or Tarry Town as they existed in 1819–1820 in all their matter-of-factness.

The effect of these imaginative settings, of these archetypal but individualized characters, of the startling reversals of plot, and of Irving's vivid poetic style is to create a world out of time and out of place: particularized as to time and place but transcending them through the magic language of fantasy. Rip Van Winkle is a desultory, casual, idle, inconsistent, drifting figure, and, like his author, is "unfitted for any periodically recurring task or any stipulated labor of body or mind." He has been criticized for all of these deficiencies as well as for failing to understand the meaning of his own bizarre adventure. But how could he have understood it—beset, as he was, by both the enigma of his long dream and the clamoring ideological fanatics who confront and confuse him. In place of the old Dutch village inn is the Union Hotel. In place of the great tree shading it is the tall pole with the red liberty cap of Revolution. In place of the sign of King George is that of General Washington. Gone are the sage Nicholas Vedder and the schoolmaster Van Brummel. Present are these Yankees, like Jonathan Doolittle, who politick incessantly, insist on political correctness, and denounce the traditionalist who has other interests in life: "A tory! A tory! A spy!" Irving, a Federalist, had little sympathy for these leveling-downward Yankees who had induced the scandalous Jefferson to destroy the American economy —and the well-being of families like the Irvings—for the sake of the embargo of 1807. If politics were a game of the rascal and fool, through art lay Irving's pathway to immortality. In his extraordinary experience in the mountains, Rip rises, along with his creator, above human time and into immortal memory. He attains this achievement, like Shakespeare, as an artist, a storyteller:

> He used to tell his story to every stranger that arrived at Mr. Doolittle's Hotel. He was observed at first to vary on some points, every time he told it, which was doubtless owing to his having so recently awakened. It at last settled down precisely to the tale I have related [reports Diedrich Knickerbocker] and not a man, woman, or child in the neighbourhood but knew it by heart. Some always pretended to doubt the reality of it, and insisted that Rip had been

out of his head, and that this was one point on which he always remained flighty. The old Dutch inhabitants, however, almost universally gave it full credit—Even to this day they never hear a thunder storm of a summer afternoon about the Kaatskill, but they say Hendrick Hudson and his crew are at their game of nine pins; and it is a common wish of all henpecked husbands in the neighbourhood, when life hangs heavy on their hands, that they might have a quieting draught out of Rip Van Winkle's flagon (*SB*, 41).

Irving's emphasis here, in the final paragraph of the story, is on the art of narrative, on imaginative invention and variation, on the universal provenance of storytelling, on mystery and strangeness, and on the readiness of a certain kind of mind—here associated with the old Dutch inhabitants (as opposed to the practical-minded and politically obsessed Anglo-Saxons)—to credit the imagination's capacity to penetrate to a truth about life that lies beyond the faculty of mundane thought and ordinary reality. In this respect the Dutch—or rather their descendants—had no reason to complain of Irving's treatment of them: the readiness of the individual to grasp the truths of the mythological, the openness of the mind to latent truths that may be encoded in storytelling, here has all of Irving's sympathy.

Lacking his sympathy, as a Middle States man, were those Yankees, of course—New Englanders who had flooded his region and brought with them not only commercial instincts and materialistic values but a certain readiness to coerce everyone else into accepting their combative egalitarian politics. If politics, as we see in *A History of New York,* is the comic pastime of knaves and buffoons, in *The Sketch Book* the demand for political correctness becomes socially coercive and oppressive. But beyond his aversion to the Yankee, which Irving shared with James Fenimore Cooper and many other Middle States writers of the time, is also a resistance to the Yankees' dogmatic literal-mindedness, which by its very definition is subversive of the implicit play of literature. Symbolism, allegory, plurisignificance, the equivocality of words and language are all at risk in the presence of an insistence on the literal. Irving's criticism of this frame of mind, which demands the commonplace, ordinary, here-and-now sunshine of the democratic republic, is of a piece with the complaints of Hawthorne, Melville, Poe, and every other romancer of the century who felt the lack of mystery—of ivy, ruins, the decay of antiquity, and all of the other impedimenta of the romance form.

With the completion of *The Sketch Book,* Irving was in an agony of suspense as to its reception by the British public. His fate as a writer, his very livelihood at the moment, and his future reputation all hinged on its reaction. In his review of *The Sketch Book,* John Gibson Lockhart, writing in *Blackwood's Edinburgh Magazine,* spoke for the public, then and now, in praising these sketches and tales as "exquisite and classical pieces of writing" in a style that he called "very graceful—infinitely more so than any piece of American writing that ever came from any other hand, and well entitled to be classed with the best English writings of our day" (*SB,* xxv). This commendation heralded acceptance by the British; it was a warrant of Irving's fame in England, just the kind of response he had longed for.

But something more than elegance of style lies at the heart of these, his two best stories, and something more than reputation amongst his contemporaries followed from them. These tales reflect a wizardry of style—like that of Shakespeare—taking the writer and his audience out of quotidian time into the world of pure imagination, where the rhythms of desire always find fulfillment, where our recurrent need for freedom from the constraints of ordinary actuality finds a satisfying, if ambiguous, resolution. That generations of readers turn again and again to these stories, despite the fluctuations of political, literary, and critical dogmatism, is evidence enough of Irving's fame.

Cooper's
Damn Yankees

Shortly after the publication of *The Pioneers* (1823), the elder Richard Henry Dana, Boston editor, essayist, and poet, complimented James Fenimore Cooper on his novel but observed that New Englanders would take offense at his portraits of Hiram Doolittle and Dr. Elnathan Todd: "The voice of praise will, I doubt not, soon reach you from the other side the water, tho' it should not come to you down the Connecticut and thro' the Sound from the friends and relatives of Hiram Doolittle and Dr. Todd." Cooper's reply was to the point: "I perceive by the concluding paragraph of your letter, that those worthies, 'Hiram Doolittle' and 'Dr. Todd' are not favorites in your section of the Country—I regret it the more, because I deprecate the reason. . . . I write of men and things as I have seen them, and few men of my years, have seen the world in more of its aspects than myself—there may be a want of ability in the delineations but there is no unworthyness of motive."[1] Cooper was of course not the only critic of New England at this time. Many of the New York literati of both the Knickerbocker and the "Young America" sets did not hesitate to attack New England, nor, later, did Poe and a number of his Southern contemporaries. The focus of the attack naturally varied—New England's puritanism, its Unitarianism, its transcendentalism, its dominant national politics, its pro-British literary cosmopolitanism. As Perry Miller observes in *The Raven and the Whale*, the Episcopal Whigs who made up the Knickerbocker coterie "tried not to step unnecessarily on the toes of their New

---

1 *The Letters and Journals of James Fenimore Cooper*, ed. James Franklin Beard (Cambridge: Harvard University Press, 1960), I, 94.

England friends, but as loyal New Yorkers (especially those who came from New England) they had to dissociate themselves from any taint of Puritanism, calling it a religious radicalism happily being replaced throughout America by 'a conservative and redeeming influence.'"[2] Of the New Yorkers, Cooper and Washington Irving were doubtless the chief critics of the Yankees.

To a good many readers in New England, both a want of ability and an ungenerous motive seemed to lie beneath Cooper's portraits of Doolittle and Todd in *The Pioneers.* Cooper's purpose was ostensibly descriptive, as the epigraph of the novel, from Paulding, suggests:

> Extremes of habits, manners, time and space,
> Brought close together, here stood face to face,
> And gave at once a contrast to the view,
> That other lands and ages never knew.

But Doolittle and Todd, not to speak of Remarkable Pettibone, seemed not faithful reproductions from nature but rather spiteful distortions of the New England character.[3]

Hiram Doolittle is portrayed as "a certain wandering, eastern mechanic" who worms his way into Templeton to become Judge Temple's land agent and supervisor.[4] Posing as an architect, Doolittle designs Temple's residence in a grotesque style which will later be repudiated by the Effinghams (in *Home as Found*) as illustrative of provincial bad taste. As Templeton's justice of the peace, "Squire" Doolittle affects a dignity he does not possess and behaves deceitfully. In the economy of the plot he is the opponent and foil of Leatherstocking, with whom we are intended to sympathize. Dr. Elnathan Todd, although less obnoxious than Doolittle, nevertheless provides another expression of Cooper's prejudice against the New England character. Physically a grotesque, Todd is huge and gangling

---

2 Perry Miller, *The Raven and the Whale: The War of Words and Wit in the Era of Poe and Melville* (New York: Harcourt, Brace, 1956), p. 24. Richard E. Cunningham's dissertation, "James Fenimore Cooper and the New England Mind" (University of Illinois, 1965), should also be consulted for other responses to the region too numerous to mention here.

3 Dana did speak of Remarkable, but only as offering a servant problem, not as a regional type. He described her as "a most happy instance of one of the thousands of those beings to be found anywhere amongst us, who let themselves out to make themselves and the family as uncomfortable as possible. . . ." *Correspondence of James Fenimore-Cooper,* I, 93.

4 James Fenimore Cooper, *The Pioneers,* ed. Leon Howard (New York: Holt, Rinehart and Winston, 1959), p. 30. Hereafter, quotations from this work will be cited as *P,* in parentheses, in the text.

of limb, narrow-shouldered, pug-nosed, and bullet-headed. His training in physic is practically nil. When he is called to doctor the superficial wound of Edward Oliver-Effingham, Todd parades his vials, saws, knives, and scissors before the assembled company and then fumbles the operation. As he is about to extract the ball from Effingham's arm, the shot falls into his hand. Fortunately, Indian John (Chingachgook) relieves the incompetent doctor and thus prevents any harm to the patient: the old Mohegan's bark remedies are made out to be superior to the doctor's Yankee physic (*P,* 61–72).[5]

Remarkable Pettibone is a third unattractive New Englander. Judge Temple's housekeeper, she is a tall, shapeless, almost toothless, wrinkled snuff-taker of middle age. Envy-ridden and jealous of her mistress Eve, Remarkable must be taught the proper forms of deference to a superior. Cooper consistently presents Remarkable as an ultra-democratic leveler who wrongheadedly believes her manners and deportment to be as genteel as those of the Temples: "And as to speech, I hold myself as second to nobody out of New England. I was born and raised in Essex county; and I've always heer'n say, that the Bay State was provarbal for pronounsation" (*P,* 172).

Given Cooper's aversion to Yankees, it was something of an understatement for his daughter Susan to have later written that her father "was very far from being an admirer of Puritan peculiarities, or the fruits their principles have yielded in later times. . . ."[6] His portraits were generally so unflattering to the New England character that, when he heard that the novelist was composing *The Pilot,* Dana implored Cooper to "have some mercy on the Yankees this time."[7] Cooper confidently reassured Dana that "the hour is not far distant

5 It should be pointed out that the practice of medicine in the United States in 1793 was everywhere a primitive art and that the medical education of Dr. Elnathan Todd, "a mere empiric," could hardly be equal to that of the graduate of Leyden or Edinburgh, ineffectual as even that might be. By the end of the eighteenth century there were only three medical schools in the country. The American Revolution had interrupted medical education in New York, and the King's College medical school was not reopened until 1792. In New England, the Harvard College medical school was set up in 1783, but until 1821, when the Massachusetts General Hospital was opened, its program was limited. Of other American cities only Philadelphia, in addition to Boston and New York, could boast of any medical education. Elnathan Todd is not less funny for the primitiveness of his Yankee physic. But Cooper could hardly have attributed his medical ignorance to his New England origin. See Richard H. Shryock's *Medicine and Society in America* (New York: New York University Press, 1960), pp. 21–38; also useful is Shryock's *The Development of Modern Medicine: An Interpretation of the Social and Scientific Factors Involved* (New York: Alfred A. Knopf, 1947).

6 Susan Fenimore Cooper, *Pages and Pictures from the Writings of James Fenimore Cooper* (New York: W. A. Townsend, 1861), p. 211.

7 H. W. Boynton, *James Fenimore Cooper* (New York: Century, 1931), p. 121.

when 'Dick Barnstable' will remove the impression" that Cooper was ill-disposed toward New England. Barnstable, one of the young naval officers in *The Pilot,* is doubtless more appealing than Hiram Doolittle or Elnathan Todd. But as James F. Beard has rightly observed, "Long Tom Coffin, the Nantucket whaler in *The Pilot,* is a greater compliment to New England character than Barnstable, the naval captain and lover in the tale."[8]

II

The simple fact is that despite Cooper's occasional attempts to portray an attractive New Englander in his social fiction—and to do so required a deliberate effort—Cooper was fundamentally suspicious of Yankees and chronically incapable of controlling his antipathy when he wrote about them in fiction. Even the historical romance *Lionel Lincoln,* a tale of the American Revolution, fails because, as historian Alexander Cowie has said, "Cooper's fundamental and ineradicable antipathy toward 'Yankees' prevented his entering con amore upon a narrative of New England of the period of Lexington, Concord, and Bunker Hill."[9] Another historical romance about King Philip's War, *The Wept of Wish-ton-Wish,* is also a failure, Thomas Lounsbury has argued, because Cooper could not control his irritation sufficiently to portray the Puritan character.[10] In addition, Robert E. Spiller has remarked that "toward New Englanders he [Cooper] had an instinctive antipathy because he realized that the middle class ideal had been brought to America by the Pilgrim and Puritan fathers," an ideal at variance with "the social traditions of which he was a part and of which he preached the doctrine."[11] To Cooper's social theories, in relation to the New England character, I shall return. In the meantime, it is enough to note that only in *Notions of the Americans,* an anonymous piece of travel literature designed to enlighten Europe by extolling America, does Cooper deal grudgingly in the praise of New England. But even here Cooper is unconvincing because he could not resist making sarcastic asides, though Cowie is right in saying that "New Englanders, generally the butt of Cooper's satire, are here given a grand puff."[12]

---

8 *Letters and Journals of James Fenimore Cooper,* I, 95n. It should be noted that, however realistic for the region, neither Coffin nor Barnstable is a complimentary name.
9 Cowie, *The Rise of the American Novel* (New York: American Book Co., 1951), p. 130.
10 Lounsbury, *James Fenimore Cooper* (New York: Houghton Mifflin, 1883), p. 75.
11 Spiller, *Fenimore Cooper: Critic of His Times* (New York: Minton, Balch, 1931), p. 313.
12 Cowie, *The Rise of the American Novel,* p. 133.

The superior tone that marks the portrayal of so many of Cooper's New England characters is more conspicuous in his social novels than in the romances of the forest and sea.[13] For it is in these novels that Cooper develops most explicitly the social principles on which his regional prejudice ultimately rests. (This dislike of Yankees is mostly latent in the romances; little, for example, is made of the New England origins of the genial psalm-singing David Gamut of *The Last of the Mohicans*. Still, the half-wit *is* a Yankee.)

In *Homeward Bound* and *Home as Found*—novels of manners designed to show that "the governing social evil of America is provincialism"[14]—Cooper portrays the Yankee gossipAbijah Gross and the journalist Steadfast Dodge as ignorant, pretentious, ultra-leveling provincials. About Dodge's regional origins Cooper is not specific, but the implications of his remarks are clear: "Mr. Dodge came from a part of the country in which men were accustomed to think, act, almost to eat and drink and sleep, in common; or, in any other words, from one of those regions in America in which there was so much community that few had the moral courage, even when they possessed the knowledge, and all the other necessary means to cause their individuality to be respected."[15] Observations such as these, scattered throughout the two novels, inescapably suggest that Dodge is a Yankee. As Lewis Leary put it, "Though never given an identifiable habitation, Steadfast (of 'pious ancestry') can be supposed to be a New Englander come to New York. . . ."[16]

III

Although Cooper never specifically identifies Dodge's region, his attitude toward New England is incontestably clear in so many other novels and romances that Kay Seymour House has summarized what was, for Cooper, "The Case Against New England." New Englanders were narrowly provincial, intolerant, nosy and intrusive, egotistical, "law honest," litigious, tyrannical, hypocritical, ignorant and vain-glorious of their superficial schooling.[17] Cooper makes so much of the

---

13 There is, incidentally, no reason why we should not regard *The Pioneers* as a social novel, what Leon Howard has rightly called "a semi-historical novel of manners on the American border" ("Introduction," *The Pioneers*, p. viii).

14 Cooper, *Home as Found*, ed. Lewis Leary (New York: Capricorn Books, 1961), p. xxviii.

15 Cooper, *Homeward Bound, or The Chase* (New York: D. Appleton, 1883), p. 47.

16 Lewis Leary, "Introduction," *Home as Found*, p. xvii.

17 House, *Cooper's Americans* (Columbus: Ohio State University Press, 1965), pp. 144–145.

Yankees' pretension to learning that we need to remember that Cooper was expelled from Yale in 1805 for a schoolboy prank. Did he harbor resentment against New Haven for the expulsion? If so it would be ironic, for the bulk of the Cooper manuscripts, as well as the fine naval portrait of him, were deposited by the family in the Yale University Library.

It would be tedious, in any case, to detail every instance of Cooper's frequently expressed bias. Instead, I want to focus on the most representative and significant attack on Cooper's Yankee neighbors as a way of getting at the political and cultural values that Cooper thought were appropriate for America in his time. That attack—waged in the Littlepage Manuscripts, a trilogy of anti-rent novels composed of *Satanstoe* (1845), *The Chainbearer* (1845) and *The Redskins* (1846)—offers a key to understanding the ongoing tension in America over the need for a gentry to set the standard for social and cultural development. In describing "The Family of Littlepage" books, Cooper told Richard Bentley that the trilogy

> will form three complete Tales, each perfectly distinct from the others as regards leading characters, love story &c, but, in this wise connected. I divide the subjects into the "Colony," "Revolution" and "Republic," carrying the same family, the same localities, and the same *things* generally through the three different books, but exhibiting the changes produced by time &c. In the Colony, for instance, the Littlepage of that day, first visits an estate of wild land, during the operations of the year 1758, the year that succeeded the scenes of the Mohicans, and it is there that the most stirring events of the book oc[c]ur. In the "Revolution" this land is first settled, and the principles are developed, on which this settlement takes place, showing a book, in some respects resembling the Pioneers, though varied by localities and incidents—In the "Republic" we shall have the present aspect of things, with an exhibition of the Anti-Rent commotion that now exists among us, and which certainly threatens the destruction of our system.[18]

The titles of the novels were changed in the course of composition, but this scenario suggests how long Cooper had brooded on landlords, tenants, and Yankees since the publication of *Wyandotté* (1843). *Satanstoe,* the first volume in the series, set in the 1750s, narrates the founding of two estates (Ravensnest and Mooseridge) by

---

18 See *Letters and Journals of James Fenimore Cooper,* ed. James Franklin Beard (Cambridge: Harvard University Press, 1968), V, 7.

the Mordaunt and Littlepage families. These estates, which will later become the bone of contention between the landlord and tenants, are more or less united at the end of the novel by the marriage of Cornelius Littlepage and Anneke Mordaunt, a pair of genteel Dutch-English New Yorkers. *The Chainbearer*, set shortly after the Peace of 1783, deals with the troubles caused by squatters who have illegally settled on these estates of Mordaunt Littlepage, son of Corny and Anneke. *The Redskins*, which brings the history of these estates and of the Littlepage family down into the 1840s, deals with the resistance of the tenants to the terms of their leases and with the violence they perpetrate upon the person and property of Hugh Roger Littlepage (Mordaunt's grandson) and his household.

Cooper became involved in the conditions which led up to the anti-rent controversy, in a tangential way, almost immediately upon his return to the United States from Europe in 1833. I have no interest in the psychobiographical reading of Cooper, according to which the legal issues he dealt with for the next ten or fifteen years manifest an identity problem.[19] The notorious "Three Mile Point" controversy at Cooperstown, Cooper's war with the Whig press, the libel trials which he initiated, the publication of satires like *Homeward Bound* and *Home as Found* in 1838, and the publication of *The American Democrat* (1838), a political treatise published in Cooperstown and directed at his neighbors—all of these events and the Cooper publications which grew out of them were intended to insist on the protection of property as a democratic right guaranteed by the Constitution. Although they did involve Cooper's own rights, their implications extended far beyond his own particular relationship with his neighbors and included the whole anti-rent controversy.

This controversy between landlords and tenants over the payment of rents, which simmered for decades and finally came to a violent turn between 1839 and 1846, has already been thoroughly documented,[20] and the major literary features of this trilogy of novels have also been studied in some detail by earlier literary critics concerned

---

19 I have in mind Charles Hansford Adams's claim that there is a distinctive "configuration of law and identity" that dictated Cooper's sense of himself and the shape of his litigations and his literary career. See *"The Guardian of the Law": Authority and Identity in James Fenimore Cooper* (University Park: Pennsylvania State University, 1990), p. 113.

20 See, for example, David M. Ellis, *Landlords and Farmers in the Hudson-Mohawk Region, 1790-1850* (Ithaca: Cornell University Press, 1946) and Ellis's "The Coopers and New York State Landholding Systems," in *James Fenimore Cooper: A Reappraisal* (Cooperstown: New York State Historical Association, 1954), pp. 44–54. Also *ad rem* is Edward P. Cheyney's *The Anti-Rent Agitation in the State of New York, 1839–1846* (Philadelphia: Porter and Coates, 1887). Neither of these historians ascribes the troubles at this time to the regional origin of the leaseholders.

with such novelistic issues as theme and form.[21] But an oft-neglected aspect of these books is the extent to which Cooper charges the controversy to the work of outside agitators from New England bent on destroying the old-established social and economic institutions of the Middle States. The principal New England villains in the Littlepage trilogy are these: in the first two novels, *Satanstoe* and *The Chainbearer*, Jason Newcome, the newcomer or invader from New England; in the second novel, *The Chainbearer*, Aaron Thousandacres, a Yankee squatter on the vast Littlepage patent who pays no rent but steals and sells Littlepage timber and in other ways profits from the private property of his betters; and, in the last novel, *The Redskins*, Seneca Newcome, the ultra-leveling grandson of Jason who, in committing arson on the property of the Littlepage family, embodies the absolute perversion of principle first apparent in the grasping and envious attitude of his conniving grandfather.

Cooper establishes the basis for differentiating colonial New Yorkers from Yankees at the beginning of *Satanstoe,* and from that point on to the end of *The Redskins* we can be in no doubt as to how the malign influence of the original Yankee immigrant Jason Newcome will work itself out over several succeeding generations. Here is Cornelius Littlepage, a Middle States man and property owner, reflecting on regional differences in the opening chapter of *Satanstoe*:

> There was and is little sympathy, in the way of national feeling, between the colonies of New England and those which lie farther south. We are all loyal, those of the east as well as those of the southwest and south; but there is, and ever has been, so wide a difference in our customs, origins, religious opinions, and histories, as to cause a broad moral line, in the way of feeling, to be drawn between the colony of New York and those that lie east of the Byram River. I have heard it said, that most of the emigrants to the New England states came from the west of England, where many of their social peculiarities and much of their language are still to be traced, while the colonies farther south have received their population from the more central counties, and those sections of the island that are supposed to be less provincial and peculiar. I do not affirm that such is literally the fact, though it is well known that we of New York have long been accustomed to regard our neighbors of New England as

21 See James Grossman's *James Fenimore Cooper* (New York: W. Sloan Associates, 1949), pp. 200–219; Donald A. Ringe's "Cooper's Littlepage Novels: Change and Stability in American Society," *American Literature,* 32 (1960), 280–290; and Warren S. Walker's "Cooper's Yorkers and Yankees in the Jeffersonian Garden," in *James Fenimore Cooper: His Country and His Art* (Oneonta, N.Y.: SUNY College Press, 1981), pp. 71–80.

very different from ourselves, whilst, I dare say, our neighbors of New England have regarded us as different from themselves, and insomuch removed from perfection.[22]

These differences are embodied in the New Yorker Corny Littlepage, a graduate of Princeton, and Jason Newcome, A.B. Yale, the neighborhood pedagogue from New England. Jason is provincial in dialect and attitude, ignorant of the forms of polite breeding, envious, shrewd but sneaking, nosy and hypocritical. He is contemptuous of New York, deferential to money, has "overweening notions of moral and intellectual superiority," but fawns before the titled aristocracy. Worst of all, according to Cooper, "Jason was ultra levelling in his notions of social intercourse" (*S,* 39). As *The American Democrat, Homeward Bound, Home as Found,* and these "Littlepage Manuscripts" abundantly reveal, there is no greater sin in the Cooper decalogue than harboring ultra-leveling sentiments in social (not political) relations.

The distance that separates Corny from Jason is tellingly revealed in a paragraph in *Satanstoe* in which Corny reflects on Jason's character in the light of the proprieties obtaining in every polite society, of which Jason seems to have no knowledge whatsoever:

In this respect Jason was always a moral enigma to me; there being an absolute absence in his mind, of every thing like a perception of the fitness of things, so far as the claims and rights of persons were connected with rank, education, birth and experience. Rank, in the official sense, once possessed, he understood and respected; but of the claims to entitle one to its enjoyment, he seemed to have no sort of notion. For property he had a profound deference, so far as that deference extended to its importance and influence; but it would have cost him not the slightest qualm, either in the way of conscience or feeling, to find himself suddenly installed in the mansion of the patroons, for instance, and placed in possession of their estates, provided only he fancied he could maintain his position. . . . I have mentioned this propensity of Jason's at some length as I feel certain, should this history be carried down by my own posterity as I hope and design, it will be seen that this disposition to regard the

---

22 James Fenimore Cooper, *Satanstoe,* eds. Robert E. Spiller and Joseph D. Coppock (New York: American Book Co., 1937), pp. 11–12. Hereafter, quotations from this text will be cited as *S,* in parentheses, in the text. For an interesting discussion of the dividing *line* of the Byram River, as well as boxes, circles, and other tropes in these Littlepage Manuscripts, see H. Daniel Peck's *A World by Itself: The Pastoral Moment in Cooper's Fiction* (New Haven: Yale University Press, 1977).

whole human family as so many tenants in common of the estate left by Adam, will lead in the end, to something extraordinary (*S,* 274–275).

IV

What Jason's leveling propensity leads to is evident in the successive novels of this trilogy. Between the events of the 1750s in *Satanstoe* and those of the 1780s in *The Chainbearer,* "The plot has thickened." [23] Cooper actually uses, if not invents, the phrase, a thickening that develops, by the way, at the expense of *Satanstoe's* marvelous element of "pastoral enchantment." [24] Some of the immigrants who have leased farms on the Littlepage patent have begun to balk at their rent payments—even though the original terms were quite generous. Jason, now the Littlepage land agent, is one of the first to hedge on his obligations and to claim rights to the property that have no foundation in law. But even worse, he passively permits the Littlepages to be cheated by the Yankee squatter Aaron Thousandacres, who slips onto the property and cuts timber for his own profit. The old squatter's justification for this lawlessness is the doctrine of possession: "There's two rights to all the land on 'arth, and the whull world over. One of these rights is what I call a king's right, or that which depends on writin's, and laws, and sichlike contrivances; and the other depends on possession. It stands to reason, that fact is better than any writin' about it can be. . . ." (*C,* 384). To rid the patent of this evil principle costs the lives of both Thousandacres and his foil—Andries Coejemans, the old Dutch chainbearer, whose verdict, apparently assented to by the novel as a whole, is that "Yankee religion and Tutch religion cannot come out of t'e same pipe" (*C,* 334). Newcome and Thousandacres have no respect for Cooper's belief that "all the knowledge, and all the arts of life that the white man enjoys and turns to his profit, come from the rights of property" (*C,* 123).

Much was made, in nineteenth- and early twentieth-century criticism, of Cooper's love of the free life of Hawkeye in the woods, of his profound respect for the Native American, and of his guilt at the violent displacement of the Indian as American civilization moved westward. On this reading, Cooper shared in the romantic primitivism of the age and, especially in *The Last of the Mohicans,* mourned

---

23 Cooper, *The Chainbearer, or The Littlepage Manuscripts* (New York: D. Appleton, 1883), p. v. Hereafter, quotations from this text will be cited as *C,* in parentheses, in the text.
24 Robert E. Long, *James Fenimore Cooper* (New York: Frederick Ungar, 1990), p. 153.

the passing of the red man and the horrific cost in human life of the advancement of civilization. That view seems to have been replaced, in recent years, by a new cynicism, according to which demystifying left-wing critics of the-white-man-is-a-killer school have ridiculed Cooper's feeling for the Indian and have condemned him as an out-and-out racist. However much Cooper may have felt nostalgia for the boyish adventures of Hawkeye and the nomadic freedom of the Indian, Stephen Railton is right in remarking that the Littlepage Manuscripts "affirm that clearing the forest for society is unequivocally good, and that the men who lead this enterprise, the landlords, are the very capital on the column of American civilization."[25] These landlords, incidentally, are not Yankees but long-settled upstanding Middle States men who embody the progress of civilization.

Yet even though he has personally been cheated by a pair of Yankees, the landlord Mordaunt Littlepage, Corny's less biased son and the narrator of *The Chainbearer*, concedes some virtue to New Englanders. Writing of the post-Revolutionary invasion of Yankees into New York, Mordaunt says:

> We of New York have our prejudices against the Yankees, and have long looked upon them with eyes of distrust and disfavor. They have repaid us in kind, perhaps; but their dislikes have not been strong enough to prevent them from coming to take possession of our lands. For my own part, while I certainly see much in the New England character that I do not like (more in their manners and minor ways, perhaps, than in essentials), I as certainly see a great deal to command my respect (*C*, 126).

Though Yankee civilization is not of a very high order as regards tastes, sentiments, and the nicer feelings, Mordaunt concedes that it *is* based on common sense and a respect for practical learning. Consequently the spread of New Englanders into New York has not been altogether bad because it has had "a more salutary influence on its practical knowledge, on its enterprise, on its improvements, and consequently on its happiness." In this concession to Yankee practicality, Mordaunt goes farther than his father or grandfather would have gone and even foresees a more liberal attitude on the part of his sons. Nevertheless, he passes on some serious advice to Yankees then

---

25 See Stephen Railton, *Fenimore Cooper: A Study of His Life and Imagination* (Princeton: Princeton University Press, 1978), pp. 241–242. For a discussion of Cooper's view of the role of private property in the development of civilized societies, see Grant Morrison's "James Fenimore Cooper and American Republicanism, *Modern Age*, 34 (Spring 1992), 220–221.

in New York—advice that still has pertinence whenever a multicultural country is flooded with illegal (or even legal) immigrants:

> Our immigrant friends should remember one thing, however, and it would render them much more agreeable as companions and neighbors which is this: he who migrates is bound to respect the habits and opinions of those whom he joins; it not being sufficient for the perfection of everything under the canopy of heaven, that it should come from our own little corner of the earth.

And, he adds, half facetiously, "Even the pumpkin-pies of the Middle States are vastly better than those usually found in New England" (*C*, 127).

These concessions represent an ineffectual attempt by Cooper to deal objectively with the facts of New York social history and to right the imbalance his prejudices tended to create. In the long run, he could not sustain the balance. As a spokesman for a conservative social viewpoint, he often delivers with tongue in cheek what he seriously believes. Thus in the following passage from the Preface to *The Chainbearer*, Cooper, speaking in his own voice, is both facetious and serious in explaining why the Littlepages are so hostile to New Englanders:

> In the first place, we do not pretend to be answerable for all the opinions of those whose writings are submitted to our supervision [Cooper is ostensibly only the "editor" of the Littlepage Manuscripts], any more than we should be answerable for all the contradictory characters, impulses, and opinions that might be exhibited in a representation of fictitious characters, purely of our own creation. That the Littlepages entertained New York notions, and, if the reader will, New York prejudices, may be true enough; but in pictures of this sort, even prejudices become facts that ought not to be altogether kept down. Then, New England has long since anticipated her revenge, glorifying herself and underrating her neighbors in a way that, in our opinion, fully justifies those who possess a little Dutch blood in expressing their sentiments on the subject. Those who give so freely should know how to take a little in return; and that more especially, when there is nothing very direct or personal in the hits they receive (*C*, vii).

Cooper thus justifies ethnic satire when it is not personal or "direct." How different it is today, when any ethnic satirist can be condemned for "hate speech" and remanded to the psychiatrist or the keepwarden. Since he denies that he himself has any Dutch blood,

Cooper disclaims a side in the argument. As "editor," he describes himself as only "a bottle-holder to one of the parties in this set-to." But Cooper's irritation betrays itself on every page of the trilogy. Though his Dutch characters may at times be as much the butt of satire as his Yankee characters, the Dutch still retain Cooper's sympathy and speak for him in every significant exchange between Dutchman and New Englander. Corny may be more prejudiced than his son and grandson will be, but each of the three novels leads us to believe that the distinctions between Jason and Guert Ten Eyck, an unschooled young Dutch boy killed while defending the Mordaunts in an Indian raid, hold true for New Yorkers and Yankees throughout the historical evolution of New York as a whole:

> Notwithstanding, all the books in the world could not have converted Guert Ten Eyck into a Jason Newcome, or Jason Newcome into a Guert Ten Eyck. Each owed many of his peculiarities, doubtless, to the province in which he was bred and born, and to the training consequent on these accidents; but nature had also drawn broad distinctions between them. All the wildness of Guert's impulses could not altogether destroy his feelings, tone, and tact as a gentleman; while all the soaring, extravagant pretentions of Jason never could have ended in elevating him to that character (*S,* 414).

This passage reflects some of Cooper's deeply held feelings about the potential distinctions "in nature" between New Yorkers and New Englanders. And even though Cooper tries to be more objective about New Englanders in the succeeding novels, he really does not sustain the attempt. None of the Yankees of the Littlepage Manuscripts is elevated to the character of a gentleman. Even Mordaunt, whom Cooper makes out to be more generous than his father, loses his good temper a great deal and in one outburst rants scornfully: "There is among us a set of declaimers, who come from a state of society in which little distinction exists in either fortunes or social conditions, and who are incapable of even seeing, much less of appreciating, the vast differences that are created by habits, opinions, and education, but who reduce all moral discrepancies to dollars and cents" (*C,* 251–252).

There is no doubt that this set of declaimers is of New England origin. Mordaunt's view is not simply an historical attitude Cooper has revived for the purposes of verisimilitude in fiction. It is his own view. And the fact that this view is intended to apply to the social and economic conditions of the 1840s in New York is evident in the Preface to *The Chainbearer.* There, in a defense of his already no-

torious "undue asperity on the subject of the New England character" in the earlier *Satanstoe,* Cooper remarks: "In our judgment the
false principles that are to be found in a large portion of the educated
classes, on the subject of the relation between landlord and tenant,
are to be traced to the provincial notions of those who have received
their impressions from a state of society in which no such relations
exist" (*C,* 7). In other words, from New England. How different
Cooper is from the Yankee Emerson here. If the Concord writer
vested everything in the originary force of the present moment and
dreamed the future as merely new barriers to overleap, Cooper
reminds us, in the words of Edgar A. Dryden, that "today stands
fully revealed only when it is illuminated by the light of yesterday.
The reality of his characters, therefore, is shaped not by their future
possibilities but by the shadows of their pasts."[26]

V

The decay of political principle, the growing disrespect for the rights
of property, the attempts by renters to defraud the landlords of their
rents, the anti-rent violence raging throughout the countryside — all
of these are thus ultimately traceable, Cooper suggests, to outside
agitators from New England who seek to overthrow, by force if
necessary, the ancient social and economic institutions of the Middle
States. The anti-rent controversy that Yankees have provoked, in the
words of John P. McWilliams, "is the gravest threat to the republic in
its sixty-year history because, for the first time, the fundamental principles of republicanism are being flouted by groups that organize
lawlessness."[27] This most serious charge Cooper sought to dramatize
in *The Redskins.* Here the anti-renters, dressed in calico as Injins, are
led by Seneca Newcome, the conniving and dishonest grandson of
old Jason. The anti-renters' crimes extend from evading payment,
threats, and intimidation of landlords to arson and attempted murder. Speaking through Hugh Roger Littlepage, Mordaunt's grandson, Cooper's fury rises: "I write warmly, I know, but I feel warmly;
and I write like a man who sees that a most flagitious attempt to rob
him is tampered with by some in power, instead of being met, as the
boasted morals and intelligence of the country would require, by the
stern opposition of all in authority. Curses — deep, deep curses — ere

---

26 See Edgar A. Dryden's impressive "History and Progress: Some Implications of Form
in Cooper's Littlepage Novels," *Nineteenth-Century Fiction,* 26 (1971), 49–64.
27 John P. McWilliams, Jr., *Political Justice in a Republic: James Fenimore Cooper's America*
(Berkeley: University of California Press, 1972), p. 306.

long, will fall on all who shrink from their duty in such a crisis. Even the very men who succeed, if succeed they should, will, in the end, curse the instruments of their own success."[28]

As angry as he occasionally was, Cooper had calmer moments when he saw the land problem steadily, even if he did not see it whole. In these calmer moments Cooper could not bring himself absolutely to indict New England for the political troubles that had befallen New York. That he could not constitutes a failure of control over his material and creates a disturbing ambivalence in his fiction: he accuses the Yankees and then half ridicules his own accusation, as if he did not really seriously intend it. In *The Redskins*, Hugh's mother formulates perfectly the charge that Cooper has implied all along: "I apprehend, Roger, that we owe this anti-rent struggle, and particularly the feebleness with which it is resisted, to the difference of opinion that prevails among the people of New England, who have sent so many immigrants among us, and our own purely New York notions." Hugh's Uncle Ro agrees with her view of the cause of their troubles, although he admits that "New Yorkers, by descent, are not wanting to sustain the innovation." Uncle Ro, Cooper's spokesman, argues that, while the renegade Middle States' men act from motives of cupidity or popularity, the New England immigrants "are influenced by the notions of the state of society from which either they themselves, or their parents, were directly derived." (This is the same argument that Cooper had first advanced, *in propria persona*, in the Preface to *The Chainbearer*.) Uncle Ro explains that "the relation of landlord and tenant as connected with what we should term estates, is virtually unknown to New England; though Maine may afford some exceptions." But when Hugh tries to pin him down ("Am I to understand you, sir, to say that anti-rentism is of New England origin?"), Uncle Ro begins to hedge:

> Perhaps not. Its origin was probably more directly derived from the devil, who has tempted the tenants as he is known once to have tempted the Saviour. The outbreak was originally among the descendants of the Dutch, for they happened to be the tenants, and, as for the theories that have been broached, they savor more of the reaction of European abuses, than of anything American at all; and least of all of anything from New England, where there is generally a great respect for the rights of property, and unusual reverence for the

---

28 James Fenimore Cooper, *The Redskins, or Indian and Injin* (New York: D. Appleton, 1883), p. 227. Hereafter, quotations from this text will be cited as *R*, in parentheses, in the text.

law. Still, I think we owe our greatest danger to the opinions and habits of those of New England descent among us (*R,* 457–458).

This passage shows Cooper in full and disorganized retreat from a sociopolitical thesis that he had been dramatizing throughout three long novels, each one more insistent than the last, and all intended to warn New Yorkers against the confiscatory dangers of the envious populace and its venal politicians. He wished to preserve rights of property that had been guaranteed by the Dutch crown to the patroons, by the English kings to their subjects, and by the Constitution to American residents of the new Republic. In some part of his mind he understood that the system of feudal leaseholds was an incendiary vestige of Old World class arrangements. But the law of contracts and property had a sanctity for him that exceeded even the bitter testing it had received in the Three Mile Point Controversy. But even if Yankees were not the origin of the anti-rent sentiment, the thesis that New York's troubles were of New England origin—as the last sentence of the passage above suggests—gave Cooper a convenient scapegoat.

VI

To establish the causes of the anti-rent agitation required more historical objectivity than Cooper could muster in the trying decade of the 1840s. He was perfectly convinced that the fundamental political contest of his time was "between those who would place power in the hands of an elite, either hereditary or financial, and those who would entrust it to the mass of the people themselves."[29] But, aroused as he was, he could only reduce the complex phenomena of New York social history to a theory based on his personal biases, dramatize the theory as an additional instance of social disorder, and then turn ambivalently from it. Cooper argued passionately against the tendency of events because they threatened what to him was the ideal American social order. New Englanders were a threat to the *status quo* because they came from a state of society in which every husbandman might be the owner in fee of his farm instead of the tenant of a feudal leasehold, and thus could be the social equal of his neighbors. Yankees, Cooper feared, were destroying the possibility of establishing more securely a landed gentry in New York.

Cooper held that in a country like the United States not small

---

29 Donald A. Ringe, "Introduction" to *The Bravo* by James Fenimore Cooper (New Haven: College and University Press, 1963), p. 9.

freeholders but "a landed gentry is precisely what is most needed for
the higher order of civilization . . ." (*R,* 462). Composed of Epis-
copalian ladies and gentlemen (no dissenters here), this class would,
as the repository of genteel manners and enlightened opinion, elevate
and establish the general tone of society. It would, in addition,
provide models of perfection for the lower orders who would be
properly subservient to the claims of relative wealth, property, and
merit in a republican society. As Uncle Ro points out, a landed gentry
"is the very class which, if reasonably maintained and properly
regarded, would do the most good at the least risk of any social caste
known" (*R,* 462). But the idea of a landed gentry, even if it constituted no political risk, was alien to the social ideal of those Yankees
(and Europeans) who migrated westward looking for an equal share
in the evolving Jacksonian social order. Like Edith Wharton, who attacked the Midwestern businessmen and the post–Civil War "lords of
Pittsburgh" for invading and destroying the urbane social aristocracy
of old New York, and like Faulkner, who bitterly satirized the
Snopses for overpowering the ordered civility of the genteel South,
Fenimore Cooper sought through his fiction to prevent the anti-rent
faction from destroying his social dream. But, ironically, even as
Cooper was criticizing the anti-renters as influences foreign to the
spirit of New York social and political institutions, the State Assembly of New York was formulating legislation that would effectively break up the huge manorial estates.[30] This legislation made it
possible for small farmers, of whatever regional origin and social
class, to own their own farms in fee and to shape for themselves a
destiny equal to their capacities.

30 For a discussion of Democrat and Whig party maneuvering as the New York Assembly
moved to break up the huge estates, see Dorothy Waples, *The Whig Myth of James
Fenimore Cooper* (1938; reprinted Hamden, Conn.: Archon Books, 1968).

Poe:
The Quest for
Supernal Beauty

I have sometimes amused myself by endeavoring to fancy what would be the fate of any individual gifted or rather accursed, with an intellect *very* far superior to that of his race. Of course, he would be conscious of his superiority; nor could he (if otherwise constituted as man is) help manifesting his consciousness. Thus he would make himself enemies at all points. And since his opinions and speculations would widely differ from those of *all* mankind —that he would be considered a madman, is evident. How horribly painful such a condition! Hell could invent no greater torture than that of being charged with abnormal weakness on account of being abnormally strong.
—Edgar Allan Poe, *Marginalia*

Edgar Allan Poe (1809–1849) may be the most misunderstood and perhaps the most disliked of serious writers to have made anything like a deep impact on the American public. This is in part the consequence of his sensational and morbid affects: hysteria, hallucinations, catalepsy, metempsychosis, premature burial, the odd impulse, the bizarre fetish, the split personality, the paranoid delusion, insane revenge, and bestial murder. Such material may estrange or alienate us from the writer, depending on the relationship of author to his characters. But more important than confusion occasioned by his texts is the fact that Poe's reputation is the unfortunate consequence of persistent errors of fact and interpretation that have twisted the public view of Poe from the very beginning. Just four years after Poe's death, the Reverend George Gilfillan proclaimed:

> Poets as a tribe have been rather a worthless, wicked set of people; and certainly Edgar A. Poe, instead of being an exception, was probably *the* most worthless and wicked of all his fraternity. . . . He was no more a gentleman than he was a saint. His heart was as rotten as his conduct was infamous. . . . He had absolutely no virtue or good quality, unless you call remorse a virtue, and despair a grace . . . . He was, in short, a combination in almost equal proportions, of the fiend, the brute, and the genius.[1]

Granted that poets sometimes stray from the straight and narrow, what could Poe have conceivably done to warrant such accusations? For one thing, Poe had had the bad judgment to select as his literary executor another minister, the Reverend Rufus Wilmot Griswold, who had literary ambitions and whose view of Poe was intermixed with malice and jealousy. Poe naïvely regarded him as a friend, as a sponsor of his work. But the jealous Griswold, a minor literatus, had never gotten over Poe's candid criticism of one of his anthologies, and he harbored a thirst for revenge worthy of Montresor in "The Cask of Amontillado." At Poe's death, Griswold simply assassinated the poet's character, leaving an image of Poe as the archetype of the immoral, self-indulgent, and socially subversive writer whose work was without redeeming (i.e., ideologically useful) moral or social value. Scarcely was the body cold when Griswold, under the pseudonym "Ludwig," spewed out his calumnies in an obituary published in the New York *Daily Tribune* for October 9, 1849.

> Edgar Allan Poe is dead. He died in Baltimore the day before yesterday. This announcement will startle many, *but few will be grieved by it.* The poet was well known personally or by reputation, in all this country; he had readers in England and in several of the states of Continental Europe; *but he had few or no friends;* and the regrets for his death will be suggested principally by the consideration that in him literary art lost one of its most brilliant, but erratic stars.

---

1 Quoted in Arthur Hobson Quinn, *Edgar Allan Poe: A Critical Biography* (New York: Appleton-Century-Crofts, 1941), p. 681.

Turning to "the character of Mr. Poe," Griswold called him an un-balanced misanthrope who "walked the streets in madness or mel-ancholy, with lips moving in indistinct curses, or with eyes upturned in passionate prayers." Taking Poe's works as revelations of the writ-er's own character, Griswold described him as cynical, devoid of faith in man or woman, contemptuous of the social system, shrewd, angry, envious, irascible, coldly repellent, and the dupe of villains:

> There seemed to him no moral susceptibility; and what was more remarkable in a proud nature, little or nothing of the true point of honor. He had, to a morbid excess, that desire to rise which is vul-garly called ambition, but no wish for the esteem or the love of his species; only the hard wish to succeed—not shine, not serve —succeed, that he might have the right to despise a world which galled his self-conceit.[2]

The attitudes here expressed (and reprinted at the time in many other American newspapers) were further elaborated in Griswold's "Mem-oir of the Author," which he had the malice to attach to his four-volume edition of the writer's works in 1850. With such a sponsor, is it any wonder that for a century Poe was roundly condemned by ministers, temperance advocates, high-school teachers, and other guardians of public morality?[3]

II

Given the promise of such fantastic sensationalism, biographers have sometimes played fast and loose with the facts. Still, there have been a good many serious biographies in the nearly century and a half since Griswold's memoir. But many of the better ones—including Hervy Allen's *Israfel: The Life and Times of Edgar Allan Poe* (1934), Arthur Hobson Quinn's *Edgar Allan Poe: A Critical Biography* (1941), Edward Wagenknecht's *Edgar Allan Poe: The Man Behind the Legend* (1963), and N. Fagin Bryllion's *The Histrionic Mr. Poe* (1967) —have been based, as John Carl Miller has shown, on the materials and methods of Poe's first important admirer, John Henry Ingram, an Englishman who amassed an important collection of biographical materials (now at the University of Virginia Library) and launched serious Poe studies with *Edgar Allan Poe: His Life, Letters, and Opin-*

---

2 See *The Recognition of Edgar Allan Poe: Selected Criticism Since 1829,* ed. Eric Carlson (Ann Arbor: University of Michigan Press, 1966), pp. 28, 32–33.
3 For an account of the life of Griswold, see Joy Bayless, *Rufus Wilmot Griswold: Poe's Literary Executor* (Nashville: Vanderbilt University Press, 1943.)

ions (1880).[4] And it has of course been *de rigueur* for modern biographers—ever since Camille Mauclair's *Le Génie d'Edgar Poe* (1926), Joseph Wood Krutch's *Edgar Allan Poe: A Study in Genius* (1926), and Marie Bonaparte's *Edgar Poe: étude psychanalytique* (1933)—to do some psychoanalysis of the writer; and to the psychological approach we owe some of the wildest (and most riveting) literary interpretations ever to have been penned by human hand. Even so, that it is possible to offer a tactful analysis of Poe's psychic configuration and his preoccupation with morbid themes is evident in Kenneth Silverman's splendid *Edgar A. Poe: Mournful and Never-ending Remembrance* (1991), which posits bereavement at the loss of his mother and the failure of adjustment in mourning as the key to much that seems obscure, macabre, or sensational in the poet.[5]

Thanks also to Dwight Thomas and David K. Jackson, we can now see the writer's life with a different kind of clarity that none of his contemporaries (and only a very few subsequent biographers) have been able to attain. In *The Poe Log: A Documentary Life of Edgar Allan Poe, 1809–1849*, Thomas and Jackson presented as complete a written record of Poe's activities, of his family, friends, and acquaintances, of his publications and reception, as we are likely ever to have in one volume.[6] It was a splendid, massive, compendious work of biographical research—a deep probe into newspapers, magazines, published and unpublished letters and journals, business account books, school and medical records, military communiqués, rent receipts, and the like. If you want to know what it cost Poe's step-father to mend the seven-year-old's linen and to supply his shoe-strings at the Misses Dubourg's school in London in 1816, the answer is there: three shillings.

I confess to a special liking for the day-by-day, month-by-month, year-by-year summary of a writer's life. Books like *The Poe Log*, Jay Leyda's *Melville Log*, and Leyda's *The Years and Hours of Emily Dickinson* are not conventional biographies. They are simply compendia of facts—all or most of the known facts, facts without interpretation, the facts marshaled in a calendar sequence. To read through such books is to experience a "diary" of the unfolding events of a writer's inner and outer life and the way these events were perceived by his

---

4 On the history of the Poe lives, see John Carl Miller's *Building Poe Biography* (Baton Rouge: Louisiana State University Press, 1977), pp. 1–18.

5 Kenneth Silverman, *Edgar A. Poe: Mournful and Never-ending Remembrance* (New York: HarperCollins, 1991), especially pp. 76–78.

6 Dwight Thomas and David Jackson, *The Poe Log: A Documentary Life of Edgar Allan Poe, 1809–1849* (Boston: G. K. Hall, 1987). Hereafter, citations from this work will be given as *PL*, in parentheses, in the text.

contemporaries. Perhaps the clearest way to suggest what such books contain is to present some typical listings for Poe's life. In December 1846 Poe had fallen dangerously ill in Fordham with what was commonly believed to be a "lesion of the brain"; his wife Virginia was dying of tuberculosis; and, with no income from his writing, they had been reduced to abject poverty and destitution. News of their plight was published in the New York *Morning Express* on December 15. (In the following entries, I have deleted some repetitive material and the documentation.)

DECEMBER OR LATER. James Watson Webb, editor of the [New York] *Morning Courier*, collects "fifty or sixty dollars" for Poe at the Metropolitan Club. Sylvanus D. Lewis, a Brooklyn lawyer, donates "a similar sum" after reading "the statement of the poet's poverty."

16 DECEMBER. *The Evening Mirror* reprints the report of Poe's illness from yesterday's *Morning Express*. Hiram Fuller [the editor and a critic of Poe's satirical sketches of the New York literati] comments: "Mr. Poe is undeniably a man of fine talents, and in his peculiar vein has written stories unequalled. We have no doubt but that with a fair field for exertion, he could produce a series of tales in grotesqueness and force equal to those of the German Hoffman. His friends ought not to wait for publishers to start a movement in his behalf, and if they do not, we, whom he has quarreled with, will take the lead."

AFTER 16 DECEMBER. PHILLIPS, MAINE. [Friend George] Eveleth receives Poe's 15 December letter, mailed on 16 December. He writes Louis A. Godey [the publisher of *Godey's Lady's Book*] in Philadelphia, stating that Poe has told him his reason for discontinuing the "Literati" articles.

18 DECEMBER. BROOKLYN. In the *Daily Eagle* Walt Whitman reports: "It is stated that Mr. Poe, the poet and author, now lies dangerously ill with the brain fever, and that his wife is in the last stages of consumption.— They are said to be "without money and without friends, actually suffering from disease and destitution in New York."

19? DECEMBER. NEW YORK. Mrs. Hewitt writes Mrs. Osgood in Philadelphia: "The Poes are in the same state of physical & pecuniary suffering—indeed worse than they were last summer, for now the cold weather is added to their accumulation of ills. . . ."

BEFORE 23? DECEMBER. LOWELL, MASSACHUSETTS. Mrs. Jane Ermina Locke . . . sends Nathaniel P. Willis her poem "An Invocation for Suffering Genius," inspired by press reports of Poe's illness. . . .

23 DECEMBER. NEW YORK. The *Home Journal* for 26 December contains Willis' editorial . . . [proposing] that there should be an institution to assist educated and refined persons who become disabled or impoverished. . . .

23 DECEMBER. Willis writes Poe at Fordham, enclosing his editorial, the anonymous letter mentioned in it, and apparently Mrs. Locke's poem. . . .

26 DECEMBER. BOSTON. The *Bostonian,* a weekly paper, comments: "Great God! is it possible, that the literary people of the Union, will let poor Poe perish by starvation and lean faced beggary in New York? . . ."

30 DECEMBER. FORDHAM. Poe writes Nathaniel P. Willis: "The paragraph which has been put in circulation respecting my wife's illness, my own, my poverty etc., is now lying before me; together with the beautiful lines by Mrs. Locke and those by Mrs. —— to which the paragraph has given rise, as well as your kind and manly comments in 'THE HOME JOURNAL.'" Since the private affairs of Poe's family have been "thus pitilessly thrust before the public," he must make a statement clarifying "what is true and what erroneous in the report alluded to." It is true that his wife is hopelessly ill and that he himself has been "long and dangerously ill." Because of his illness Poe has been in want of money, but he has never suffered from privation beyond his powers of endurance. The statement that he is "without friends" is a complete falsehood: "Even in the city of New York I could have no difficulty in naming a hundred persons, to each of whom—when the hour for speaking had arrived—I could and would have applied for aid." Poe is now recovering his health: "The truth is, I have a great deal to do; and I have made up my mind not to die till it is done" (*PL,* 673–677).

To read about Poe in this way, day by day, week by week, is to get to know the author partly from the inside, partly from the outside; to apprehend the unfolding of his experience as it occurs—without much biographical flashback or foreshadowing; to move forward with him "without knowing" where he is heading; but, at the same time, to register the anxieties felt when the fortunes of an acquaintance begin to fluctuate. The effect is a salutary antidote to lives where the biographer structures events in advance—according to Piaget's theories of childhood development or Freud's Oedipus Complex or Marx's notion of social determinism and class warfare. The method of such intellectual or ideological constructions has the merit of clarity, but it is a clarity purchased at the expense of truth and is invariably reductive of the rich complexity of an author's actual lived experience.

At the same time, such a calendar makes one aware that Poe indeed had many friends, that he had a Southerner's point of honor and sense of chivalry, that if he had ambition it was a passion to create enduring masterworks of literature and to elevate the aesthetic taste of his country and time, and to perceive that his death was deeply mourned by those who knew him well. Poe, it is true, was often destitute and suffered the humiliation of begging or borrowing money. Sometimes he lied, drank to excess, and became surly. There is no doubt that his hard-hitting reviews alienated powerful people and that he had many enemies. But he was by no means the moral monster his enemies made him out to be. Henceforth there ought to be a special circle in Dante's hell reserved for every high school English teacher who neglects to read *The Poe Log* and goes on presenting Poe's work as if the author were one of his own demented personae, leering in the visage of Vincent Price.[7]

III

The difficulties of Poe's life were at times overwhelming. His parents, well-known thespians in the East, died when he was two. Taken in by the successful Virginia merchant John Allan, Poe grew up in comparative ease in Richmond and in England. In all respects he seems to have had a normal youth. He had many friends, was an excellent student, and had the gifts of a superior athlete in swimming, running, and boxing. But in his adolescence his literary aspirations began to estrange him from his practical foster father; they quarreled continually; and, when young Poe ran up gambling debts at the University of Virginia in 1826, he was temporarily cut off. Obliged to subsist by his own wits, he joined the army in 1827, served a hitch, was honorably discharged, and thereafter won an appointment to West Point. But the youth who had already published two books of poetry

---

7 Mine is a conviction that Poe was an artist more or less always in command of his material and therefore at a distance from his oft-deranged narrators. Yet lately the dubious idea of the identity of author and narrator seems to be making a comeback. I have in mind Jonathan Auerbach's surprising claim that Poe is to be identified with his narrators because his failures of artistic control over his "I" in many of the tales (the incapacity of the narrator fully to understand the tale that he is telling) is a sign of the confused "authorial investment" of Poe in his "fictional surrogate." Auerbach's claim can be found in *The Romance of Failure: First-Person Fictions of Poe, Hawthorne, and James* (New York: Oxford University Press, 1989), p. 25.

by the age of twenty was dissatisfied with the life of a penniless cadet and contrived to get himself dismissed. And when John Allan died in 1834, Poe was omitted entirely from the will.

After the grinding vicissitudes of an irregular life, Poe's luck took an upward turn when he joined the impoverished family of his aunt Maria Clemm, a household that included her daughter Virginia, her mother, and her nephew Henry Poe, the poet's brother. With that modicum of domestic stability, Poe began in the early 1830s to sell his short stories in Baltimore; he won some literary prizes; and he came to the attention of a local reading public. This success led to an editorial appointment on *The Southern Literary Messenger,* which gave him a ready outlet for his poetry, fiction, and criticism. In his creative and editorial capacity, Poe almost single-handedly made that journal the most important literary magazine of its time. By May 1836 he felt financially secure enough to marry his cousin Virginia, a beautiful young girl not quite fourteen at the time. Thereafter, between 1838 and 1844, he performed editorial work for *Burton's Gentleman's Magazine* and *Graham's Magazine* in Philadelphia, and then removed with his family to New York, where he wrote for Willis's *Evening Mirror* and other periodicals.

In many respects these were the happiest years of Poe's life. He was deeply and tenderly in love with his young bride.[8] Virginia's mother gave "Eddy" a maternal sympathy and love he had never had in childhood; his book reviews established him as the best literary critic in America; and his virtually unique short stories ("Ligeia," "The Fall of the House of Usher," "William Wilson," "The Murders in the Rue Morgue," "The Masque of the Red Death," "The Pit and the Pendulum") and his exotic poems ("The Raven," "Tamerlane," "Al Aaraaf," "To Helen," "Lenore," "Israfel") established him as perhaps the most brilliant and absorbing man of letters in America. Everyone, it semed, knew Poe's work.

Furthermore, his critical observations—scattered throughout his essays, reviews, and letters—established him as one of the foremost romantic literary theorists of his time. His emphasis on pleasure rather than on truth in art, on the indefinite image rather than on the discursive statement, on the priority of music and sound over

---

8 In view of the ethereal character of their love, it is bizarre to see William Bittner remark that "The only reason they could have had for getting married was that they wanted to go to bed together." See Bittner's *Poe: A Biography* (Boston: Little Brown, 1962), p. 275. But such is the animosity that characterizes Poe criticism. It should be remarked that a girl's marriage in her early teens was quite common in the 1830s in America and that there was no taboo against marriage to a distant cousin.

sense—all of these *obiter dicta,* however unoriginal, inspired his work, dazzled his contemporaries, and helped to lay the groundwork for aestheticism, surrealism, and symbolism in the *fin de siècle.* In emphasizing mood and feeling, especially melancholy and pathos, he touched the nerve of his century. Even in our era of polemical feminism, it is not difficult for many people to regard "the death of the beautiful young woman" as that artistic subject "which most induces the pleasurable excitement of melancholy."[9] Thus readers still seek in him the affective states that Poe cited as the end of art. Nor can there be any doubt that the preoccupation today with the lyric form owes much to his theory that true poetry inheres in a pleasurable excitement of the soul, or the intensity of an emotional affect, that can be achieved only in a brief lyric. He thought a rhymed poem, not an hour in length, was about all the excitement one could take in a single sitting. And his formalist insistence on a preconceived unity of effect in art has been one of the foundations of the New Criticism as practiced by Ransom, Tate, Brooks, and Warren. Poe's was essentially a jerry-built aesthetic, manufactured from piecemeal and not always fully understood reading, but in the era of Longfellow's pious moralizing and Emerson's didactic meter-making arguments in verse, it had the impact in America of a revelation of genius.

There are many evidences of Poe's high celebrity in the years in which he flourished. In December 1835, James Kirke Paulding told White of *The Southern Literary Messenger* that "Your publication is decidedly superior to any Periodical in the United States, and Mr. Poe is decidedly the best of all our going writers. I don't know but I might add all our Old Ones, with one or two exceptions" (*PL,* 184). In 1839 the St. Louis *Commercial Bulletin* commented on Poe's editorship of *Burton's:* "There are few writers in this country—take Neal, Irving, & Willis away and we would say *none*—who can compete successfully, in many respects, with Poe. With an acuteness of observation, a vigorous and effective style, and an independence that defies control, he unites a fervid fancy and a most beautiful enthusiasm. His is a high destiny" (*PL,* 269). Few would have disagreed with Park Benjamin, who in 1842 remarked in the New York *New World*: "EDGAR A. POE—We regard this gentleman as one of the best writers of the English language now living" (*PL,* 368). Furthermore, Poe's editorial duties at these journals and his residence in Richmond, Baltimore, Philadelphia, and New York had brought him into

---

9 "The Philosophy of Composition," in *Selected Writings of Edgar Allan Poe,* ed. Edward H. Davidson (Boston: Houghton Mifflin, 1956), p. 458.

contact with the major writers of his time—Albert Gallatin, Washington Irving, James Fenimore Cooper, Fitz-Greene Halleck, James K. Paulding, William Cullen Bryant, Charles King, Lewis Gaylord Clark, James Russell Lowell, and George Lippard. It is true that he made many enemies in New England, for he dared to criticize the fuzzy-minded transcendentalists and to accuse Longfellow of plagiarism. But nearly everywhere else, at the peak of his career, Poe was held in the highest regard.

But Poe's too frequent job-hopping was symptomatic of deep troubles, both personal and professional. At each of the magazines where he worked he was but an employee, and although at times he virtually controlled the literary department and dramatically improved the circulation, he was often at odds with the publisher about what the magazine ought to contain. And he never earned enough. Although he issued a continuous stream of reviews, articles, stories, and poems throughout the period, Poe was poorly paid and could not decently support his family. The absence of a satisfactory international copyright law made his works easily pirated and widely reprinted at no profit to him. Thus his fame increased, but not his store. In fulfilling his editorial duties, he was obliged to drudge for up to six hours a day, reviewing trivial and transient authors and handling correspondence, proofreading, printing, and production. These chores bored him and left him little fresh time for creative work, and he sometimes sought refuge in drink. At times he failed to proofread an issue or to supply sufficient copy and alienated his bosses; and he could be nasty and egotistical when drunk. He wanted and needed a journal of his own, and for a period of years sought backers for a new magazine of literature and criticism. But the economic conditions in the 1840s were not propitious.

We must add to these professional problems the tragedies of his personal life. His wife and mother-in-law, whom he loved with a tenderness and devotion truly remarkable, were constantly in want. Mrs. Clemm did what she could as his messenger, delivering manuscripts and review copies and receiving payments. But there was never enough money. Virginia came down with tuberculosis in 1842 and, during the next five years, her hemorrhages were recurrent and progressive, culminating in her death in 1847. The emotional ordeal of watching her die sent Poe into a profound depression. Those closest to him felt keenly the tragedy of Virginia's recurrent hemorrhages and Poe's recurrent disintegrations. Her death, they all knew, was a fated event. George R. Graham, the publisher, remarked:

I shall never forget how solicitous of the happiness of his wife and mother-in-law he was, whilst one of the editors of Graham's Magazine—his whole efforts seemed to be to procure the comfort and welfare of his home. Except for their happiness—and the natural ambition of having a magazine of his own—I never heard him deplore the want of wealth. The truth is, he cared little for money, and knew less of its value, for he seemed to have no personal expenses. What he received from me in regular monthly instalments, went directly into the hands of his mother-in-law. . . . His love for his wife was a sort of rapturous worship of the spirit of beauty which he felt was fading before his eyes. I have seen him hovering around her when she was ill, with all the fond fear and tender anxiety of a mother for her first-born—her slightest cough causing in him a shudder, a heart-chill that was visible (*PL,* 390).

As a consequence of these pressures, Poe drank—irregularly but sometimes to excess. He went through long periods of cold sobriety but could fall off the wagon at any time and be found wandering the streets in a state of delirium. Some of his "sprees" were publicly reported in the press and circulated throughout the country; and, in an era of aggressive temperance reform, Poe was condemned as immoral rather than seen as the victim of a disease. After reports of his drinking had been circulating for some time, he tried to defend himself to his friend Joseph Snodgrass.

It is, however, due to candor that I inform you upon what foundations he [the publisher Burton] has erected his slanders. At no period of my life was I ever what men call intemperate. I never was in the *habit* of intoxication. I never drunk drams, &c. But, for a brief period, while I resided in Richmond, and edited the *Messenger,* I certainly did give way, at long intervals, to the temptation held out on all sides by the spirit of Southern conviviality. My sensitive temperament could not stand an excitement which was an everyday matter to my companions. In short, it sometimes happened that I was completely intoxicated. For some days after each excess I was invariably confined to bed. But it is now quite four years since I have abandoned every kind of alcoholic drink—four years, with the exception of a single deviation, which occurred shortly *after* my leaving Burton, and when I was induced to resort to the occasional use of *cider,* with the hope of relieving a nervous attack (*PL,* 322).

These remarks are the rationalizations of an alcoholic, but it is doubtless true that Poe became intoxicated exceptionally easily. He told his friend George W. Eveleth that when Virginia began to hem-horrage and he despaired of her life, he

> took leave of her forever & underwent all the agonies of her death. She recovered partially and I again hoped. At the end of a year the vessel broke again—I went through precisely the same scene. Again in about a year afterward. Then again—again—again & even once again at varying intervals. Each time I felt all the agonies of her death—and at each accession of the disorder I loved her more dearly & clung to her life with more desperate pertinacity. But I am con-stitutionally sensitive—nervous in a very unusual degree. I became insane, with long intervals of horrible sanity. During these fits of ab-solute unconsciousness I drank, God only knows how often or how much (*PL,* 716).

If this is true, it is likewise the case that he led a generally ab-stemious life, "a studious and literary life," as he called it, that was not seen by the public. But, shattered personally and professionally, he did succumb to the compulsion to drink. And while traveling through Baltimore in 1849, Poe fell in with some bibulous acquain-tances and was discovered on October 3 at Gunners Hall, a local tavern, drunk and incoherent. It was Election Day, ballots were cast in the tavern, and the ward heelers had made sure that drinks were plentiful. Neilson Poe, the poet's cousin, later told Griswold that Poe had "passed, by *a single indulgence,* from a condition of perfect sobriety to one bordering upon the madness usually occasioned only by long continued intoxication . . ." (*PL,* 844). However that may be, Poe was carried to a Baltimore hospital, where he died on October 7 in a state of *delirium tremens* brought on by the fatal effects of toxic withdrawal. After his interment, J. Alden Weston, a young admirer, remarked:

> The burial ceremony, which did not occupy more than three minutes, was so cold-blooded and unchristianlike as to provoke on my part a sense of anger difficult to suppress. . . . In justice to the people of Baltimore I must say that if the funeral had been post-poned for a single day, until the death was generally known, a far more imposing escort to the tomb and one more worthy of the many admirers of the poet in the city would have taken place (*PL,* 848).

Poe's defense of his studious life has considerable merit. A total sot could not have produced such a large and important literary *oeuvre.* And it may be true that a single drink triggered these toxic reactions. Was liquor a poison rooted in the family's physiological constitution? Did Poe have an hereditary "predisposition" toward alcoholism? William Poe, the brother of Edgar's grandfather, seemed to think so, for he issued this warning to the poet in 1843: "There is one thing I am anxious to caution you against, & which has been a great enemy to our family, I hope, however in yr case, it may prove unnecessary, 'A too free use of the Bottle.' Too many & especially Literary Characters, have sought to drown their sorrows & disappointments by this means, but in vain, and only, when it has been too late, discovered it to be a deeper source of misery" (*PL,* 415). Perhaps there is another basis for the idea of a predisposition brought on in childhood. Jane Scott Mackenzie later remembered that when she had visited Poe's dying mother in 1811, she found that "the children [Poe and his sister Rosalie] were thin and pale and very fretful. To quiet them, their old nurse . . . took them upon her lap and fed them liberally with bread soaked in gin, when they soon fell asleep." The nurse confessed to Mrs. Mackenzie that for more than a year she had "freely administered to them gin and other spirituous liquors, with sometimes laudanum, 'to make them strong and healthy,' or to put them to sleep when restless . . ." (*PL,* 14).[10]

IV

If the moral objections to Poe's character were not enough to sink him, another kind of criticism has subsequently affected the poet's critical reputation. This is the view that Poe's is essentially a puerile sensibility that appeals to the juvenile. Henry James, in his comments on Baudelaire's *Les Fleurs du Mal,* said in 1876 that to take Poe

> with more than a certain degree of seriousness is to lack seriousness one's self. An enthusiasm for Poe is the mark of a decidedly primitive stage of reflection. Baudelaire thought him a profound philosopher, the neglect of whose golden utterances stamped his native land with infamy. Nevertheless, Poe was the much greater charlatan of the two, as well as the greater genius.[11]

T. S. Eliot likewise remarked in "From Poe to Valéry" that "If we examine his work in detail, we seem to find in it nothing but slipshod

---

10 For a rich (if confusing) meditation on Poe that deals with many other matters more philosophically transcendent than the poet in his cups, see Marion Montgomery's strange compendium *Why Poe Drank Liquor* (La Salle, Ill.: Sherwood Sugden, 1983).
11 Henry James, "Charles Baudelaire," *Literary Criticism: French Writers, Other European Writers. . .,* ed. Leon Edel (New York: Library of America, 1984), p. 154.

writing, puerile thinking unsupported by wide reading or profound scholarship, haphazard experiments in various types of writing, chiefly under the pressure of financial need, without perfection in any detail."[12] Eliot thought that Poe's verse and fiction appealed to some primitive domain of the psyche and, although his work stuck, it is not work of the kind to which we return again and again. This is reminiscent of James Russell Lowell's comment in "A Fable for Critics":

> There comes Poe, with his raven, like Barnaby Rudge,
> Three-fifths of him genius and two-fifths sheer fudge. . . ."[13]

Eliot was dismayed at the high reputation of Poe in France—particularly in the criticism of Baudelaire, Mallarmé, and Valéry. For, indeed, it was through this Gallic admiration that Poe's reputation was partly sustained after his death and even revivified in the twentieth century, thanks to deeper interest in France in *l'art pour l'art* aestheticism, surrealism, oneiric literature, and psychoanalysis.[14] In calling attention to Poe in France, Baudelaire told Théophile Thoré that "The first time that I opened one of his books I was shocked and delighted to see not only subjects which I had dreamed of, but SENTENCES which I had thought and which he had written twenty years before."[15] Baudelaire translated a good many of Poe's tales, and, in *Edgar Poe, sa vie et ses oeuvres* (1856), he represented him as *le poète maudit,* an outcast artist in materialist America whose critical ideas in "The Poetic Principle" and "The Philosophy of Composition" had outlined a brilliant aesthetic formed in opposition to the coarse con-

---

12 Eliot, "From Poe to Valéry," in *The Recognition of Edgar Allan Poe: Selected Criticism Since 1829,* pp. 205, 207–208.

13 James Russell Lowell, "A Fable for Critics," in *The Romantic Triumph: American Literature from 1830 to 1860,* ed. Tremaine McDowell (New York: Macmillan, 1949), p. 679.

14 On the French view of Poe and Anglo-American stupefaction with it, see also Celestin Pierre Cambiaire's *The Influence of Edgar Allan Poe in France* (New York: G. E. Stechert, 1927), Léon Lemonnier's *Edgar Poe et la Critique Française de 1845 à 1875* (Paris: Presses Universitaires de France, 1928), Patrick F. Quinn's *The French Face of Edgar Poe* (Carbondale: Southern Illinois University Press, 1957), and, more recently, John Weightman's "Poe in France: A Myth Revisited," in *Edgar Allan Poe: The Design of Order,* ed. A. Robert Lee (London: Vision Press, 1987), pp. 202–219. For a modern French view of Poe (in the light of Derrida, Lacan, and the usual Parisian suspects), see Jefferson Humphries' rather polysyllabic *Metamorphoses of the Raven: Literary Overdeterminedness in France and the South Since Poe* (Baton Rouge: Louisiana State University Press, 1985), which supplies its own glossary of arcane terms—*aporia, aseity, semiosis*—yet still fails of lucidity.

15 Baudelaire, *Correspondance Générale,* Letter 844 (IV, 277); quoted in *Baudelaire on Poe: Critical Papers,* trans. Lois and Francis E. Hyslop, Jr. (State College, Pa.: Bald Eagle Press, 1952), p. 30.

temporary political ideologies and arrant didacticism in art.

Poe's opposition to the didactic was refined in many public lectures on poetry and criticism in many cities along the Eastern seaboard, occasionally to audiences as large as two thousand listeners. On August 21, 1849, in the Richmond *Semi-Weekly Examiner,* the reviewer John M. Daniel remarked that Poe's lecture exploded "what he very properly pronounced to be the poetic 'heresy of modern times,' to wit: that poetry should have a purpose, an end to accomplish beyond that of ministering to our sense of the beautiful." There appears to have been an excessive number of ideological poets then operative: Daniel complained of "the poets of humanity and poets of universal suffrage, poets whose mission it is to break down corn laws and poets to build up workhouses." Poe's aestheticism was thus a refreshing reaction to the moralizing milieu in which he wrote. Literary taste in American culture had also been corrupted by an overweening nationalism. Emerson had complained in 1836 that we had listened too long to "the Courtly muses of Europe"[16] and said that we ought to have a properly appreciated indigenous American art; and the book reviewers—according to the Washington *National Intelligencer* in the same year—began to give "exorbitant and indiscriminate praise to every American book." The nationalistic spirit was so pernicious that, "no sooner was a novel, poem, or any work of any species, published as the production of an American author, than the periodical press, unanimously, throughout the land, were occupied in singing its praises; and in this manner many a spurious and utterly untenable reputation has been attained" (*PL,* 231).

That book reviewing then (as now) was a game of puffery and back-scratching is suggested by the career of Griswold himself, who told J. T. Fields, of the Boston publisher Ticknor & Company, that "I puff your books, you know, without any regard to their quality" (*PL,* 377). Although Poe himself was not guiltless of this vice, especially where good-looking female writers were concerned, he was generally appalled at the state of criticism in his time and the corruption of literary standards. Interwoven into his reviews and essays is a sometimes implicit, often explicit expression of the principles by which a literary criticism ought to emerge. In his practice as a reviewer, however, this insistence on sound principles sometimes produced *ad hominem* criticism. As the *National Intelligencer* put it, Poe

boldly took up the cudgels against so pernicious an evil, and suc-

---

16 Ralph Waldo Emerson, "The American Scholar," in *Ralph Waldo Emerson: Essays & Lectures,* ed. Joel Porte (New York: Library of America, 1983), p. 70.

ceeded in shaking the throne of popular faith to its centre, by a series of attacks, bold, well-directed and irresistible, against a number of the most popular authors of the day. The system, too, has been followed up ever since with an industry so untiring, and impartiality so unimpeachable, an ability so undeniable, as to have extorted admiration from all sources . . . (*PL*, 231).

But if at first readers liked Poe's critical objectivity, he eventually developed the reputation of excessive bile, of tomahawking defenseless incompetents, and the effect of his criticism was rather like that of John Simon today. Meanwhile, his poems and stories came to be seen as brilliant productions but "without any redeeming admonition to the heart." For such complaints against him, Poe of course cared little. As he remarked in the Preface to *The Raven and Other Poems* (1845), "With me poetry has been not a purpose, but a passion; and the passions should be held in reverence; they must not—they cannot at will be excited with an eye to the paltry compensations, or the more paltry commendations, of mankind."[17]

V

Poe's grand indifference to the opinions of mankind suggests that profound dissatisfaction with the conditions of this world voiced in so many of his otherworldly works. *Eureka: A Prose Poem,* "the summary and apotheosis of his beliefs,"[18] in particular elaborates the sources of his strange preoccupation with the paradisal otherworldly life beyond the grave. Dedicated to Alexander von Humboldt, and reflecting his reading in LaPlace, Newton, Ferguson, Coleridge, and others, *Eureka* ascribes Creative Volition to the deity, Simplicity to the Divine Nature, and Original Unity as the primal condition. Creation was the fracturing of the Original Unity into the Many. While through diffusion multiplicity occurs, there is a necessary reaction to diffusion in the tendency of disunited particles or atoms to want to return to the oneness prior to the phenomenal creation. Poe invokes mathematics, science, and romantic intuition to assert that "each soul is, in part, its own God—its own Creator:—in a word, that God—the material *and* spiritual God—*now* exists solely in the diffused Matter and Spirit of the Universe; and that the re-gathering

17 *The Complete Works of Edgar Allan Poe,* ed. James A. Harrison (1902; reprinted New York: AMS Press, 1965), p. xlvii.

18 Margaret Alterton and Hardin Craig, "Introduction," *Edgar Allan Poe: Representative Selections* (1935; reprinted New York: Hill & Wang, 1962), p. xxxv.

of this diffused Matter and Spirit will be but the re-constitution of the *purely* spiritual and individual God." Daniel Hoffman has rightly remarked that "Half a hundred years before *le malaise du fin du siècle,* Poe had understood, had intuited, had *felt* as true the undeniable principle that we, and our universe, contain within ourselves, intrinsic with our very being, the seeds of our own destruction—which we unconsciously *long for*."[19] The protagonists of Poe's art are projections of this longing and this vision; they are men of imagination, exiles from a primal Paradise, voyagers in a strange land—this disease of our material existence. They have their real being in an Ideal World marked by a Unity and Oneness occurring in some primordial far-off antiquity. Thus there is next to no social context in Poe's tales and poems.

Although he lived at a particularly turbulent time in America—while the westering movement was afoot, immigration was constant, urbanization was dawning, abolitionism and slavery were gearing up for the Civil War—Poe was never interested in giving reportorial or journalistic accounts of the sociological features of American life. For Poe, the artistic vision that might capture an intuition of paradise was the only thing that mattered. It was his passionate means of trying to unify the fragmented world of fallen reality, to recover from the primal alienation produced by the creation itself. He therefore trafficked in the nostalgia of loss, in an ideality known only in dreams, his substitute for the horrifying actuality of the quotidian life. "Israfel," "Ligeia," "The Fall of the House of Usher," *Pym,* "Annabelle Lee," and "Lenore" all allegorize a longing for immortality, for this lost world of Ideal Existence before birth. Accompanying this nostalgia is a concomitant fear of death and annihilation, with obsessive brooding about physical and psychological decay—the grim phantasm of fear afflicting the reason and bringing it to the point of madness, a fear reflected in his characters' preoccupation with dreams, trances, hypnosis, catalepsy, and metempsychosis. Above all, he longed for a love that survives death, bodily dissolution, and the grave. Art, whether created or appreciated, was a means of transcending the paltry circumstances of the actual and attaining the effect of an intimation of immortality. As he put it in "The Poetic Principle," the faculty of ideality in us creates a thirst that is not a mere

appreciation of the Beauty before us—but a wild effort to reach the

---

19 Daniel Hoffman, *Poe Poe Poe Poe Poe Poe Poe* (Garden City, N.Y.: Doubleday, 1973), p. 287.

Beauty above. Inspired by an ecstatic prescience of the glories beyond the grave, we struggle by multiform combinations among things and thoughts of Time to attain a portion of that Loveliness whose very elements perhaps appertain to Eternity alone. And thus when by Poetry—or when by Music, the most entrancing of the Poetic moods—we find ourselves melted into tears—we weep them —not as the Abbate Gravina supposes—through excess of pleasure, but through a certain petulant, impatient sorrow at our inability to grasp *now*, wholly, here on earth, at once and for ever, those divine and rapturous joys, of which *through* the poem, or *through* the music, we attain to but brief and indeterminate glances.[20]

Thus through art we are meant to get a glimpse of that supernal beauty, existent before the fall into birth, that is our eventual destiny.

Poe's relation to these materials is poorly understood, for his speculative cosmology is the incoherent thought of an overworked autodidact. Readers with an interest in ideas in literature have tried to find in his antihumanist worldview a coherent philosophic statement, but without complete success.[21] Poe's grandly elaborated impatience with this valley of unrest seems to appeal most to Freudian critics, for the single perceiving self (the subject of the great works) is a self in quest of its own annihilation. And from Marie Bonaparte onward, we have had a string of psychobiographies (those of J. W. Krutch, J. W. Robertson, and David M. Rein, for example), each one so bizarre that, as Geoffrey Rams has remarked, they "must be disregarded except as curiosities, so tenuous is their command of the rules of evidence, and so ready to accept hearsay, and to treat their own speculations as fact."[22] Yet works like *The Poe Log* and Kenneth Silverman's *Edgar A. Poe: Mournful and Never-ending Remembrance* bring us back to the practicing journalist, poet, and fiction writer, to the man who lived in a material world of editors and publishers, books and manuscripts. Such biogaphical records also wonderfully tether Poe's wild flights in the actualities of his life and show us the romantic rhapsode in the context of the hurried polemical journalism of his own time. They make intimate to us the husband and son-in-law "Eddy" behind the self-created myth of the tortured romantic artist.

---

20 "The Poetic Principle," in *Selected Writings of Edgar Allan Poe*, p. 470.
21 The most brilliant exposition of Poe's cosmology will be found in Richard Wilbur's "Introduction to Poe," in *The Laurel Poe* (New York: Dell, 1959).
22 Geoffrey Rams, *Edgar Allan Poe* (Edinburgh and London: Oliver and Boyd, 1965), p. 101.

Howells
and the Manners
of the Good Heart

William Dean Howells (1837–1920) will probably always be of interest to the student of the novel of manners in America because of the considerable art with which he embodied the democratic egalitarian social assumptions of the developing West in which he grew up. The son of a backcountry Ohio newspaperman, Howells spent his youth in small-town newspaper offices unconsciously assimilating the Western egalitarianism that marked the politics of Jackson and Lincoln. Later, when as a young man he came to have a wider knowledge of the world, "the vision of the West as the ideal land of freedom, equality and purity was constantly present in his mind and could only occasionally be blurred by dark events. It became a constant source of inspiration to him," as Olov Fryckstedt has rightly observed, and "it is only from this experience that we can fully understand the enthusiasm and the loving care with which he depicted the commonplace realities of American life in novel after novel."[1] Even after Howells had become a well-known novelist, the editor of the *Atlantic Monthly,* and the intimate friend of the New England Brahmins who constituted the arbiters of taste in America, he did not repudiate his Western egalitarian values. As Henry Steele Commager has rightly suggested of the mature Howells, "the dictator of literary Boston and, eventually, of literary America, Howells never forgot his frontier origins or abandoned his democratic

---

1 Olov Fryckstedt, *In Quest of America: A Study of Howells' Early Development as a Novelist* (Upsala: Dissertation Upsala University, 1958), pp. 38–39.

simplicity."[2] This point deserves to be made and made emphatically because in the years immediately following his death, Howells was accused of toadying to the genteel aristocracy of the East. When we consider that Howells had by this time become (of all things) a *socialist,* the idea of his capitulation to some Eastern aristocratic standard is of course arrant nonsense.

One form of this old charge appears in Arthur Boardman's claim that Howells romanticized the upper classes, identified with their values, and asserted the glamour and superiority of the aristocracy with "the effect of contradicting the egalitarian theme Howells expressed in the novels protesting great social injustices."[3] This form of revisionism strikes me as no more creditable than the earlier attacks on Howells in the generation of H. L. Mencken and Sinclair Lewis. The fact is that few men of his time were more capable than Howells of representing accurately in fiction the social contradictions that characterized American life in the last twenty-five years of the nineteenth century. His canvas was never a large one, but he understood what he saw. And what he saw was the spectacle of simple Westerners like himself thrown up against hypercivilized Boston snobs, of provincial country folk deracinated and struggling to find themselves in the developing cities, of the underworld of the urban laboring poor, and of newly rich millionaires trying to crash polite society—in other words, a broad spectrum of manners and mores which could be sympathetically brought into dramatic relief through the medium of the travel narrative and the novel of manners.

His first two novels—*Their Wedding Journey* and *A Chance Acquaintance*—employ the travel structure to bring into apposition the variety and multiplicity of American manners in Boston and the provinces and the differences between the commonplace world of America and the picturesque antiquities of the Canadian scene. His use of the travel structure is not surprising. "I was a traveller long before I was a noveler," Howells once noted, "and I . . . mounted somewhat timidly to the threshold of fiction from the high-roads and by-roads where I had studied manners and men."[4] Perhaps more by accident than design, Howells discovered in the travel narrative one of the most effective devices in the novel of manners: the neutral setting

2 Henry Steele Commager, "The Return to Howells," *The War of the Critics over William Dean Howells,* eds. E. H. Cady and D. L. Frazier (Evanston: Row, Peterson, 1962), pp. 191–192.

3 Arthur Boardman, "Social Point of View in the Novels of William Dean Howells," *American Literature,* 39 (1967), 42.

4 Howells is quoted in J. Henry Harper's *The House of Harper: A Century of Publishing in Franklin Square* (New York: Harper and Brothers, 1912), p. 326.

which brings together characters from a variety of social backgrounds and generates its action out of the conflict of opposing manners. *A Chance Acquaintance* and *The Lady of the Aroostook* particularly employ this device, explore the social contradictions of American society, and permit Howells the opportunity to affirm the social value of the democratic social and political ideal.

II

In *A Chance Acquaintance,* Colonel Ellison and his wife Fanny, from Milwaukee, who are traveling up the Saguenay to Quebec and down again to Boston with their niece, Kitty Ellison of Eriecreek, New York, accidentally make the acquaintance of Miles Arbuton, a rather reserved Bostonian whom they mistake for an Englishman. In the course of the long trip in the novel, Miles and Kitty—despite what Howells calls the "incompatibility of Boston and Eriecreek tradi- tions"—fall in love.[5] Although they have practically nothing in com- mon except their youth and good looks, they head back to Boston betrothed. The critical moment in the relationship of Miles and Kitty occurs on the porch of an inn where Miles unexpectedly meets two Boston ladies whom he knows. Stupefied at seeing them so far from home, Miles at first neglects to introduce them to Kitty, and, as the women draw Miles farther and farther down the piazza, Miles feels "obliged" to leave Kitty sitting on the porch alone and to accompany the ladies all the way down to their boat. This scene is one of great embarrassment to Kitty. It turns, she at first believes, on a point of manners: "Why, how stupid I am!" she thinks. "Of course a gentle- man can't introduce ladies; and the one thing for him to do is to ex- cuse himself to them as soon as he can, without rudeness, and come back to me" (*CA,* 260).

But the real issue, as she eventually perceives, is that Miles is too ashamed to introduce Kitty to his fashionable Boston friends because she is too countrified. When he finally comes back, and her shame convicts him of his rudeness, he has the honesty to recognize that his manners have been outrageous. "He saw it with paralyzing clearness; and, as an inexorable fact that confounded quite as much as it dis- mayed him, he perceived that throughout that ignoble scene she had been the gentle person and he the vulgar one" (*CA,* 267). Arbu- ton—with his exquisite and aristocratic bearing, his sophisticated and

---

5 William Dean Howells, *A Chance Acquaintance* (Boston: J. R. Osgood, 1872), p. 242. Hereafter, quotations from this work will be cited as *CA,* in parentheses, in the text.

civilized style, his "fastidious good looks and his blameless manners"—is shown to be proud of place, arrogant of social distinctions, and deficient in human feeling—the feeling of common humanity. By his rudeness to Kitty, in fact, he has proved himself to be "all gloves and slim umbrella,—the mere husk of well-dressed culture and good manners" (*CA*, 152).

To bring *A Chance Acquaintance* into political focus, in terms of the distinction between the Jeffersonian *aristoi* and the Jacksonian common man, is not at all to distort the social significance of the novel. Howells was distressed enough at the superciliousness of the *aristoi* in Boston to create in Kitty a truly democratic heroine, a girl meant to be the lovely average of American girlhood capable of putting to shame the so-called civilized Boston snob. As Kitty writes of Miles to one of her girlfriends in Eriecreek: "He has been a good deal abroad, and he is Europeanized enough not to think much of America, though I can't find that he quite approves of Europe, and his experience seems not to have left him any particular country in either hemisphere." In addition, he "believes in 'vulgar and meretricious distinctions' of all sorts, and . . . hasn't an atom of 'magnanimous democracy' in him. In fact," she goes on,

> I find, to my great astonishment, that some ideas which I thought were held only in England, and which I had never seriously thought of, seem actually a part of Mr. Arbuton's nature or education. He talks about the lower classes, and tradesmen, and the best people, and good families, as I supposed nobody in *this* country *ever* did,—in earnest (*CA*, 134–135).

Kitty has no experience with exclusionary attitudes of this type; they strike her as the stuff of sentimental English romances, not facts of American life, and she can hardly believe that Arbuton seriously means what he says.

Kitty's inability to understand Arbuton's snobbishness is to be accounted for by the republican conditions of American life and history that have shaped her sense of values. Howells makes Kitty out to be the daughter of a small country editor, a Free Soil man in Kansas before the Civil War who was murdered in one of the border feuds. Taken in by an uncle back in Eriecreek, she grew up among a family of ardent abolitionists whose house was a stopover for slaves on the underground railroad to Canada. She had sat in the lap of Osawatomie John Brown and heard him sing "Blow ye the trumpet, blow!" For Kitty and her family, Boston represented a place of "humanitarian pre-eminence," the home of the great New England abolitionists, "of the author of the 'Biglow Papers,' of Senator Sumner, of Mr. Whittier, of Dr. Howe, of Colonel Higginson, and of Mr. Garrison" (*CA*, 9). For the Ellisons, Boston was "not only the birthplace of American liberty, but the yet holier scene of its resurrection." When he learns that Kitty is going to Boston, her uncle reminds her that

> there everything that is noble and grand and liberal and enlightened in the national life has originated, and I cannot doubt that you will find the character of its people marked by every attribute of a magnanimous democracy. If I could envy you anything, my dear girl, I should envy you this privilege of seeing a city where man is valued simply and solely for what he is in himself, and where color, wealth, family, occupation, and other vulgar and meretricious distinctions are wholly lost sight of in the consideration of individual excellence (*CA*, 10).

Kitty's presuppositions about the glory of New England are destroyed in her encounter with Miles Arbuton. And it is a mark of her intelligence that she comes to understand very quickly the exclusiveness of this quasi-aristocracy and to recognize that she and Miles could never be happy together as man and wife. Her rejection of Miles, then, is an affirmation of democratic American manners. Arbuton might not have been titled, but Kitty's refusal of marriage tells as convincingly for American social values as Bessie Alden's rejection of Lord Lambeth in James's "An International Episode" (1878) or Isabel's refusal of Lord Warburton in *The Portrait of a Lady* (1881). In fact, it is possible to say that James saw in *A Chance Acquaintance* how the Howellsian comedy of manners could be employed to assert distinctively American social values.

Some years ago, in *William Dean Howells: The Development of a Novelist,* George N. Bennett claimed that "*A Chance Acquaintance* did not need to be narrowly interpreted as a novel of manners."[6] He said this because a good many contemporary critics, following the lead of Lionel Trilling in *The Liberal Imagination,* wrote off the novel of manners as a form pertinent to American social experience. Still, I can see no other way to penetrate to the social significance that lies at the heart of the novel—the moral superiority of "natural nobility" to artificial forms of gentility—than to recognize at the outset that the novel turns on the question of manners. Arbuton's bad manners

---

6 George N. Bennett, *William Dean Howells: The Development of a Novelist* (Norman: University of Oklahoma Press, 1959), p. 21.

occur in a context where we cannot possibly mistake Howells's affirmation of egalitarian political and social values. To recognize this is not to narrow its significance but rather to get to the heart of Howells's conception of the relation of manners and values. The informed historical critic can never forget that Howells cherished the novel of manners, that he loved its potential for the realistic notation of our commonplace, democratic, middle-class American life, and that his greatest achievements—*A Modern Instance, The Rise of Silas Lapham,* and *A Hazard of New Fortunes*—distinguish the form. Until he turned to the economic romance in the 1890s, Howells's achievement suggests how skillfully he charged the novel of manners with those implied political and social considerations that brought the form to a high level of artistic competence.

The indictment of aristocratic manners in *A Chance Acquaintance* was certainly not lost on his Boston readers. Quite a few Bostonians thought Howells a Western upstart who had never known a gentleman or who knew only one kind of Bostonian. But his most sensitive critics recognized how Howells's treatment of manners here constituted "the first of a long series of attacks on Proper Boston."[7] Thomas Sergeant Perry, who by an odd coincidence was in part the model for Arbuton, commended Howells's "national spirit" in the *Century Magazine*. He praised "the way Mr. Howells shows the . . . emptiness of convention and the dignity of native worth." It is "one of the main conditions of American, if not of modern, society," Perry observed, "that inborn merit has a chance to assert itself." And this possibility was nowhere more tellingly asserted than in the comparison of Kitty and Arbuton. If the old lines were being destroyed, Perry observed, it was because "the democratic hero" had done much in literature to speed up the process. "After all, what can realism produce but the downfall of conventionality. Just as the scientific spirit digs the ground from beneath superstition, so does its fellow-worker, realism, tend to prick the bubble of abstract types. Realism is the tool of the democratic spirit, and Mr. Howells's realism is untiring."[8]

Henry James, whose attitudes toward America were rather like Arbuton's, was less complimentary to the novel, finding it a slight affair. But he did believe that Kitty was a real creation and that "in bringing her through with such unerring felicity, your imagination

7 Edwin Cady, *The Road to Realism: The Early Years, 1837-1885, of William Dean Howells* (Syracuse: Syracuse University Press, 1956), p. 183.
8 T. S. Perry, "William Dean Howells," *Century Magazine*, 33 (1882), 683. See also Virginia Harlow's *Thomas Sergeant Perry* (Durham: Duke University Press, 1950).

has *fait ses preuves.*" [9] Miles, he thought, was a straw man. Howells agreed that the situation between his couple was contrived, but "well- or ill-advisedly," he rejoined, he had

> conceived the notion of confronting two extreme American types: the conventional and the unconventional. These always disgust each other, but I amused myself with the notion of their falling in love, which would not be impossible, if they were both young and good looking. Now conventionality is, in our condition of things, in itself a caricature; and I did my best for the young man, but his nature was against him, and he is the stick you see.

Howells always felt that the rituals of aristocratic society were artificial, and he could not help representing them as play-acting, a kind of drawing-room theatrical, an elaborate charade of the European conventionalities, or—better yet—a stage farce which couldn't be taken very seriously by anyone. He concluded by saying that he felt he had "learnt a great deal in writing the story" and that if it didn't destroy his public he would be "weaponed better than ever" for a career in fiction.[10]

In view of Howells' assault on the genteel Boston gentleman, his manifest preference for the natural simplicities of democratic small-town life, it is surprising that so many critics have misunderstood him. One can do nothing with Bernard Smith's claim that when Howells found in Boston "the culture, the temper, the manners he admired, he gave himself to it unreservedly and was stamped genteel for life" or with C. Hartley Grattan's claim that Howells "accepted the New England environment at Boston's evaluation and took Boston's judgments as his own." [11] These views grossly oversimplify a complex attitude toward the several interconnected Bostons. Howells principally admired the Boston that stood for plain living and high thinking, the "cleanly decencies" of American life, the high attainments of American writing, and the pure simplicity of an unassuming social organization. Family counted for something in Boston, certainly, he later wrote, "but family alone did not mean position, and the want of family did not mean the want of it." Money, still less than family, commanded: "one could be openly poor in Cambridge

9 *The Letters of Henry James,* ed. Percy Lubbock (New York: Scribner's, 1920), I, 34.
10 *Life in Letters of William Dean Howells,* ed. Mildred Howells (Garden City, N.Y.: Doubleday, 1928), I, 174–175.
11 Bernard Smith, "Howells: The Genteel Radical" (p. 172), and C. Hartley Grattan, "Howells: Ten Years After" (p. 159), in *The War of the Critics over William Dean Howells.*

without open shame, or shame at all, for no one was very rich there, and no one was proud of his riches." Howells's real Boston interests were "the intellectual interests, and all other interests were lost in these to such as did not seek them too insistently." [12] The Boston Howells did not like, as *A Chance Acquaintance* makes clear, was "a Boston of mysterious prejudices and lofty reservations; a Boston of high and difficult tastes, that found its social ideal in the Old World, and that shrank from the reality of this; a Boston as alien as Europe"; a city

> that seemed to be proud only of the things that were unlike other American things; a Boston that would rather perish by fire and sword than be suspected of vulgarity; a critical, fastidious, and reluctant Boston, dissatisfied with the rest of the hemisphere, and gelidly self-satisfied in so far as it was not in the least the Boston of her [Kitty's] fond preconceptions (*CA*, 151–152).

III

A Foregone Conclusion (1875), *The Lady of the Aroostook* (1879), and *A Fearful Responsibility* (1881) also employ the travel narrative designed to bring into dramatic relief manners and values, but in these novels Howells Europeanizes the setting in order to take advantage of the international theme. Each documents the minutiae of international manners—the quaint Italian custom of cutting up all of one's meat beforehand; the American breakfast of hot beefsteak and fried potatoes; the scandal of European fingernails; the custom of tucking one's napkin into his collar—and for each the plot turns in some crucial way on the expression of national manners. In these as well as in the earlier novels I have mentioned, his technique was to lift people out of the environments which separate them, free them of their "baggage," confine them aboard a ship or in a train or boardinghouse, put them into some sort of dramatic juxtaposition, and study how their manners and values are modified under the pressure of the experience.

The strategy of *The Lady of the Aroostook* is to put his characters in apposition aboard a ship. The novel recounts the journey from Boston to Venice of Lydia Blood, an upcountry schoolmarm from South Bradfield, Massachusetts, who is as lovely and charming as Kitty El-

---

12 William Dean Howells, *Literary Friends and Acquaintance: A Personal Retrospect of American Authorship* (New York: Harper and Brothers, 1900), p. 286.

lison, and of Staniford, a Europeanized Boston gentleman who is traveling abroad with his friend Dunham. The point at issue in the novel, a question of manners, is that Lydia is the only woman aboard, unchaperoned and unescorted, at a time when the proprieties simply forbade such freedom.

At the beginning of the voyage of the *Aroostook,* when Staniford perceives that Lydia "has been placed in a position which could be made very painful to her," he suggests to Dunham that "it's our part to prevent it from being so. I doubt if she finds it at all anomalous, and if we choose she need never do so till after we've parted with her. I fancy, " he wagers, "we can preserve her unconsciousness intact."[13] Being Americans, "they knew how to worship a woman" (*LA,* 95), Howells ironically observes, and all of the men aboard, including the crew, make her the object of chivalrous attention. Lydia, like the "unsuspecting" Daisy Miller, never knows how improper her position has been until after she has arrived in Venice.

If Lydia is a version of Kitty Ellison, Staniford is a Miles Arbuton bound for pleasure in Europe. Sophisticated, intelligent, a good talker and a handsome fellow, Staniford regards himself as much too civilized for the society of a country girl like Lydia; he therefore avoids her company aboard ship and is content to gossip with those who do socialize with her. Facetious, he conjectures that "she has never known anything like society," and he doubts that she has ever seen "anything livelier than a township cattle show, or a Sunday-school picnic, in her life." "They don't pay visits in the country," Staniford observes, "except at rare intervals, and their evening parties, when they have any, are something to strike you dead with pity." This supercilious conception of the social life of small-town America is not wholly serious on Staniford's part, but Howells has Staniford lay it on thick because he wants occasion to demonstrate just what the effect might be on Lydia of this alleged meagerness of the social experience of provincial life. Howells was almost surely reaching back into his youth in Ohio when Staniford describes how "they used to clear away the corn-husks and pumpkins on the barn floor, and dance by the light of tin lanterns. At least, that's the usual thing. The actual thing is sitting around four sides of the room, giggling, whispering, looking at photograph albums, and coaxing somebody to play on the piano." Staniford concludes, "I wonder our country people don't all go mad" (*LA,* 70–71).

---

13 Howells, *The Lady of the Aroostook* (Boston: Houghton, Osgood, 1879), pp. 57–58. Quotations from this novel will hereafter be cited as *LA,* in parentheses, in the text.

Staniford's prejudices arise from the fact that all of the social rituals of the upper class in Boston (the society luncheon, the tea, the "at home," the formal dinner and dance) derive from European social customs. Howells genuinely regretted that the American aristocracy regarded as "low class" all of the native American social rites adapted to the simpler life of small towns—the Thanksgiving Day turkey, the corn-husking, the apple bee, the sugar party, the spelling matches, the church socials. As one of Howells's spokesmen observes in *Through the Eye of the Needle:* "As soon as people become at all refined they look down upon what is their own as something vulgar. But it is peculiarly so with us. We have nothing national that is not connected with the life of work, and when we begin to live the life of pleasure we must borrow from the people abroad, who have always lived the life of pleasure."[14]

Staniford amuses himself during the early part of the voyage by imagining what Lydia's past is like and then comparing notes with Dunham, who has made her acquaintance. Staniford gives her the countrified name of Lurella and notices that she behaves "like a lady," that is, she "eats with her fork." He notes that although the men are all "sunk in barbaric uses," one sometimes *does* find country women "practicing some of the arts of civilization." He develops a real curiosity "to know what a girl of her traditions thinks about the world when she first sees it," for he imagines that "her mind must be in most respects an unbroken wilderness" and that "she can't have had any cultivation" (*LA,* 82–83).

What he learns about her destroys his stereotype of the country hoyden and constitutes an implied warning to readers who judge people in terms of their imputed regional or social limitations. For Lydia is far from being a hoyden from the sticks. As Howells conceives her, Lydia *is* a lady, and his aim in portraying this American lady is just as serious as James's in creating Isabel Archer. Clothed with "the stylishness that instinctive taste may evoke, even in a hill town, from study of paper patterns, *Harper's Bazar,* and the customs of summer boarders," Lydia is sensitive, intelligent, and sweet-tempered. Although she hasn't gone to a Female Academy and Finishing School, she carries herself with high spirit and personal dignity. Above all, she has a native confidence in her own judgment and the American girl's "ability to take care of herself under any circumstances." As her Aunt Maria says on the eve of her journey, "I

---

14 See William Dean Howells, *Through the Eye of the Needle* (New York: Harper and Brothers, 1907), p. 67.

guess Lyddy'd know how to conduct herself wherever she was; she's a born lady, if ever there was one" (*LA,* 7, 49, 46).

In the course of the voyage, freed of the conventions associated with Boston, thrown together under conditions of unusual freedom and intimacy, Staniford and Lydia fall in love. A matter of some delicacy, a point of manners, prevents him from proposing to her. He knows that she is receptive, but he feels that under the circumstances, he must postpone his proposal until Lydia is safely in the care of her aunt and uncle in Venice. Owing to Dunham's illness on reaching port, however, Staniford is not able to accompany her to Venice. After a mix-up, and under the misapprehension that he has been trifling with her, Lydia enters the ordeal of Venetian society alone.

"What would she do with these ideals of hers in that depraved Old World,—so long past trouble for its sins as to have got a sort of sweetness and innocence in them, where her facts would be utterly irreconcilable?" (*LA,* 216). This question Staniford asks himself as he contemplates Lydia's introduction to Venetian society. Clearly the innocent American girl suddenly planted in the Old World was bound to have a nasty shock. Her initiation into the manners and customs of the Venetians, the British, and the Europeanized Americans there is quick. She is told that she cannot go out alone in public, even to church, because it would be scandalous. She cannot remain alone in the company of a man. Yet she is introduced to a married countess who has many lovers, to a young lady about whose real father there is some question, and to a fashionable English lady whose husband had abandoned her under circumstances which presumably the New York divorce court would then have approved. And in her own aunt's drawing room she meets the hussar officer who propositioned her on the train from Trieste to Venice. Lydia is of course appalled at the laxity of Old World morals, and when Staniford finally appears and properly proposes, they marry hastily and return to America, settling eventually in California (could she have been happy in Boston or he in South Bradfield?), where Staniford becomes a rancher.

The conclusion of the novel suggests Howells's own response to Venetian society in the early 1860s, when Lincoln appointed him to the American consulate in Venice. Shortly after arriving there in 1861, he wrote to his sister that "no one knows how much better than the whole world America is until he tries some other part of the world."[15] Howells was impressed by the beauty of Venice but he could not help seeing the poverty and squalor, the aristocratic distinctions of

---

15 *Life in Letters of William Dean Howells,* I, 47.

rank, the arrogance of the Austrian military who controlled the city, and the public vice that everywhere affronted his exceptionally pure sensibilities. "Young ladies *never* receive calls," he wrote to Victoria, "and a young lady cannot go upon the street unless accompanied by her mother or brother. If she went alone she would lose her character." The natural consequence of the social system in Venice, he observed, was that "the young men are beasts and the women what you might expect them. O Vic, Vic! prize America all you can," he adjured her. "Try not to think of the Americans' faults—they are a people so much purer and nobler and truer than any other, that I think they will be pardoned the wrong they do." He said that he was "getting disgusted with this stupid Europe" and was "growing to hate it. What I have told you of society here in Italy is true of society throughout the continent. Germany is socially rotten—and the Germans have a filthy frankness in their vice, which is unspeakably hideous and abominable to me." He told his sister that "the less we know of Europe, the better for our civilization; and the fewer German customs that take root among us, the better for our decency."

This is a remarkable statement since Ohio was so full of immigrants in the 1860s that the state laws had to be printed in German. Wanting to be the Heine of the Western Reserve, Howells had in fact studied German with an immigrant watchmaker who became the model of Lindau in *A Hazard of New Fortunes*. "You will read the lies of many people who say that life in Europe is more cheerful and social than ours," he went on to Victoria. "Lies, I say—or stupidities, which are almost as bad. There is no life in the whole world so cheerful, so social, so beautiful as the American." And "the pleasure which we have innocently in America, from our unrestrained and unconventional social intercourse, is guilty in Europe—brilliant men and women know something of it; but they are also guilty men and women." And he added that when he returned home from his stint in Venice he thought he would "go to Oregon—and live as far as possible from the influence of European civilization." European life might be denser, richer in picturesque effects, and possibly more pliable in the artist's hands (at least Henry James thought so), but, as he told Victoria, "I can scarcely have patience with my former impertinent and stupid ideas."[16] He told his friend and fellow poet J. J. Piatt in America that "though you make much of the pictures and the palaces, and the ruins, I doubt if they could console you; for I assure you that our American freedom, social, intellectual, and political, is

---

16 *Life in Letters of William Dean Howells*, I, 58–59.

better than all the past and present slavery of Europe, however glorious in art and history that may be." He said that he looked back upon "the careless, independent life I led at Columbus as something too good to be altogether true," and he wrote that "when I remember it I bow to the European conventionalities with a groan of profound regret."[17]

Howells's conception of the good life in the New World was based on the social and political organization of small towns in the West like Jefferson and Columbus. He had known no other life. The effect of his discovery of Europe was to suggest to him that "this civilization, old and rich, was more wholly destitute of art and the things that reveal and reflect the beautiful than even that new order of the West, which truly has made the wilderness to blossom like the rose, but has not as yet found time to adorn its usefulness with the final grace of art." Casting himself in the role of the disappointed sentimentalist for whom Europe had failed to live up to its reputation, he charged that even the inhabitants of Europe felt nothing for the fabled antiquities amidst which they lived and he doubted that they lived "a more *thorough* life than Americans, even though they had a thousand years of history behind them."[18]

Charles Eliot Norton, the *arbiter elegantarium,* the touchstone of taste in New England, complained that the "old tradition and inherited culture" of New England (the saving remnant) were being undermined by Howells's West. Composed of people "ignorant, rude, careless of social obligations, lawless in disposition, and of dull moral sense," Westerners, Norton felt, tended to "arrogance and self-assertion," had "few ideals of an ennobling sort," were "little instructed in the lessons of history," and had "underdeveloped imaginations and imperfect sympathies." The question Norton posed was "whether our civilization can maintain itself, and make advance, against the pressure of ignorant and barbaric multitudes; whether the civilized part of the community is eventually to master the barbaric, or whether it is to be overcome in the struggle."[19] But Howells, for all his admiration of some of the intellectual achievements of the New England tradition, could not help believing that the West offered the highest opportunities for self-fulfillment and social and material advancement. "Society in Columbus at that day," he wrote of the 1850s, "had a pleasant refinement," an intellectual tone, a good deal of charm and a mixture of Northern, Southern and Middle

---

17 Quoted in *The Hesperian Tree,* ed. John J. Piatt (Columbus, Ohio, 1903), p. 426.
18 William Dean Howells, "A Little German Capital," *Nation,* 2 (1866), 12.
19 Norton, "Some Aspects of Civilization in America," *Forum,* 20 (1896), 644, 649.

Western traits which made for the pleasant manners and customs of the city. The social life of Columbus

> had the finality which it seems to have had nowhere since the war; it had certain fixed ideals, which were none the less graceful and becoming because they were the simple old American ideals, now vanished, or fast vanishing, before the knowledge of good and evil as they have it in Europe, and as it has imparted itself to American travel and sojourn.[20]

Norton was not insensible of the political value of a democracy; he knew the significance of the expanding frontier. But for Norton, what America needed was just precisely "a renewed sense of continuity with Europe and the traditions of the past."[21] Howells, however, left Europe after three years saying, "I have seen enough uncountryed Americans in Europe to disgust me with voluntary exile, and its effects upon character."[22] Did I err, he asked in his essay "A Little German Capital,"

> in reverting to an opposite faith, and prizing above history, art, and the poetry of association that social and civil order which permits every life to be at once grand and simple, that makes man superior to classes and only subject to freedom? Was I wrong to hold the darkest probability of the American future at greater worth than all the past and present of Europe?[23]

Critics and novelists like Norton, Henry James, and Edith Wharton would have said yes: Howells *was* wrong to reduce the problem to such an equation. But, joined by such pugnacious democrats as Thomas Wentworth Higginson and E. L. Godkin, Howells was little disposed, in the 1860s, to celebrate or appreciate the artistic by-products of a feudal aristocratic society. When he returned to America, Howells was pleased to find "a young, free, energetic society" in which "love . . . was innocent; a society in which the relation between man and woman was simple and pure. Here, I thought, are the materials for novels. Why should I go to the people of bygone ages and of lands not my own?"[24] Indeed, why? *The Lady of the Aroostook* proved at least the wisdom of his choice of subject and set-

---

20 Howells, *Literary Friends and Acquaintance*, p. 2.
21 Kermit Vanderbilt, *Charles Eliot Norton: Apostle of Culture in a Democracy* (Cambridge: Harvard University Press, 1959), p. 149.
22 *Life in Letters of William Dean Howells*, I, 85.
23 Howells, "A Little German Capital," p. 12.
24 George Arms and William Gibson, "Five Interviews with Howells," *Americana*, 37 (1943), 292.

ting, if not the accuracy of his sociological and aesthetic judgments of the European scene.

If Howells idealized the social arrangements of American life, the question may also be raised as to whether his novels of manners in the 1870s depict these social arrangements in a realistic and convincing way, whether, that is, his novels achieve that verisimilitude he claimed for them. Could backcountry girls like Kitty and Lydia Blood really be as "cultivated" as Howells made them out to be? Was their speech as pure as the dialogue renders it? Were their personal manners as winsome as we readers find them to be? These are difficult questions for criticism, for, although literature reflects life, often in comprehensive sociological detail, the novel is not really history, and despite Howells's implied generalizations about these young women, we are essentially presented with individual instances rather than types of the provincial American girl of that time.

As to the manners of Kitty and Lydia, there is no doubt that Howells wished us to respond warmly and sympathetically to them, not as the heroines of sentimental romance but rather as illustrations of a distinctively short-lived social phenomenon—"the innocently adventuring, unconsciously periculant American maiden," like Daisy Miller or Bessie Alden in James's *An International Episode,* a type of young woman whom one saw everywhere in the 1860s and 1870s but who had disappeared as a social fact by the 1880s.[25] James, it seems to me, was more "realistic" than Howells in portraying the American girl's not merely ignorance of but also indifference to the regulations of a conventional European society. Nevertheless, James never descended into slang or dialect as a constant way of characterizing the American girl's speech. While James was innocent of Howells's open egalitarianism, Howells felt that the defense of simple democratic manners was worth a slight loss of verisimilitude suffered in the literary act of refining and purifying their manners and speech. His thinking was rather like that of Colonel Higginson, the abolitionist celebrated in *A Chance Acquaintance.* Higginson pointed out in "On a Certain Humility in Americans" that Americans in the presence of Europeans were often wrongly humble about their manners:

> During the last French Empire it used to be held at Newport and New York that there was no standard of good breeding but in Paris,

---

25 William Dean Howells, "Introduction," *Daisy Miller and An International Episode* (New York: n. p., n. d.), p. iii. Howells's awareness of the transience of the type that he and James had captured (on the wing, as it were) is one of the most engaging aspects of his introduction to James's stories.

as if the best-bred American society were not of older tradition as well as better strain than the dynasty of the Napoleons. The truth is that the finest American manners are indigenous, not imported. You will find such manners in little towns in Virginia and Kentucky, where not a person has ever seen Europe, and where to have been to Philadelphia or New York is to be a great traveller.[26]

In the service of this conception of simple Christian democratic manners, as the natural expression of the innocent personality, Howells idealized Kitty and Lydia Blood. He hardly ever rendered their conversation in dialect, for example, as he always did when he wished to expose ignorance or uncouthness or when he wished to emphasize the differences in the social levels of his characters. In *The Lady of the Aroostook,* some of Howells' best writing contains those finely modulated notations of the speech of South Bradfield, "the conscientiously-cunningly-reluctant, arbitrarily emphatic Yankee *manner* of Lydia's grandfather and aunt." [27] Lydia's speech is purified of the grossness of dialect, but it is not exceptionally idealized. What tips off Staniford and Dunham about Lydia's upcountry background is precisely her speech. When Staniford publicly remarks the hotness of the weather, Lydia replies, "I want to know!" (*LA,* 55). This is a dead giveaway. She fails what Higginson called "the test of talk." Higginson reminds us of Coleridge's well-known anecdote about "the stranger at the dinner table who would forever have remained a dignified and commanding figure," full of possible distinction and apparent elegance, "had not the excellence of the apple-dumplings called him for a moment forth from his shell to utter the fatal words, 'Them's the jockeys for me.'" After that, Higginson observed, "the case was hopeless." [28] He might have been a saint or a hero for all anybody knew, but he had betrayed his humble origins in five words, and, so far as the test of talk went, it was conclusive.

Howells loved to deal with episodes in which appearances are deceiving, in which the fake is betrayed by some dead giveaway like the test of talk. In one of the most charming episodes in *Their Wedding Journey,* for example, Basil and Isabel March encounter "a tall, handsome young man, with a face of somewhat foreign cast, and well dressed, with a certain impressive difference from the rest in the cut of his clothes," wearing a "large cross, set with brilliants, and sur-

26 Thomas Wentworth Higginson, "On a Certain Humility in Americans," *Women and Men* (New York: Harper and Brothers, 1888), p. 98.

27 *Life and Letters of William Dean Howells,* I, 269.

28 "The Test of Talk," *Book and Heart: Essays on Literature and Life* (New York: Harper and Brothers, 1897), pp. 218–219.

mounted by a heavy double-headed eagle in gold." Isabel is convinced that he is some foreign nobleman decorated with a royal
order, perhaps from a legation at Washington. "Never tell me, Basil,
that there's nothing in blood!" cried Isabel, who, Howells observes,
"was a bitter aristocrat at heart, like all her sex, though in principle
she was democratic enough." But when, at the ship's table, the
hungry young aristocrat comes out, in an unmistakable New York
accent, with "Pretty tejious waitin', ain't it?" the test of talk is conclusive.[29] Even the gold cross turns out to be fake, an emblem of the
fifty-fourth degree of his secret society. The manner of speech tells,
therefore, a great deal about the culture of the speaker.

The test of talk, however, is conclusive only as far as it goes. To
think of Lydia as only a provincial country girl who need not be
taken seriously is precisely the mistake that Staniford makes. For the
test of talk doesn't go far enough. Our feelings about dialect, slang,
and Americanisms are apt to prejudice our appreciation of the person
speaking. Lionel Trilling once remarked how superficial is the American's interest in manners and how little, beyond our dialects, are
the real differences that separate us. But Howells realized that our
prejudices against dialect are so deep—it is the characteristic mode of
ridicule for native American humorists—that, given his purposes, he
would have to avoid rendering Lydia's and Kitty's speech realistically.
That he purified their dialect indicates the extent to which he was
willing to surrender verisimilitude to his larger purpose—to demonstrate the superiority of simple American manners over the veneer of
conventionality that conceals the moral corruption of European
society.

This purpose, paradoxically, is reinforced in Charles Eliot Norton's essay "Good Manners," in which he argued that "though the
standard varies, the best of good manners is unchanging, for it is
derived from the moral principles of human conduct. Bad manners
indicate ill morals, good manners are the expression of good morals,
and the best manners are those of the best men." This sounds like the
usual New England oversimplification between manners and morals.
But Norton believed that the false notions about manners still
prevalent in America "derived mainly from the feudal conditions of
European society, in which, men being divided into classes, there
were introduced many factitious and conventional relations, a due
regard for which constituted a large part of the manners of courts of

---

29 See William Dean Howells, *Their Wedding Journey* (Boston: J. R. Osgood, 1878), pp.
187–188.

society." Norton held that "the traditions of the past in regard to manners, as in regard to other arts, are not to be held in too high respect." But he argued that in our country, where the relations of men are simple, natural, and humane, we must revise "the old codes of manners" because these codes "were part of the laws by which the false distinctions among men were maintained." The "superior manners" of the aristocracy were, in his view, its safeguard against social mobility. But "in our society the only conventionalisms in manners which are important and require to be preserved are those which long experience has shown to be requisite or desirable as aiding to place men in equal relations with each other in a mixed society."

Norton's definition here of the function and character of manners in a democratic society is a significant one. Far from serving as an instrument to separate men, "conventionalisms in manners serve to bring all the company upon a common level, to set each man at ease with his neighbor, and to prevent each from giving unwitting offence"—even though they may be ignorant of "each other's special tastes, foibles, inclinations, and capacities." He went on to say that "it is a part of good morals to make one's self familiar with these conventionalisms." "It is of the nature of a duty to society and to ourselves. It is selfishness to neglect them."

Norton and like-minded observers of American social life in the post–Civil War period knew that "the tendency of American life" was "not altogether favorable as yet to the production and general cultivation of good manners." The massive immigration into this country of diverse peoples alien in speech, language, customs, and manners portended a degree of ignorance and a level of consequent incivility that undermined the amity of public life. The rowdiness and even savagery of the wide-open frontier was also a constant check upon the development of harmonious and distinguished ways of interacting. Norton said that he hoped that "the manners of men will constantly improve," becoming "simpler, more considerate, more conformed to the absolute test of morals than the manners of other peoples." He believed that Americans had rightly jettisoned many of the empty forms that derived from the political and social institutions of aristocratic society. But clearly he feared that the really valuable customs in American social life were going to be destroyed by those new postwar forces that were changing America:

> the loose organization of our society, the sturdy individualism which
> it has developed, the absence of any social stability, the low standard
> for the most part of the cultivation of our most cultivated people, the

rude life and habits of backwoodsmen, emigrants, and frontiersmen, which react upon our most civilized and refined classes; the immense flood of half-barbarian foreigners who draw together in degraded masses in our cities—these are among the circumstances which combine to affect ill our manners as a nation.[30]

Norton's feelings about democracy and democratic manners were never simple. A few years earlier he had regarded "with regret and dismay this universal eager demand for popular liberty"; he had asserted that the *demos* could not be looked to for leadership in America; and he had argued that we must rely on and be guided by "the few who have been blessed with the opportunities, the rare genius, fitting them to lead."[31] But the Civil War and the emergence of Westerners like Lincoln radically altered Norton's aristocratic political assumptions, realigning his views with those of Howells. And Norton did not hesitate to propose Lincoln as the foundation of democratic manners, a model for every American:

> Mr. Lincoln possessed the essentials of good manners. He showed us what manners an American "railsplitter" might have. They were the manners of a good heart, that trusted itself to other men. Upon such a foundation we may build whatever superstructure of beauty, grace, and art we choose. And though our manners be uncouth and unconventional today, they shall to-morrow—a hundred years hence—be the noble manners of men not only gentle in heart but of refined and elegant cultivation.[32]

Howells would heartily have agreed. In the limited realism of his portraits of Kitty Ellison and Lydia Blood, he affirmed his faith in the manners of the good heart.

---

30 Charles Eliot Norton, "Good Manners," *Nation*, 2 (1866), 571.
31 Charles Eliot Norton, *Considerations on Some Recent Social Theories* (Boston: Little, Brown, 1853), pp. 3–4, 19–20.
32 Charles Eliot Norton, "Good Manners," p. 571.

Henry James
and the
Venice of Dreams

That Venice has had, almost from the very beginning of American travel to Italy, a very special place in the consciousness of our writers is suggested by a book recently published by the American novelist Gore Vidal, the author of *The City and the Pillar, Myra Breckinridge, Burr,* and *Lincoln.* Principally a book of beautiful photographs of the city of Venice, meant for the Christmas trade and the coffee table, *Vidal in Venice* is spiced, as one might have foreseen, by Gore Vidal's unique, witty, and ironical view of Venetian history, politics, society, art, and particularly her sexual mores. In view of Vidal's interest in Henry James, in novels about the European scene, in the felicities of a cultivated social style and a distinguished literary manner—such as Henry James preeminently illustrates—some preliminary comments about Vidal's book may not be wholly irrelevant.

Vidal in Venice appears to have been motivated by a genealogical impulse. One of Vidal's elderly aunts passed on to him a family legend that the Vidals had important connections in Venice—in fact, that three of Venice's ancient doges were Vidals. (Like many Americans, Vidal has spent a lifetime avidly identifying himself with one aristocracy or another, commercial American or titled European, while offering the condescension of his wit to the common people, the democratic institutions, and the middle-class values of America.) In the case of *Vidal in Venice,* he did not find any Vidals, although there are some Vitales, but he did find evidence of the name in the Church of San Vidal, with the Rio de San Vidal, the little canal running along behind it. Most depressing, the family name did not appear in "The Golden Book," the list of names of the distinguished ancient families in Venice. And of the three doges referred to by the aunt, only the first name was Vidal, not the last or family name. This did not deter Principe Vidal from having his photograph taken, for the jacket of the book, sitting on the doge's throne. I take this genealogical search of Vidal's to be a very common thing with Americans. It reflects an old theme, that of "the American claimant" to European aristocratic status—to use the title of Mark Twain's book of 1892.

Almost from the very beginning, Anglo-Americans have come to Venice wishing to lay claim to the city, to take possession of it, to appropriate the city to their private uses. This is clearly evident in the language of the book jacket of *Vidal in Venice,* the advertising copy of which reflects a typical attitude: "Today Venice exists for the tourists: it is a living museum, a Disneyland, a mirror that reflects the image of the beholder. . . ." This idea that Venice exists for visitors and tourists effectively annihilates the thousands of people who live and work in Venice, in labor and love, getting and spending, reading and writing, giving and being given in marriage, rearing children, and so on. It is no wonder, then, that Venetians may look askance, in resignation and dismay, at the American traveler, in his contemporary or historical character, and want to seal off the city at Mestre. Was Henry James such a traveler?

II

My subject is not so much Henry James as the image of Venice occurring in those literary works, principally American, that James knew or might have known, works that constitute, taken together, something of the available myth of Venice for the late-nineteenth-century writer. I am interested here in the gathering body of fiction, poetry, and travel writing that mentions or describes Venice. I can, of course, allude only to a fraction of it. This body of work, nevertheless, forms a matrix of allusions and attitudes that may be said to constitute a shaping influence on the writer's conception of a specific place, quite independent of his own personal discovery of the place, travel to it, or temporary residence in it. The literary image of a city is thus a lens through which a well-read traveler will partly see the cityscape. In fact, given the pervasiveness of associationist psychology in the nineteenth century, the literary vision of a place is sometimes felt to be superior to the reality of the place itself. For some nineteenth-century writers with idealist propensities, mental associations and imaginative re-creations of a setting are often accompanied by a radical devaluation of the actuality of it. In the older romance tradition of American writing, the admixture of imagination with reality always produced an effect said to be superior to reality. Hawthorne, whose life James wrote, illustrates this claim in "The Birthmark," where the optical phenomena conjured up by Aylmer's art led Hawthorne to write: "The scenery and the figures of actual life were perfectly represented, but with that bewitching yet indescribable difference which always makes a picture, an image, or a shadow so much more attractive than the original." This observation represents the romantic view of the creative personality's improvement on actuality. When Hawthorne saw the Roman Coliseum he was rather disappointed and remarked: "Byron's celebrated description is better than the reality."

Henry James was prepared by such cultural attitudes to find discrepancies between the literary images of Italy—and particularly Venice—and the actuality of the place when he got to it. He was an American claimant himself in exulting to his family: "I take possession of the old world—I inhale it—I appropriate it." He might go reeling and moaning through the streets of Rome, in a fervid ecstasy of aesthetic rapture. But after a year in Italy, in the early 1870s, he had, he complained to Grace Norton, "hardly spoken to an Italian creature save washerwomen and waiters. This, you'll say, is my own stupidity; but granting this gladly, it proves that even a creature addicted as much to sentimentalizing as I am over the whole *mise en scène* of Italian life, doesn't find an easy initiation into what lies behind it. Sometimes I am overwhelmed with the pitifulness of this absurd want of reciprocity between Italy itself and all my rhapsodies about it."

Something of this difficulty of initiation into what lies behind the surface of Italian life has inevitably been the complex fate of the American imagination in Italy. For this reason, travel works like Giuseppe Baretti's *Account of the Manners and Customs of Italy*, John Moore's *A View of Society and Manners in Italy*, Arthur Young's *Travels*, Antonio Gallenga's *Italy, Past and Present*, Gautier's *Italia*, Hester Thrale Piozzi's *Glimpses of Italian Society in the Eighteenth Century*, not to speak of Casanova's *History of My Life* and the ubiquitous Baedeker, have been essential preparatory reading.

What evolves out of such readings, for the American writer in the nineteenth century, is an image of Venice that has its archetypal symbolism fully elaborated by the time Henry James arrives on the scene.

Characteristically, it is enriched, reinforced, counterpointed, and sometimes contradicted by other writings of poets and novelists, some of whom were James's contemporaries and even friends. I have in mind works like Hawthorne's *The Marble Faun*; Howells's *Venetian Life, Italian Journeys* and *Tuscan Cities*; Charles Eliot Norton's *Notes of Travel and Study in Italy*; Goldoni's *Memoirs*; Vernon Lee's *Studies in Eighteenth Century Italy*; Pater's *The Renaissance*; Ruskin's *The Stones of Venice*; Edith Wharton's *Italian Villas and Their Gardens* and *Italian Backgrounds*; as well as the writings of Bernard Berenson and many others. The symbolism of Venice, the myth attendant upon the city, inherited by James and the rest of us, is a complex myth, with many layers, and one can touch upon only two or three aspects of it here.

III

A part of the myth, for Americans, inheres in the ancient politics of Venice, as a republic, something American revolutionists aspired in their own way to create. Venice therefore commanded attention, as a possible paradigm of our national political life. Ambassador Dolfin, who served the Venetian Republic in Paris at the time of Benjamin Franklin, was assiduous in cultivating diplomatic relations with the new country, in 1783, remarking that he wanted Americans to be "well disposed at all events to uphold not only the interests, but the regards due the Venetian flag. . . ." These negotiations, however, were doomed, as Antonio Pace has shown in *Benjamin Franklin in Italy,* by Napoleon's delivering the republic in bondage to Austria. As the American colonies had recently been in bondage to a foreign power, the history of the Republic of Venice, its political organization, its decay and fall, and its occupation by Austria, gave pause to early American observers.

The fall of the Venetian Republic was a very serious blow to all nineteenth-century republicans, not only to the new American nation. Wordsworth's poem "On the Extinction of the Venetian Republic" echoed American attitudes and shaped them as well:

And what if she had seen those glories fade,
Those titles vanish, and that strength decay;
Yet shall some tribute of regret be paid
When her long life has reached its final day;
Men we are, and must grieve when even the Shade
Of that which once was great, is passed away.

This is of a piece with Byron's lament of the fall of Venice in *Childe Harold's Pilgrimage*:

> Statues of glass—all shivered—the long file
> Of her dead Doges are declined to dust;
> But where they dwelt, the vast and sumptuous pile
> Bespeaks the pageant of their splendid trust;
> Their sceptre broken, and their sword in rust,
> Have yielded to the stranger: empty halls,
> Thin streets, and foreign aspects, such as must
> Too oft remind her who and what enthrals,
> Have flung a desolate cloud
> O'er Venice's lovely walls.

Knowing Byron's life and work, and familiar with Venetians connected to Byron (like the Countess Gamba, niece by her husband of Byron's lover, the Countess Guiccioli; and the Countess Pisani, whose father was Byron's physician), Henry James was primed, in *The Aspern Papers,* to make a compelling fiction out of these empty halls, thin streets, and foreign aspects.

In any case, there begins to enter American writing in the early nineteenth century not merely the image of the former grand pageantry of Venice in her era of glory but the theme of decay and desolation, impoverishment, decline, and the tyranny of a foreign political power. All of these were resonant themes in America, where there was full consciousness, in the beginning, that no republic had ever survived the audacity of the experiment of a government founded on the consent of the governed. Early American travel writing emphasized the ruins of Venice. And indeed, it is not irrelevant to remark that ruins even came to be foregrounded in the visual art of early American landscapes, as the theme of civic and personal virtue was acclaimed as the only way to effect the survival of the young American republic. Venice was, in one respect, a cautionary instance of where a republic could go wrong, and James Fenimore Cooper's novel *The Bravo* (1831), set in Venice, was intended to illustrate the moral that "any government in which the power resides in a minority conduces to oppression of the weak and perversion of the good."

IV

A second theme appears almost simultaneously in American writing about Italy, it seems to me, and that is the theme of the happiness, sunniness, poetry, gaiety, and laughter that characterize the land.

What was needed for American writers was a countermyth to the theme of decay, perhaps a compensation for it. Here it is harder to separate Venice from the larger myth of Italy as a whole. (Most American writers did not make nice cultural distinctions amongst the several regional centers of the country.) Henry Wadsworth Longfellow expressed this second theme in a tribute to Italy in his Harvard lecture of 1851: "To the imagination, Italy has always been, and always will be, the land of sun, and the land of song; and neither tempest, rain nor snow will ever chill the glow of enthusiasm that the name of Italy excites in every poetic mind. Say what ill of it you may, it still remains to the poet the land of his predilection, to the artist, the land of his necessity." As seems evident, the *reality* of Italy does not matter very much; in fact, despite the reality, Italy as the scene of sun and song is a necessary myth or symbol, essential to the operations of the American poetic imagination. Longfellow's remark alludes obliquely to the probability that something "ill" might justifiably be said about Italy (a notion to which I shall return), but it is clear that the necessity of the myth of "the spirit of the South," as Henry James was to call it, transcended, in some measure, any moral criticism of the country.

How, in the older American romantic imagination, the myth could differ from the reality is suggested in the response to Italy of James Fenimore Cooper. When he first abandoned "the sublimity of desolation" in Switzerland in 1828, and passed over the Simplon Pass heading for Venice, and the coachman cracked his whip and called out "Italie," Cooper wrote that "I pulled off my hat in reverence." It was not, as C. Waller Barrett makes plain in *Italian Influence on American Literature,* a gesture to the warmer weather but to the imaginative meaning of the country to the American literati.

Cooper served in the United States Navy and wrote a good deal of sea fiction, but Venice was an unexpected maritime experience for him: "Everything was strange," he wrote; "though a sailor and accustomed to water, I had never seen a city afloat. It is now evening; but a fine moon shedding its light on the scene rendered it fairy-like." Here Venice by moonlight displaces, for a moment, the land of sun and song, so as to become almost Hawthorne's "neutral territory," a fairy-tale setting: Venice is an unreal city. Although it bothered Cooper that he knew no one in Venice (and thus spent only a short time there), he declared that "no other place struck my imagination so forcefully." In fact, he said that it "seized" his fancy with such a "deep hold" that he had to "disburthen" it in a novel—which, as I have remarked, he did in *The Bravo.* Cooper was critical of Venice in those periods of its worst political excess, but his almost two years of residence in Italy, in the late 1820s, led him to say of Italy that "The very name excites me, for it is the only region of the earth that I truly love." And in *Gleanings from Europe: Italy* (1838), he gave extended expression to his love for the country. As Nathalia Wright has rightly said in her book *American Novelists in Italy,* "From the beginning Italy represented to Cooper the ideal civilization, to which he would have had American civilization comparable."

When we talk of Henry James's response to Venice, we are of course speaking of an ongoing response over nearly a half-century, with the inevitable alterations, changing nuances, refinements of perception, and so on. At times he found his experience in Venice "rather too abnormal for my eminently natural habits," but that was ordinarily when the social whirl of his hosts, the Curtises, interfered with his writing. But at the beginning, before he came to be a guest at the Palazzo Barbaro on so many occasions, something of Cooper's sense of the fairy-tale quality of the "sea city" was James's first impression. Venice, he told John LaFarge in 1869, was "perfectly *Italianissima*": "Venice is quite the Venice of one's dreams, but it remains strangely the Venice of dreams, more than of any appreciable reality. The mind is bothered with a constant sense of the exceptional character of the city: you can't quite reconcile it with common civilization. It's awfully sad too in its inexorable decay." To his brother William he remarked that the city was "the Venice of romance and fancy," but he complained that "it is a cold and foreign mass—never to be absorbed and appropriated. The meaning of this superb image is that I feel I shall never look at Italy—at Venice, for instance—but from without." It made him feel, he said, "more and more my inexorable Yankeehood."

Of course after repeated visits to Italy, James came to appreciate more fully the spirit of the South and to imagine himself in fuller possession of the interior life of the country. Certainly he came to value "the rest, the leisure, the beauty, the sunsets, the pictures" as "more than compensation" for the social opportunities in London that he missed while visiting the Curtises and others in Italy. He could even tell Mrs. Isabella Stewart Gardner in 1892 that he was "utterly homesick for Venice"; and he remarked to Grace Norton in the same year that the prospect of a return to Venice promised the blessing that "Italy remains firm while other things come and go—remains, on the whole, I mean, the sweetest impression of life." What remained most firm was the high style in which James was entertained in Venice, particularly by the Daniel Curtises and their friends, who lionized and pampered him at the Palazzo Barbaro. Indeed, Leon Edel has observed in *Henry James: Letters III* that "the ducal splendors of the Palazzo Barbaro, its frescoes and sculptured and painted ceilings, and the ease provided by the attendant gondoliers and servants" represented "the grand style that James's innate aristocratic sense loved. The gilt and grandeur ministered to his feelings for past and present, the fruits of ripe civilization. He brought back to London a feeling of liberation and ease."

The Curtises and others might very well have created this atmosphere of elegant well-being for James in Italy, but it is worth observing that it was a milieu of mostly English and Americans in which he moved; and we may very well question, therefore, how deep was his involvement with Venetians themselves. In his "inexorable Yankeehood," how deeply did he penetrate what might be called the inner life of Venetians in their own *milieux*? James might remark in 1907, to Jessie Allen, that "One dreams again so of some clutched perch of one's own here," but he pronounced that wish "the most drivelling of dreams"; and he always returned to London or Rye, where the "cold and foreign mass" was so much more easily assimilable.

V

James's remark about his "inexorable Yankeehood" suggests the third component of the myth of Venice—in addition to the cultural significance of its fall and its mythic unreality as an actual city. Part of the inexorable Yankeehood of Americans traveling in Italy was of course that complex of ideas and ideals that is connected to the relations between the sexes and their social expression. After Americans first began to travel in numbers to Italy, something of a crisis afflicted the American sensibility, for nearly a century, in relation to Italian sexual mores and their social forms. Irving is one of the first important American writers to experience a moral shock at the differences between America and Italy in the permissible relations between the sexes, particularly in connection to the courtship of unmarried girls and the freedoms permitted to married women. On his trip to Italy in 1804, remarking on the large number of handsome women there, Irving observed: "The innocent familiarities that prevail in America and England are unknown in this country and to press the ruby lips of a fair damsel would be a howling abomination. Such favors are only bestowed by the married lady—in private." This turns the "natural" but "innocent" forms of relation between the unmarried

American boy and girl upside down, while the Italian social system seemed to authorize intimacies between men and women who are married—but not to each other. In this respect, both Americans and the English, taking the high moral ground, were culturally unprepared to understand the meaning, for Italians, of the nature of chastity and marriage in relation to the consolidations of property, class and status, and the degree of romantic love and fidelity that might, or might not, be a motive for and in marriage.

Of particular horror, to the Anglo-American moral sensibility, was the old custom of cicisbeism, in which the married lady was everywhere attended, on social occasions, by a gallant or lover not her husband. To the vestigially Puritan mind, this custom of the country was a transparent cover for adultery, and for many travelers it apparently was a real question as to whether this old custom might still informally obtain. Thus for the American abroad there enters into the image of Italy, and particularly of Venice, a suspicion of illicit sexual passion, marital intrigue, and infidelity, a frank sensuality rooted in Italy's pagan past and uneradicated by the Christian superimposition, a sensuality symbolized by Italian art, with its ubiquitous nudes, both in painting and statuary. "Goats and monkeys" is the way Iago in *Othello* had taught Americans to think; they're all doing it; *così fan tutte*. Such is, it seems to me, what Longfellow implied by speaking ill of Italy. And with this suspicion comes a resistance to Italy: the potential for moral, particularly sexual, corruption that Venice communicates through this myth. As William Dean Howells put it in *Venetian Life,* "The charm of the place sweetens your temper but corrupts you." Venice might be beautiful, but life there dulled, even subverted, the Anglo-American moral sense.

Howells, a close friend of Henry James, illustrated several features of this developing mythology. Amongst these early travelers, Howells had perhaps the longest sustained experience of Venice—four years as American consul in the city. Out of his Italian experience came not only his nonfiction works *Venetian Life* (1866), *Italian Journeys* (1867), *Tuscan Cities* (1886), *Modern Italian Poets* (1887) and *Roman Holidays* (1908) but also some five novels wholly or largely set in Italy, and some fifteen others where an Italian connection is significant. Howells even wanted to write a history of Venice, a project to which he returned again and again, but he could never finish it.

One of the striking things about Howells's work is the way in which he sought to deflate the fairy-tale myth of Venice, a form of the older romanticism, and to present the city, and the dramatic action of the fictions laid there, in a vein more realistic than past writers had done. *A Foregone Conclusion* (1874), with its portrait of the Venetian priest driven by sexual passion but bound by the vow of celibacy, is one of these tales. *The Lady of the Aroostook* (1879), with its naïve American girl chafing under the constraints of chaperonage in a city filled with designing and worldly-wise Venetians, is another. Indeed, Lydia Blood, the heroine, is not unlike James's Daisy Miller in Roman society, although James is never as inclined to moralize so fatuously as Howells.

Howells, James, and Twain were all, in varying degrees, trying to put Venice on a more realistic footing, to dispose of the fairy-tale myth. The general objectives of American realism, as a self-conscious project, extended even into these writers' images of Venice. But in actuality they tended to utilize what by their time had become recurrent and familiar Venetian stereotypes. Twain certainly explodes the ideal image of Venice in *Innocents Abroad,* with his burlesque portraits of the croaking gondolier, the hearse-like gondola, the sadistic barber, the mauseoleum-like architecture, and the one million identical pictures of bald-headed monks, in coarse robes, "gazing heavenward with countenances which I am informed are full of 'expression.'" After Twain, no one could conceivably look at St. Mark's the way that Cooper, Byron, Norton, Ruskin, and others had lovingly described it. Of St. Mark's, Twain wrote:

> One's admiration of a perfect thing always grows, never declines; and this is the surest evidence to him that it is perfect. St. Mark is perfect. To me it soon grew to be so nobly, so augustly ugly, that it was difficult to stay away from it, even for a little while. Every time its squat domes disappeared from my view, I had a despondent feeling; whenever they reappeared, I felt an honest rapture—I have not known any happier hours than those I daily spent in front of Florian's looking across the Great Square at it. . . . Propped on its long row of low thick-legged columns, its back knobbed with domes, it seemed like a vast warty bug taking a meditative walk.

But both Howells and Twain, Western and irreverent as they could be—the one in his supposed realism, the other in his burlesque buffoonery—shared in the general American queasiness with the pervasive nudity of the artwork and the intimations of sensuality and sexuality which their hyperdeveloped antennae detected everywhere. One of the things Howells most liked about Carlo Goldoni, whose drama he virtually introduced to Americans, is suggested in his remark in *Recent Italian Comedy* that "Goldoni wrote, in an age of unchaste literature, plays which a girl may read with as little cause to blush as would be given by a novel of Dickens. At a time when in England only the tedious Richardson wrote chaste romances, Goldoni produced plays full of decent laughter, of cleanly humor and amiable morality, in that Venice which we commonly believe to have been Sodomitic in its filth and wickedness." Sodom by the Adriatic? That phrase seems rather strong, but we must see in this attitude the prudishness and gentility that Howells, Twain, and even James himself shared with their countrymen. Americans, like Victorian Englishmen, thought of themselves as upholding a standard of sexual purity that might redeem the Italians. Browning, who was staying in Venice at the time Howells's *The Lady of the Aroostook* was published in America and who read it with great pleasure, presents something of this view of the historic "wickedness" of Venice in "A Toccata of Galuppi's." In that poem, the carnival atmosphere, the gay insouciant hedonism, the *carpe diem* sensuality of Venice is brought under a moral censure. Browning projects the censure onto Galuppi himself, who is dismayed at the hedonism of his time. In fact the poet seems to suggest that wrinkling and age, decay and death, are almost indeed the price of Venetian sexual abandon:

> As for Venice and its people, merely born to bloom and drop,
> Here on earth they bore their fruitage, mirth and folly were the crop.
> What of soul was left, I wonder, when the kissing had to stop?
> "Dust and ashes!" So you creak it, and I want the heart to scold.
> Dear dead women, with such hair, too—what's become of all the gold
> Used to hang and brush their bosoms? I feel chilly and grown old.

Closely interrogated, however, Browning's passage is ambivalent about Venice. The speaker, meditating on such beauty, such vitality, such *joie de vivre* as Galuppi's music is made to condemn, lacks the heart to scold and is chilled, even aged, by the suspicion of his own irrelevant moralism.

The literary image of Venice, available to James in the literary culture and supplemented by his own direct observations, suggested that Venice was a place of enchantment, an unreal city. For visual beauty, for the quaint, the picturesque, the charming, it had few European equals. For the historical pomp and majesty, for the poignance of a vanished power and greatness, for the sense of a dense, deep, rich, old world culture, it had few peers. Yet at the same time, contemporary Venice was for James, as for Ruskin, one of time's ruins, marked by its visible poverty and decay, its dissolution and decline. Mixed in with the beauty and decay were the felt vestiges of the sensuality and hedonism of the old carnival spirit.

VI

How, then, do these impressions attain figural significance in the novels? In his 1882 essay "Venice," James said, "There is notoriously nothing more to be said on the subject," but in his more than twelve thousand words of additional commentary he formulated some elements of this myth of Venice that may guide us in understanding his treatment of the city in *The Aspern Papers, The Princess Casamassima, The Pupil,* and *The Wings of the Dove.* I have space here to touch upon only some of the most obvious ways in which his sense of Venice translated into character and setting.

If, in the essay "Venice," he remarks on the poverty and misery of Venetians, their decayed habitations, light pockets, and scant opportunities, Venice seems a fit setting for the collapsing fortunes of the devious and dishonest Moreen family, in "The Pupil," who, unable to marry off a daughter to an aristocrat, end little Morgan's life in pawning him off on Pemberton his tutor. The cold November weather, the roaring wind, the rain-lashed lagoon, the stately decay of the rented residence, its absence of fire and furniture, the cold scagliola floors and high battered casements are all symbols of "a blast of desolation, a portent of disgrace and disaster," that will end the story in the pupil's death.

If Venetians, as James wrote in the essay, steer "a crooked course not to your or my advantage—amid the sanctities of property," what better place than Venice to have Merton Densher make up to a dying girl in order to get her fortune and so marry the woman Kate Croy, who has already vulgarly become his mistress? Property and the despoliation of it, under mercenary motives of the coarsest acquisitiveness, are the driving energy of Kate Croy, whose *cupiditas,* abetted by Densher's betrayal, makes Millie turn her face to the wall. Even the portrait of Eugenio is written so as to emphasize his mercenary avidity: "She had judged him in advance, polyglot and universal, very dear and very deep, as probably but a swindler finished to the finger-tips; for he was forever carrying one well-kept Italian hand to his heart and plunging the other straight into her pocket, which, as she had instantly observed him to recognise, fitted it like a glove." The multiple claims upon Millie's property, even upon her person so as to *get* her property, are sufficiently communicated by the Venetian setting. On the other hand, if Venice is historically linked with the passion of love, what better place to bring Milly Theale, who in her resemblance to the dear dead Lucrezia Panciatichi in the Bronzino portrait, is the living incarnation of all the beautiful women of past Italian glory?

Browning's "A Toccata of Galuppi's" asks what of soul was left when the kissing had to stop, what had become of the women with such passion, such hair of gold that used to hang and brush their bosoms. In the elderly Miss Bordereau, in the Julia of *The Aspern Papers,* we have the answer: the relic of a once-grand passion. James remarks in the essay on Venice that the city "hasn't a genius for stiff morality, and indeed makes few pretensions in that direction." What better setting than Venice, therefore, to recall not only a vivid illicit romantic passion, now preserved only in the memory of the jealous old woman and in the letters of the poet Aspern, a passion voyeuristically pursued by the publishing scoundrel, whose making up to the plain Miss Tita to get the letters is a travesty of love altogether?

Two concluding remarks. First, James's principal characters are not Venetian. Since Venice had always lain on his soul as a mass not to be assimilated, since it resisted easy appropriation, he "covered" himself by writing about Anglo-American national types, whom he understood. If the older romantic myth of Venice is exploited, though now somewhat modified by the project of American realism, James has enough awareness of his own limitations not to ascribe to Venetians themselves the motives, passions, and purposes of the characters whose stories he tells. Even so, Venice is exploited for its stock associations, and in the portrait of Eugenio we see James falling back on a stereotype of the Italian swindler that represents a failure of imaginative invention.

And, finally, those American writers I have mentioned—all of whom expressed some degree of dismay, shock, or horror at the political fate of Venice, her poverty and decay, and her reputation for what James in the essay called "loving if not too well at least too often"—all of them were nevertheless inveterate Italophiles. All of them express their love for the place by personifying and feminizing Venice as a lovely, seductive woman: "Italy," James Fenimore Cooper wrote to Greenough in 1838, "haunts my dreams and clings to my ribs like another wife. . . ." (He could not say "mistress," but the necessary release from social and sexual repressions experienced at home is clearly symbolized by Italy.) Likewise, Howells wrote to James in 1872 from America: "O my lagoons of Venice. . . . *Ricordati di me*—when you lie there in your boat, and at least say, Poor Howells, he liked Venice, though perhaps he didn't understand her." And James elaborates this feminine symbolism in full in his essay:

> It is by living there from day to day that you feel the fulness of her charm; that you invite her exquisite influence to sink into your spirit. The creature varies like a nervous woman, whom you know only

when you know all the aspects of her beauty. She has high spirits or low, she is pale or red, grey or pink, cold or warm, fresh or wan, according to the weather or the hour. She is always interesting and almost always sad; but she has a thousand occasional graces and is always liable to happy accidents. You become extraordinarily fond of these things; you count upon them; they make part of your life. Tenderly fond you become; there is something indefinable in those depths of personal acquaintance that gradually establish themselves. The place seems to personify itself, to become human and sentient and conscious of your affection. You desire to embrace it, to caress it, to possess it; and finally a soft sense of possession grows up and your visit becomes a perpetual love-affair.

Never, it seems to me, has the erotic passion been displaced so elaborately and projected onto a city; it is testimony of James's profound love of Venice.

According to Nathalia Wright, James visited Italy some fourteen times and set 6 of his 22 novels and 18 of his 112 stories wholly or partly in Italy. Still, in my judgment, whatever the claims for his having "represented" the place in some realistic way, these tales constitute "a city of words," to use Tony Tanner's phrase, a construct of language, an invention of the imagination in which much of the actuality of Venice is repressed or omitted, and in which what is given is slanted toward the necessities of aesthetic form. Even so, enough of the real Venice survives to make it evident that Venice is the only place in which one who is the heir of all the ages might appropriately live—and die. Italy was, as James put it, "quella terra santa," that Paradise that makes every other place a purgatory at best. And near the end of his life, on his last trip to Italy, he said of Venice that "Never has the whole place seemed to me sweeter, dearer, diviner." Given the fulness of his love for the place, perhaps Venetians will not mind too much how Venice served the imagination of *this* American claimant.

Henry Adams:
Politics and
Friendship

A man is known by the company he keeps and the friends who will claim him, and in this respect few men were more fortunate than Henry Adams (1838–1918). For so dour a pessimist he had a great many friends, for he had much to give. His relationships emerge for us, out of a richly documented past, in overlapping circles, interrelated cliques, and diverse coteries. As a native son of New England, he had many intimates in Boston and Cambridge, where he grew up and where he taught for many years at Harvard. Thanks to his father's diplomatic service in England during the Civil War, he formed quite a large number of British friendships that were sustained by letter and transatlantic travel. And in Washington he knew a great many journalists and important figures in government. Some years ago Ernest Scheyer constituted the circle of Henry Adams as an aesthetic set and circumscribed it to the architect H. H. Richardson, the painter John LaFarge, and the sculptor Augustus Saint-Gaudens.[1] This was a useful lens through which to look at Adams, though it was too limited.

Another such lens is "The Five of Hearts," a group made up of Adams's favorites. This inner circle included his wife Marian (familiarly known as "Clover"); John Hay, secretary of state, and his wife Clara, who were central to the political and social life of Washington in the late nineteenth century; and Clarence King, the geologist who

---

[1] Ernest Scheyer, *The Circle of Henry Adams: Art and Artists* (Detroit: Wayne State University Press, 1970).

knew all about gold and silver mines, charted the 40th parallel, and wrote a very popular account of the West called *Mountaineering in the Sierra Nevada* (1872). Even though this was Adams's most intimate set, the special character of the group in relation to politics cannot be grasped without taking into account others who came and went within the magic circle. And these included Henry James, the novelist, who had known Clover Hooper before her marriage to Adams; John LaFarge, the painter; Mrs. Donald Cameron, the beautiful Washington society hostess; and many others who had a recognized place in the literary, political, scientific, and social life of his time—including Charles Eliot Norton, Charles Milnes Gaskell, Henry Cabot Lodge, Oliver Wendell Holmes, and Charles W. Eliot. Adams and his friends, in the words of Patricia O'Toole, formed an elite group who in their public lives "helped to define American culture and politics in the years between the Civil War and World War I." But she has quite rightly remarked that Adams's personal relationships disclose an equally compelling story of "abounding love, the riches of friendship, tenderness, loyalties verging on passion, generosity," as well as "a story of secrets, loneliness, betrayal, madness and suicide."[2]

In *The Education of Henry Adams,* privately published in 1907, Adams was to thematize the failure of his education (in politics, law, science, literature, and society) to prepare him for the life of his time. But in 1858, at age twenty, he wrote to his brother that he had "a theory that an educated and reasonably able man can make his mark if he chooses," and he predicted that "if I know myself, I can't fail."[3] With its distinguished pedigree of presidents and diplomats, failure in that family could only have been construed in a political context. The family teased him him about a life in politics and wondered aloud as to what exalted post Henry might come to fill. He played the game with gay indifference, telling his mother in 1860 that "As for having the 'Presidency' in view I hardly think it's desirable with the present occupant's fate before one's eyes [a hostile Congress was investigating President Buchanan's "abuse" of federal patronage]; I aspire to the leadership in the lower House and the Departments" (*SL,* 22). Yet he knew himself to be most adapted to "literary pur-

---

2 Patricia O'Toole, *The Five of Hearts: An Intimate Portrait of Henry Adams and His Friends, 1880–1918* (New York: Clarkson N. Potter, 1990), pp. xii–xiii. Quotations from this work will hereafter be cited as *FH,* in parentheses, in the text.

3 *Henry Adams: Selected Letters,* ed. Ernest Samuels (Cambridge: Harvard University Press, 1992), p. 8. Hereafter, citations from this volume of letters will be given as *SL,* in parentheses, in the text.

suits," and given his family's importance, he decided at the beginning that what he had to write would have historical significance. In an 1860 letter to his brother—written from Washington, where he was serving as private secretary to his father—he remarks:

> I propose to write you this winter a series of private letters to show how things look. I fairly confess that I want to have a record of this winter on file, and though I have no ambition nor hope to become a Horace Walpole, I still would like to think that a century or two hence when everything else about us is forgotten, my letters might still be read and quoted as a memorial of manners and habits at the time of the great secession of 1860. At the same time you will be glad to hear all the gossip and to me it will supply the place of a Journal (*SL*, 31).

To examine Adams's relationships with family and friends is to discover that the famous Adams irony, self-deprecation, and skepticism were there from the very beginning. And they form his principal gift to his friends. In 1863 he tells his brother Charles Francis that all of his readings in science and philosophy confirm his belief in "our own impotence and ignorance. In this amusement, I find, if not consolation, at least some sort of mental titillation" (*SL*, 63). Later he responds to William James's argument for free will by remarking to him that "A few hundred men represent the entire intellectual activity of the whole thirteen hundred millions. What then? . . . Not one of them has ever got so far as to tell us a single vital fact worth knowing. We can't prove even that we are" (*SL*, 167). His letters certainly left proof of his existence, but for us they constitute a compendium of Walpolean gossip, his own version of table talk, and a journal of sorts recording his impressions of people, political and social developments, his travels, and his travails. Because he expected his letters to be published—no doubt about the time he ascended to the White House—his correspondence is not as intimate as that of other writers in his circle, but it nonetheless establishes the special character of Henry Adams as a friend and confidant.

After serving his father as secretary in the legation in London during the Civil War, Adams aspired to a career in journalism. He even wrote some political analyses from London. Later he edited the *North American Review* and taught history at Harvard, where he was highly esteemed. He and Clover were married in 1872, moved to a princely house on Lafayette Square in Washington, and established a salon unequaled in Washington for its high style and scintillating political talk. "I gravitate to a capital by a primary law of nature,"

Adams wrote to an English correspondent. "This is the only place in America where society amuses me, or where life offers variety."[4] In Washington Adams composed the anonymously published novel *Democracy* (1880) and, under the pseudonym Frances Snow Compton, *Esther* (1884), a study of his wife's religious conflicts. He likewise wrote a massive history of the administrations of Jefferson and Madison, *Mont-Saint-Michel and Chartres* (1904), and *The Education of Henry Adams* (1907), on which his fame as a writer principally rests.

It would almost be true to say that Adams's various circles overlapped on the grid of Washington politics. Most of his friends, even if they did not live in Washington, were treated to Adams's rich, ongoing commentary on the spectacle of what then passed for Beltway politics. As he watched the Washington political scene, Adams concluded that any young man who went into politics was the worse for it: "They all try to be honest, and then are tripped up by the dishonest; or they try to be dishonest (i.e. practical politicians) and degrade their own natures" (*SL,* 165). Although he was prepared by every consideration of birth and education to be president, Adams lacked the popular touch, was offended by the advancement of lesser men, and concluded that power was "a diseased appetite, like a passion for drink or perverted tastes"; the desire for power produced "an aggravation of self, a sort of tumor that ends by killing the victim's sympathies."[5] In 1899 he told Elizabeth Cameron that he had managed to drag on a degraded existence for more than thirty years without an office and was all the better for it. But Justice Oliver Wendell Holmes had a different opinion of Adams's relation to power: Adams wanted it all right, but he wanted it handed to him on a silver platter. In any case, Adams was forced to be content to sit on the sidelines, watching and criticizing the political system while others, such as John Hay, controlled the levers of power.

Meanwhile, Clover filled their palatial home with beautiful porcelains, oriental rugs, silver antiques, Japanese bronzes, and wonderful paintings by the old masters. And there, on Lafayette Square, she oversaw a social life that included senators and representatives, artists, intellectuals, and the social elite. Washington social life thought well of itself in this era, but in fact Washington society was full of

---

4 *Henry Adams and His Friends: A Collection of His Unpublished Letters,* ed. Harold Dean Cater (Boston: Houghton Mifflin, 1947), p. xliii.
5 *The Education of Henry Adams,* ed. D. W. Brogan (Boston: Houghton Mifflin, 1961), p. 147. Hereafter, quotations from this work will be cited as *EHA,* in parentheses, in the text.

vulgarians who would not have lasted thirty seconds in old New York or Brahmin Boston. The Adamses—whose exclusiveness was legendary—grasped this early on and quickly tired of the social procession. "The universe," Henry Adams remarked, "hitherto has existed in order to produce a dozen people to amuse the five of hearts. Among us we know all mankind. We or our friends have canvassed creation, and there are but a dozen or two companions in it;—men and women, I mean, whom you like to have about you, and whose society is an active pleasure" (*SL*, 168). In "Pandora," Henry James wrote a story in which his central character, modeled on Henry Adams, says to his wife, "Hang it, let us be vulgar and have some fun—let us invite the President." This characterization of the Adamses' social condescension was not an exaggeration.

II

John Hay, though immersed in politics, was also a man of letters. As Lincoln's assistant secretary, the young Hay had been in a position to see Oval Office decisions during the Civil War, and out of this experience came his co-authored ten-volume *Abraham Lincoln: A History* (1890). Popular with the public for his *Castilian Days* (1871) and *Pike County Ballads* (1871), Hay also published in 1884 an anonymous novel critical of the working class in the struggle between capital and labor, *The Bread-Winners*. Appointed assistant secretary of state by President Rutherford B. Hayes in 1880, the immensely wealthy Hays moved in next door to the Adamses. Afterward he was McKinley's ambassador to Great Britain and secretary of state under McKinley *and* Theodore Roosevelt. At the State Department he designed the Open Door policy in China and the Hay-Pauncefote Treaty that gave the United States control over the Panama Canal. Given the theme of the novel and the anonymity of *Democracy*, many readers thought Hay to be its author; and for a like reason people often guessed that Adams was the author of *The Bread-Winners*.

Clarence King (1842–1901) was an odd addition to this circle of intimates. A hard-driving geologist who loved nothing more than horseback riding and tenting around a campfire in the West, King had worked the mines of the Comstock lode, engaged in the survey of the Cordilleran ranges from the Rockies to California, and contributed centrally to the *Report of the Geological Explorations of the Fortieth Parallel* (1870–1880). Patricia O'Toole remarks that "the geologist's hammer was the key to El Dorado in nineteenth-century America—the only scientific means of unlocking the earth's treasure chests of gold, silver, copper, iron, and coal." King had the scientific savvy. Known as the "King of Diamonds" for exposing a scam involving a "salted" field of diamonds, he was in constant demand as a consultant on the location and worth of lodes of precious minerals. No less the snob than his friends, he wanted it engraved upon his tombstone that "I am to the last fibre aristocratic in my belief, that I think the only fine thing to do with the masses is to govern and educate them into some semblance of their social superiors" (*FH,* 70). With these superiors he hobnobbed at Lafayette Square and at his clubs, the Century and the Knickerbocker in New York. But although he had brilliant gifts in the field, King was an improvident speculator and, living in too grand a style, he died penniless. From his nickname, the King of Diamonds, the group came to call themselves "The Five of Hearts." They printed customized stationery with the embossed design of the five of hearts and corresponded with each other until their deaths. King gave them a tea service with cups shaped in the heart's design, and, as Harold Dean Cater has observed, "for about five years they amused each other at tea-table rites whenever they were in town together." [6] Adams and his friends leagued to find Clarence King a wife, even setting him up with the novelist Constance Fenimore Woolson, who, according to Hay, "loved him at sight and talks of nothing else" (*FH,* 114). But King declined the gambit: ladies of their exalted social class failed to excite him. And when hostesses in New York also tried to make a match, King would like as not remark:

> The New York girl is certainly a phenomenon. What she would doubtless call her mind is a crazy quilt of bright odds and ends. Bits of second-hand opinion cut bias, snips of polite error patched in with remnants of truth which don't show the whole pattern, little rags of scandal &c &c all deftly sewed together in a pretty chromatic chaos well calculated to please a congenital dude but fatiguing to a lover of natural women, such as I am (*FH,* 184).

King described himself as having a "pessimistic hate of civilization," which seemed odd for a member of the Century Club. But it was an expression of an idealization of the primitive that was somehow more vigorous than civilization, which had become effete and attenuated. King's feeling took the form of a detestation of the effect, on young women of his class, of Anglo-American sexual mores in the

---

6 "Introduction," *Henry Adams and His Friends: A Collection of His Unpublished Letters,* p. xliv.

Victorian Era. Praising a "grandly barbaric Congo woman" who had come to work in his mother's Newport house, King told Hay that

> Civilization so narrows the gamut! respectability lets the human pendulum swing over such a pitiful little arc that it is worthwhile now and again to see human beings whose feelings have no inflexible bar of metal restraining their swing to the limits set by civilized experience and moral law (*FH*, 186).

Such views were hardly consonant with those of the Adamses and the Hays, but the confirmed bachelor was such a genial companion that his oddities of opinion were forgiven. After his death Adams was to write that

> King had everything to interest and delight Adams. He knew more than Adams did of art and poetry; he knew America, especially west of the hundredth meridian, better than any one; he knew the professor by heart, and he knew the Congressman better than he did the professor. He knew even women, even the American woman, even the New York woman, which is saying much. . . . His wit and humor; his bubbling energy which swept every one into the current of his interest; his personal charm of youth and manners; his faculty of giving and taking, profusely lavishly, whether in thought or in money as though he were Nature herself, marked him almost alone among Americans (*EHA*, 311).

The individual lives of King, the Hays, and the Adamses are well known to students of nineteenth-century social and literary history, but the personal interrelations among them ramified outward and have an appeal equal in social interest to the Bloomsbury group or the Stein circle in Paris. One of the most interesting such ramifications was what came to be a nearly lifelong friendship of Henry Adams and Henry James. Both of them, Henry Adams thought, belonged to what Adams called the "type bourgeois-bostonien." In old age Adams had nothing but disdain for the achievements of the type—which he identified with himself, Henry James, William Wetmore Story, Emerson, Charles Sumner, Bronson Alcott, and James Russell Lowell. All of us, he told Henry James in 1903, "were in actual fact only one mind and nature; the individual was a facet of Boston. We knew each other to the last nervous centre, and feared each other's knowledge."[7] What they all knew, Adams thought, was that

---

7 *The Correspondence of Henry James and Henry Adams: 1877–1914*, ed. George Monteiro (Baton Rouge: Louisiana State University Press, 1992), p. 60. Hereafter, citations from this work will be given as *CHJ&HA*, in parentheses, in the text.

the culture of Boston and Cambridge had made them shallow; and out of this Boston matrix had arisen their profound ignorance, introspective self-distrust, and the nervous self-consciousness that vitiated them all. Neither Henry nor William James would have agreed.

Henry James—who was really a born New Yorker—did everything possible to avoid being thought a bourgeois Bostonian, as his satirical novel *The Bostonians* (1886) makes plain. And this avoidance took him to the extent of expatriating to Italy, then France, and finally England, where he became a clubman *par excellence* and bought that now-famous Lamb House in Rye. To Adams, the expatriate James was impersonating, albeit in a financially straitened way, the tone of an English earl in Sussex. James nevertheless produced a library of brilliant works of fiction that beggars most other Boston literary accomplishments—Adams's included.

Since Henry James had known Clover Adams in New England before her marriage, whenever he went to Washington, or they came to London, he settled in at their hearth for what was perhaps the best conversation in town. By all accounts Clover was a quick, intelligent, witty, sardonic personality who loved and was loved by Adams with a roughness, tenderness, and solicitude that are indeed touching.[8] She was a learned woman but also an acerbic and biting personality not always trusted by Washington matrons. Clover at times thought James made too free with their hospitality. She told her father in 1880 that "Mr. James . . . comes in every day at dusk & sits by our fire but is a frivolous being dining out nightly. Tomorrow being an off night he has invited himself to dine with us" (*CHJ&HA,* 4). Invariably they argued about the merits of life in America versus Europe. The Adamses, James told Sir John Clark, "don't pretend to conceal (as why should they?) their preference of America to Europe, and they rather rub it in to me, as they think it a wholesome discipline for my demoralized spirit." Yet their aversion to Europe he thought invidious: "One excellent reason for their liking Washington better than London is that they are, vulgarly speaking, 'someone' here, and that they are nothing in your complicated kingdom."[9]

Even so, James was enchanted with the "Clover Adamses." Clover was bright, witty, and irreverent; she seemed to James "the incarnation" of his native land. She liked James too but made it plain to the

---

8 On Clover's poignant death, see Eugenia Kaledin's excellent study *The Education of Mrs. Henry Adams* (Philadelphia: Temple University Press, 1981).

9 *Henry James: Letters,* ed. Leon Edel (Cambridge: Harvard University Press, 1975), II, 366.

novelist that he was spending too much time in Europe. If John Hay liked Henry James's novels, Clover declared that "James's trouble was not that he bit off more than he could chaw but that 'he chaws more than he bites off.'" Dismissing *The Portrait of a Lady,* she said, "I'm ageing fast and prefer what Sir Walter [Scott] called the 'big bow-wow style'" (*CHJ&HA,* 7). As their flyting went on over the adequacy of America, James told Grace Norton in 1880 that so many "cultivated Americans" lived abroad that

> it is a great refreshment to encounter two specimens of this class who find the charms of their native land so much greater than those of Europe. In England they appear to have suffered more than enjoyed, and their experience is not unedifying, for they have seen and known a good deal of English life. But they are rather too critical and invidious. I shall miss them much, though—we have had such inveterate discussions and comparing of notes. They have been much liked here. Mrs. Adams, in comparison with the usual British female, is a perfect Voltaire in petticoats.[10]

James noted that whenever he went out into society in Washington, the Adamses were avid for gossip: "they mobbed me for revelations; and after I had dined with Blaine, to meet the president [Chester A. Arthur], they fairly hung on my lips."[11] The Adamses were angling for evidence to support their condescension. Even the eminent were not spared. Watching from her Lafayette Square window on Sundays, Clover wrote of the heavyset Arthur: "There goes our chuckle-headed sovereign on his way from church! He doesn't look as if he fed only on spiritual food."[12] Of the sculptor William Wetmore Story, she said: "Oh! how he does spoil nice blocks of white marble." And observing that the retiring Clara Hay "never speaks," she remarked that it was just as well, since Mr. Hay "chats for two" (*FH,* 69).

Henry's brother Charles Francis had opposed Henry's engagement, bursting out at the news, "Heavens!—no—they're all crazy as coots. She'll kill herself, just like her aunt!" (*SL,* 187). And indeed, the Hoopers suffered what James called a "hereditary melancholia." The Hooper family had "a reputation for producing neurotic women," of whom "there were a number of medically certifiable depressives and suicides."[13] Henry Adams was fully aware of the family predisposition,

---

10 *Henry James: Letters,* II, 307.
11 Leon Edel, *Henry James: A Life* (New York: Harper and Row, 1985), p. 273.
12 Otto Friedrich, *Clover* (New York: Simon and Schuster, 1979), p. 277.
13 Peter Shaw, "All in the Family: A Psychobiography of the Adamses," *American Scholar,* 54 (1985), 505.

and told his brother that he had calculated the risks of marriage to Clover. He found the risk worth the reward and said that he intended to proceed with the marriage. Adams was also well aware of Clover's unnaturally close bond with her father, and he tried tried to make both of them happy with the marriage decision. Still, there are troubling echoes of her bouts with depression in his fiction and letters. He tried to buoy her spirits, but when her father died, Clover had no reserve of spiritual or psychological strength. She could not cope with her depression, and she ended her life in 1885 by ingestion of potassium cyanide.

I have said that the Adams record is richly detailed. Yet there are gaps, lacunae, and reticences in the record that Adams himself concealed. Years later, when he wrote *The Education,* Adams could not bring himself to mention his wife Clover, and he left void the twenty-year period touching the time of their marriage. For more than a decade afterward, Adams forbade any mention in his presence of Clover's name, much less any reference to her death. He shunned society well beyond any conventional mourning period, even for his social class and that historical period, and he grieved for her in private. The gravesite sculpture at Rock Creek Cemetery in Washington, called "The Peace of God," which Adams commissioned of Augustus Saint-Gaudens, was virtually his only comment on what Clover had meant to him in life and death. And the statue itself is eloquent in its mystery and silence. Toward the end he broke the silence and told the recent widower Lord Curzon that "I cannot talk of her. . . . Some visions are too radiant for words. When they fade, they leave life colorless. I do not understand how we bear such suffering as we do when we lose them; but we have to be silent, for no expression approaches the pain" (*SL,* 471–472). After her death, Adams said that "The world seems to me to have suddenly changed, and to have left me an old man, pretty well stranded and very indifferent to situations which another generation must deal with. . . . I have been thrown out of the procession, and can't catch up again" (*FH,* 172). He never did.

III

Hay, a Midwesterner by birth, was raised to high political position thanks to his intimacy with Lincoln and his readiness to serve the Republican Party throughout a long and distinguished diplomatic career. Marriage to Clara Stone's millions did not diminish his stature with government leaders and the social elite of Washington and

London. Henry Adams was to say in *The Education* that one of the lessons of politics is that a friend in power is a friend lost, but Hay's political eminence did not prevent him from continuously seeking Adams's counsel, a fact which Theodore Roosevelt came to resent bitterly in his secretary of state. The role John Hay played on the international political scene was not lost on him. He was prolific and creative, and subsequent generations have found him a source of wit, learning, and laughter equal to Henry Adams in almost every respect. Even so, as Hay grew older and became increasingly more refined and conservative, political life in Washington became a source of continuous abrasion, and he suffered odd, undiagnosable illnesses. About politics he told President Garfield that "The constant contact with envy, meanness, ignorance, and the swinish selfishness which ignorance breeds, needs a stronger heart and a more obedient nervous system than I can boast of" (*FH,* 72). Still, he unfailingly served his country when the call came.

Clara Hay was by all accounts a dutiful wife who served the ambassador and secretary, and their many children, with exemplary, if unintellectual, devotion. While it is clear that John Hay loved her very much, she did not satisfy his every need, and in 1887 he fell in love with Nannie Lodge, the beautiful wife of Senator Henry Cabot Lodge. Their affair was conducted by indirections so circumspect, in the gossipy Washington society of the time, that their usually "thwarted assignations" could only have caused them both continual frustration. If Clara knew about the affair, she wisely kept quiet about it and held her family together. Meanwhile the group teased one another about the anonymous novels that had been publicly ascribed to one or another of them. Some thought that Adams had written Hay's *The Bread-Winners,* others that Hay had written *Democracy.* Some thought King the author. For a while, none of them knew which of his friends had written these books. Making a game of the mystification, Hay announced that Adams must have written *The Bread-Winners,* and he told Adams, "To think that while Mrs. Hay and, Mrs. Don Cameron, sat guilelessly by your fireside and bragged about Cleveland, you were taking down our artless prattle for the use of future satire—it is too much, 75 percent too much" (*FH,* 127). *The Boston Evening Transcript* was so free with its speculations as to authorship that the wondering William Dean Howells felt it necessary to tell Hay that "I had nothing to do with it."[14]

---

14 *John Hay–Howells Letters: The Correspondence of John Milton Hay and William Dean Howells, 1861–1905,* eds. George Monteiro and Brenda Murphy (Boston: Twayne, 1980), p. 74.

Constance Fenimore Woolson thought that Hay and King had both written *Democracy* so as to make it possible for each individually to deny that he had done it. In London, Hay met a woman who delighted him "by announcing that *Democracy* and *The Bread-Winners* were the only American novels worth reading. 'I tried to make her believe I wrote them,'" he told Adams, "'but it was n.g.'" (*FH*, 223). On a trip to Cuba with Adams, Clarence King told Hay that they had discovered in their rented house "your detestable and ribald novel *Democracy*" (*FH*, 274). And in London in 1887, Hay told Adams that he had bought a number of drawings by the old masters and had spent "the last cent I got for 'Democracy' in minerals for Mrs. Hay" (*FH*, 222). Who had written which novel was great fun for all of them, while the anonymity lasted, except for King, who was so put off by *Democracy*'s satire on venality in American politics that he vowed to write a novel called *Monarchy* or *Aristocracy* to show that political life was worse in London. Adams—who had had a ringside seat at the Court of St. James during the Civil War, while Gladstone and Palmerston maneuvered with Lincoln over Confederate recognition—might have agreed.

Wealthy and famous, Adams was also the object of matchmakers after Clover's death, but as he told Lucy Baxter in 1890,

> You all abominate second marriages, yet you all conspire to bring them about. I receive admonitions constantly on the subject, and am aware that my friends take an active interest in selecting a victim to sacrifice to my selfishness. I do not care to interfere with their search. My only precaution is to show a pronounced attachment to married women, so as to preclude any attachment that could cause a rumor of other ties. It would be useless and impossible to argue the matter, or to give reasons for preferring solitude seul to solitude à deux; but the reasons are sufficiently strong, and if I ever should act in a contrary sense, it would be because I should have begun to lose my will, and was in the first stages of imbecility. Just now my only wish is to escape from the dangers that remain in life with the least possible noise and suffering (*SL*, 210).

In fact he called the period after 1885 his "posthumous" existence and never remarried.

Even so, Adams in the fall of 1881 made the acquaintance of Elizabeth Sherman Cameron, a tall, beautiful girl of twenty-four unhappily married to the rich, alcoholic Senator J. Donald Cameron of Pennsylvania. After Clover's death, Adams and Lizzie Cameron turned to each other for consolation and, though he was nearly twice her age (though younger than her husband), thus commenced a relationship that eventually set tongues wagging in Washington and Boston. There can be little doubt that the two loved each other, but it was a strange and difficult relationship. Mrs. Cameron, who valued propriety and her Washington social position, did not regard divorce as possible, and their affair remained vexingly platonic. Whatever the pleasures of their relationship, and they were many, Adams was clearly frustrated and managed his disappointment by taking off for other parts of the world.

In 1890 he went to Polynesia with the painter John LaFarge. Ostensibly he was after anthropological lore, and indeed he did write the *Memoirs of Marau Taaroa, Last Queen of Tahiti* (1893), but the expedition was meant to be therapeutic. Promised by Clarence King that he would find lascivious island beauties both available and willing, Adams and LaFarge clad themselves in the native loincloth, but he complained to Mrs. Cameron that he was left unaroused by the comely nakedness they had encountered, and neither of them had been propositioned. Later, in Japan, he and LaFarge engaged geishas, but Adams observed that sex in the Orient did not exist "except as a scientific classification." He told Hay that "I am lost in astonishment at this flower of eastern culture. . . . Absolutely the women's joints clacked audibly, and their voices were metallic" (*FH,* 174). Clearly none of the oriental beauties could match the cultivated Lizzie Cameron. Back in the United States, Clarence King was not disappointed at the indifference of Adams and LaFarge to the beautiful women of Polynesia and the Orient: "I love primal woman so madly that I should have acted with jealousy had they discerned her" (*FH,* 239). Meanwhile, Hay adjured Adams to return to Washington, where life was "dull as chelsea . . . because you are away."[15] So the congenital dude came back to Lafayette Square to a lifetime of nearly always chaperoned contacts with the tantalizing but unavailable Mrs. Cameron.

Patricia O'Toole reads Henry Adams's celebration of the Virgin Mary, in *Mont-Saint Michel and Chartres,* as a sublimation of Adams's longing for Lizzie Cameron:

> In the Virgin of the French Middle Ages he found the ideal that allowed him to transform his ungratified love into worship and to create a role for himself that was less demeaning than "tame cat" [as Chateaubriand had called himself to his friend Madame Récamier,

---

15 Quoted in Howard A. Kushner and Anne Hummel Sherrill, *John Milton Hay: The Union of Poetry and Politics* (Boston: Twayne, 1977), p. 78.

who had once been his lover]. Mrs. Cameron would be his goddess, he would be her votary. It was a noble resolution of a conflict that had tormented them both, since it seemed to settle, once and for all, the question of sex (*FH,* 336).

This reading, however, strikes me as trivializing Adams's deepest reflections on the way in which the worship of Mary turned religious ardor and spiritual devotion into complex forms of cultural energy in law, theology, art, and architecture in the Middle Ages. But resolution or not, Henry James was to say of the affair with Mrs. Cameron that it was "one of the longest and oddest American *liaisons* I've ever known. Women have been hanged for less—and yet men have been too, I judge, rewarded with more" (*CHJ&HA,* 22).[16]

IV

One of the most interesting of Adams's friends, and certainly the most unpredictable, was Clarence King. Miners in the West had noticed that King would often enough disappear from camp and be seen talking to Indian women in the settlements. And in London, while on business ventures, his open talk in the gentlemen's clubs caused gossip to circulate. He developed a reputation for indifference to the sexual proprieties of the genteel era, but he was so evident a gentleman that most of his friends dismissed his talk as mere talk. Frank Mason, an American diplomat in London, has left a description of King's shenanigans. King, he told John Hay, goes down to

> the lowest dive at Seven Dials, chirps to the pretty bar maid of a thieves' gin mill, gives her a guinea for a glass of "bittah," gets the frail simple thing clean gone on him. Then whips out his notebook and with a smile that would charm a duchess asks her to tell her story. Naturally she is pleased and fires away in dialect that never saw print which the wily ex-geologist nails on the spot. Of course she is a poor pitiful wronged thing who would have been an angel if she had been kindly treated and taken to Sunday school when she was a child.—They are all so, you know. Think, Hay, of ten such girls, with their plump red cheeks, their picturesque slang . . . corralled in one book written for a good moral purpose. . . . I suppose, rather let us

---

16 Robert L. Gale, following Leon Edel, has speculated that the setting of James's *The Sacred Fount* was Surrenden Dering, a huge manor house in Kent rented by the Camerons. If so, James may have been exploring some of the darker implications of the relationship between Adams, Mrs. Cameron, her husband, and John and Clara Hays. See Gale's *John Hay* (Boston: Twayne, 1978), p. 51.

say we *hope,* that King is walking through all these narrow, slippery places upright and unstained as an archangel (*FH,* 118).

But King was no archangel. It is Patricia O'Toole's theory that "he frequented such places because he could not feel sexually attracted to women unless they were, by nineteenth-century bourgeois standards, his social inferiors. Dark skins aroused him, as did servants, laborers, and prostitutes" (*FH,* 119). If this be true, King had in any case touched a nerve in respect to the sexual education of the white middle- and upper-class American girl; and he was no more critical of its negative effect on her than Edith Wharton was to be in *The Age of Innocence.*

But King's fortunes were even more bizarre. In 1887, at the age of forty-five, he commenced a romance in New York with a young black nursemaid of twenty-six named Ada Copeland. Seemingly a wealthy white man twice her age, King persuaded her to marry him in a ceremony that observed every rite of the sacrament except the marriage license, which could not be procured because of the law against miscegenation. None of his friends in Washington knew about this relationship. Yet during the fourteen years of their marriage, in which this primal woman bore him five children, King never told Ada his real name. He had introduced himself as one James Todd, and he accounted to her for his frequent absences—on trips to Washington and the West—by saying that he was a railroad porter from Baltimore. To his friends in Washington he explained his absences in New York, to be with Ada, as caused by mining trips or illness. King persuaded Ada to keep their marriage a secret by telling her that he stood to lose a sizable inheritance if the marriage were disclosed:

> The most important thing to us of all others is that the property which will one day come to me shall not be torn away from us by some foolish, idle person talking about us and some word getting to my old aunt. For the sake of your darling babies we must keep this secret of our love and our lives from the world (*FH,* 259).

That King loved Ada deeply cannot be doubted. He installed her in a large house in Brooklyn, complete with nurse, cook, laundress, and gardener, and cared for her with exemplary devotion. His feeling for her is suggested by this letter written during one of his mining trips to the West:

> I cannot tell you how delighted I was to see your handwriting again. To see something you had touched was like feeling the warmth of your hand. My darling, tell me all about yourself. I can see your dear

face every night when I lay my head on the pillow and my prayers go up to Heaven for you and the little ones. I feel most lonely and miss you most when I put out the light at night and turn away from the work of the day. Then I sit by my window in the starlight and look up at the dark night sky and think of you. Lonely seems my bed! Lonely is my pillow! I think of you and dream of you . . . (*FH,* 347).

But the pressures of leading this double life, and supporting two families (he was responsible also for his mother's establishment in Newport), took its toll on King. At one point during their marriage he had a nervous breakdown and was institutionalized briefly in the Bloomingdale Asylum. Shortly before his death King revealed to Ada his real identity. He reaffirmed their marriage, told her to call herself thenceforth Ada King, and made arrangements to bequeath to her and their children the substantial sum of $80,000. Unfortunately, his investments had been disastrous; he owed immense sums of money to John Hay and others. And when the will was probated, King's lawyer James Gardiner sold off his assets to satisfy the creditors. Ada and the children were legally dismissed with a meager sum of $65 a month. When she asked where this money came from, Gardiner replied that its source was an anonymous benefactor.

The surviving members of the Adams circle were stunned by the revelation of King's secret life, even as they had been stunned by Clover Adams's suicidal death. They had known each other so well, or so they thought. But the most intimate of relationships is never quite that rapturous fusion of personalities acclaimed in the nine-teenth-century cult of friendship. Tyler Dennett was later to remark that, after the revelation of this double life, King's name "was never mentioned over the 'Five of Hearts' teacups."[17] If so, at what had they taken offense? That King had had a common-law wife and il-legitimate children? That it had involved a black woman? That he had concealed it from his upper-class friends? Or that he had concealed his upper-class friends from Ada and his family? Kenton Clymer as-sumed the truth of the claim that the Five of Hearts turned against King and his memory and, unconvincingly, he has interpreted this as evidence of "Hay's lessening concern for Negroes."[18] But Clymer's at-tack on the politically conservative Hay seems doubtful. Years later, in 1933, Ada King sued the estate of her husband's lawyer, James Gar-diner, seeking a portion of her inheritance. She lost out in the courts

---

17 Tyler Dennett, *John Hay: From Poetry to Politics* (New York: Dodd, Mead, 1933), p. 157.
18 Kenton J. Clymer, *John Hay: The Gentleman as Diplomat* (Ann Arbor: University of Michigan Press, 1975), pp. 84–85.

but learned at last the identity of the benefactor who for thirty years had supported her and King's children. It was of course John Hay, who had died in 1905 but who in his will had provided a trust for her and the children.

V

It was doubtless a blow to Adams that the nation never drafted him, by acclamation, for the presidency. Yet the letters to Hay show his vicarious sense of political power and are rich in ruminations touching the imperial ambitions of Russia, Germany, France, and England. But with Hay's death in 1905, he remarked that "I've no longer any concern in politics" (*SL*, 373). Hay's death was so critical to Adams's sense of himself that he saw no other way to end *The Education* than with a long paean to his friend, now dead:

> "The rest is silence!". . . It was not even the suddenness of the shock, or the sense of void [at the news of Hay's death], that threw Adams into the depths of Hamlet's Shakespearean silence in the full flare of Paris frivolity in its favorite haunt where worldly vanity reached its most futile climax in human history; it was only the quiet summons to follow—the assent to dismissal (*EHA*, 504–505).

Yet as Charles Vandersee has noted, in tracing the slow accretion in *The Education* of *Hamlet* allusions—references expressive of "an inquiring spirit determined to find out what is going on"—Horatio's next remark in the play is equally important to its meaning: "Let me speak to the yet unknowing world / How these things came about."[19] Gradually Adams the historian, after Hay's death, immersed himself in the Middle Ages as he prepared *Mont Saint Michel and Chartres* (1904), a book descriptive of how the skeptical, scientific present had emerged. Writing was a lifelong passion with Adams, a habit and a necessity. Still, as he told Anne Palmer Fell in 1901, "though I am glad to be through with it, and to have no more responsibility for the universe, I find it still very amusing to look at, from a front box. The spectacle does not lose its interest. Far from it! What a fascinating melodrama it is, when one has time to think; and what do the Kaiser and the Czar and Edward VII and Pierpont Morgan think of it? I presume that Marian can tell you, since she was born to it. As I was born in the year 1138, I don't catch on" (*SL*, 399–400).

---

19 Charles Vandersee, "The Hamlet in Henry Adams," in *Critical Essays on Henry Adams* (Boston: G. K. Hall, 1981), pp. 199, 206.

The Education was meant to focus on what *he* thought of the meaningless spectacle of life both in his time and in its long historic sweep; and, to Henry James, he called the autobiography "a mere shield of protection in the grave. I advise you to take your own life in the same way, in order to prevent biographers from taking it in theirs" (*SL,* 488). While James found Adams's "monotonous disappointed pessimism" difficult to take, Adams (descended from a line of presidents) was what James confessed he would like to be: "a man of wealth and leisure, able to satisfy all his curiosities, while I am a penniless toiler." As James toiled along, creating his lords and ladies in *The Princess Casamassima* (1886) and *The Wings of the Dove* (1902), the brooding Adams thought James was pretending "to belong to a world which is as extinct as Queen Elizabeth," and "already as fossil as the buffalo" (*CHJ&HA,* 17–18).

But, paradoxically, as the years passed, their solitude drew James and Adams closer together, especially as their mutual friends died off. Writing about William James, Adams told Henry in 1911:

> We all began together, and our lives have made more or less of a unity, which is, as far as I can see, about the only unity that American society in our time had to show. Nearly all are gone. Richardson and St. Gaudens, LaFarge, Alex Agassiz, Clarence King, John Hay, and at the last, your brother William; and with each, a limb of our own lives cut off (*CHJ&HA,* 78–79).

With the death of so many mutual friends who had linked them, Adams clung to a friendship with James that became more epistolary than real. In 1913 Adams wrote to Elizabeth Cameron that "At about three in the morning I wobble all over the supposed universe. A little indigestion starts whole flocks of strange images, and then I wonder what Henry James is thinking about, as he is my last standard of comparison" (*CHJ&HA,* 30).

The difference between these two friends, both writers of genius who were neglected in old age, is suggested by Adams's response to James's autobiography, *Notes of a Son and Brother* (1914), published when both were in their seventies. An engaging meditation on his past, James's book recreated the world of Henry and William and Alice, growing up in the household of the elder Henry James, who had brought his family to New England and who lived near the Adamses in Cambridge. As he contemplated James's memorial of the world of the 1840s and 1850s in New England, Adams told Mrs. Cameron that "Poor Henry James thinks it all real, I believe, and actually still lives in that dreamy, stuffy Newport and Cambridge, with papa James and Charles Norton—and me! Yet why! It is a terrible dream, but not so weird as this here which is quite loony" (*CHJ&HA*, 89n). He must have expostulated to James in a similar vein in a letter no longer extant. James answered him on March 21, 1914, with, in my view, a magisterial statement of why the artist creates. James acknowledged the "unmitigated blackness" of Adams's state of mind. "*Of course* we are lone survivors, of course the past that was our lives is at the bottom of an abyss—if the abyss *has* any bottom; of course too there's no use talking unless one particularly *wants* to." But, James went on to say, "I still find my consciousness interesting," and he urged Adams to cultivate it with him.

> You see I still, in presence of life (or of what you deny to be such,) have reactions—as many as possible—& the book I sent you is a proof of them. It's because I am that queer monster the artist, an obstinate finality, an inexhaustible sensibility. Hence the reactions—appearances, memories, many things go on playing upon it with consequences that I note & "enjoy" (grim word!) noting. It all takes doing—& I *do*. I believe I shall do yet again—it is still an act of life (*CHJ&HA*, 88–89).

James, then, would not hear of Adams's throwing in the towel, of his surrendering to a pessimism of paralysis and inertia. He had the generosity and acuity to remind Adams that, despite his avowed nihilism, Adams had always continued to perform those acts of life himself—in writing those distinctive essays, books, and the ongoing letters that made him a literary master and the focus of great friendships.

Edith Wharton: The Fruit of the Tree

Edith Wharton's *The Fruit of the Tree* (1907), her third novel, was written toward the end of her residence in New York, while she was yet summering at The Mount in Massachusetts. Her publisher, Charles Scribner, wanted another best-seller just like *The House of Mirth* (1905), that is, a fresh, popular exposé of the moral bankruptcy of New York high society. But she was determined not to be typed as a high-society novelist, and she wanted nothing more than to illustrate her capacity for thematic variety. The conflict between capital and labor seemed promising.

Promising—but strange for Mrs. Wharton. Blake Nevius once suggested that Mrs. Wharton "had no community whatsoever" with "Howells and his generation,"[1] but in fact she knew Howells personally and must almost certainly have thought about *The Fruit of the Tree* in terms of *Annie Kilburn* (1889) and other popular realist novels dealing with industrial problems in the New England factory town. Howells's generation had produced a long line of popular labor novels, including Elizabeth Stuart Phelps's *The Silent Partner* (1871), Thomas Bailey Aldrich's *The Stillwater Tragedy* (1880), John Hay's *The Breadwinners* (1883), and H. F. Keenan's *The Money-Makers* (1885). In Mrs. Wharton's generation, new writers were bringing into the "Progressive Era" this older mode of writing. Ida M. Tarbell's *The History of the Standard Oil Company* (1904), Lincoln Steffens's *The*

---

1 Blake Nevius, *Edith Wharton: A Study of Her Fiction* (Berkeley: University of California Press, 1953), p. 24.

Shame of the Cities (1904), Samuel Hopkins Adams's *The Great American Fraud* (1906), and scores of nonfiction works like them were exposing corruption in business, industry, and politics that demanded urgent reform. Mary Wilkins in *The Portion of Labor* (1901), David Graham Phillips in *The Deluge* (1905), and Upton Sinclair in *The Jungle* (1906), were—like Mrs. Wharton in *The Fruit of the Tree*—following in this long procession of muckraking prose and popular labor fiction.

For one who had cast a doubtful eye on the impractical theorizing of eighteenth-century reformers in *The Valley of Decision* (1902), Mrs. Wharton's motives in writing this kind of novel seem intriguing. But if she was known as a chronicler of drawing-room society, she had also dealt in a surprisingly extensive way with poverty and its effect on the human spirit. Her first published tale, "Mrs. Manstey's View" (1891), portrayed the grimness of tenement life in New York City. Subsequent tales like "The Confessional" and "A Cup of Cold Water" also touched on the misery of the poor in the city. "Bunner Sisters"—published in *Xingu and Other Stories* in (1916)—was long thought to be one of Mrs. Wharton's later naturalistic portraits of the despair of the poor, but it was in fact drafted as early as 1891 or 1892. The world of Gerty Farish in *The House of Mirth,* and Lily's final months in the cheap boardinghouse—which stand in dingy contrast to the splendor of Bellomont and the Fifth Avenue drawing rooms—were therefore not novelties. All of these early stories suggest how sensitive was Mrs. Wharton, from the beginning of her career, to the problems of the poor.

What could be done in their behalf? Without any very specific notion about the right way to get a "square deal" for the factory worker, Mrs. Wharton turned away from the drawing room to the plight of the textile workers in small-town Massachusetts. "Heaven knows where she got her knowledge of mill-towns,"[2] Q. D. Leavis once wondered, and so may we. For Edith Wharton was a New Yorker who merely vacationed in the Berkshires. And these vacations were by and large insular affairs during which she and other New Yorkers of her class enjoyed the mountain air and exchanged visits with one another, largely avoiding the locals. But, aside from the muckraking prose then current, in which she immersed herself, she got her information about the textile mills via the innovation of the motor-car. She had her chauffeur, Charles Cook, drive her down

---

2 See Q. D. Leavis's "Henry James's Heiress: The Importance of Edith Wharton," in *Edith Wharton: A Collection of Critical Essays,* ed. Irving Howe (Englewood Cliffs, N.J.: Prentice-Hall, 1962), p. 83.

from her palatial estate at The Mount, near Lenox, to Adams, Massachusetts, where she toured the local mills to investigate factory conditions.[3] Unfortunately, the noise of the machines was so great that she couldn't hear her guide, and so the notes got scrambled. Later, when the story began to appear serially in *Scribner's Magazine,* experts wrote in to call attention to the great lady's technical errors.[4]

II

These errors seemed minor to Mrs. Wharton in view of her ambitious moral resolve. "It cannot be too often repeated," she once observed, "that every serious picture of life contains a thesis. . . ."[5] Despite her confusions of fact, Mrs. Wharton's purpose in *The Fruit of the Tree* is perfectly clear: to expose and criticize, in narrative form, an abuse of the industrial system—the irresponsibility of factory managers who fail to look after the physical and spiritual welfare of their employees. The thesis here is expressed through John Amherst, social reformer and assistant manager of the Hanaford Mills. A progressive who undertakes to reform the conditions that make mill work both dangerous and soul-destroying, Amherst seems to be different from the impractical revolutionaries of *The Valley of Decision,* whose utopian schemes destroy Pianura.

> John Amherst was no one-sided idealist. He felt keenly the growing complexity of the relation between employer and worker, the seeming hopelessness of permanently harmonizing their claims, the recurring necessity of fresh compromises and adjustments. He hated rant, demagogy, the rash formulating of emotional theories; and his contempt for bad logic and subjective judgments led him to regard with distrust the panaceas offered for the cure of economic evils.[6]

At the same time, however, Amherst is, like most of us, emotional and inconsistent. He is deeply troubled at the plight of Dillon, a worker whose arm has been mangled in a carding-room accident. If

---

3 There may be something of a reflexive and ironic self-portrait of Mrs. Wharton in Bessy Westmore, the heiress of the Westmore fortune, descending on the mills at Hanaford, to perform an inspection. But whereas Bessy had no interest in the workers and no wish to understand the conditions of their labor, Mrs. Wharton meant serious business.

4 For a discussion of these matters, see R. W. B. Lewis, *Edith Wharton: A Biography* (New York: Harper and Row, 1975), p. 181.

5 Edith Wharton, "Fiction and Criticism," p. 4; unpublished manuscript in the Beinecke Library, Yale University.

6 Edith Wharton, *The Fruit of the Tree* (New York: Scribner's, 1907), pp. 47–48. Hereafter, quotations from this work will be cited as *FT,* in parentheses, in the text.

Dillon cannot recover, shouldn't he—Amherst speculates to the nurse Justine Brent—be put out of his misery? And what can be done for Dillon's wife, whose lungs have been ruined by inhaling textile dust, or for the other seven hundred women who are working in the mills? Feeling both "the menace of industrial conditions" as a whole and the poignancy of the life of the laborers as individuals, Amherst perceives that whatever the philosophic implications of industrialism, "only through sympathy with its personal, human side could a solution be reached" (*FT,* 48). Given the explicitness of Mrs. Wharton's unmistakable theme, then, it is surprising to hear Robert Morss Lovett say that "the industrial worker" does not "appear in her pages." Quite wrongly, Lovett regarded her as unconcerned with "the relation of class with class" which, he said, *eighteen years later,* was "the vital issue of social morality today."[7]

Yet it must be stressed that *The Fruit of the Tree* does not directly address bread-and-butter economic issues. The question of the fairness of the laborer's wage or the size of the owner's margin of profit is not her point. Amherst makes it very plain that he has "no wish to criticise the business management of the mills—even if there had been any excuse for my doing so. . . ." His is a moral argument—that "the condition of the operatives could be very much improved, without permanent harm to the business, by any one who felt a personal sympathy for them; and in the end I believe such sympathy produces better work, and so benefits the employer materially" (*FT,* 100). In this respect Amherst's arguments are in support of the rights of the mill owners as a group, but he is offering them some practical wisdom as to what labor practices best conduce to the profit motive and fulfill the owners' interests. Yet oddly enough, in some criticism of this novel, Amherst's arguments are seen as expressions of a left-wing labor policy. Mrs. Wharton, however, was a lifelong opponent of socialism, as her correspondence with Upton Sinclair will suggest.

One of the greatest wrongs of the new industrial system, according to Mrs. Wharton's protagonist, is that there is no longer any familiar contact between the owner and his employee.[8] "That the breach must be farther widened by the ultimate substitution of the stock-company for the individual employer—a fact obvious to any student of economic tendencies—presented to Amherst's mind one

---

7 Robert Morss Lovett, *Edith Wharton* (New York: Robert M. McBride, 1925), pp. 57–58. One is struck with how often Mrs. Wharton's left-wing critics appear not to have read all—or indeed much—of her fiction.

8 This theme was later enlarged upon by John P. Marquand in his mid-century New England mill novel *Sincerely, Willis Wayde* (1955).

of the most painful problems in the scheme of social readjustment." It is characteristic of Amherst, however, to focus on solving the specific problems that confront him rather than those of the future. He sees his main task as bringing the owner "closer to his workers. Till he entered personally into their hardships and aspirations—till he learned what they wanted and why they wanted it—Amherst believed that no mere law-making, however enlightened, could create a wholesome relation between the two" (*FT*, 48).

Amherst's immediate project is to enlarge the floor space of the mills, so that workers like Dillon will not be endangered by the machines, and to abolish the system of tenement rents, so that workers will be able to buy homes from the mills. Green lawns, tennis courts, picnic areas, a reading room, and a gymnasium are seen as low-cost, profit-enhancing ameliorations. But Amherst finds himself handcuffed by the absentee owners. Because they are concerned with profit, they do not take a sufficient interest in the conditions in which the laborers live and work. As she looked about Adams, Mrs. Wharton could not help condemning this absenteeism in very personal —that is to say in *aesthetic*—terms. What seems to have horrified her most was the visual ugliness of the American factory town, the suburban slum that, in its visible repugnance, destroyed, she felt, the worker's moral sense:

> With sudden disgust he [Amherst] saw the sordidness of it all—the poor monotonous houses, the trampled grass-banks, the lean dogs prowling in refuse-heaps, the reflection of a crooked gas-lamp in a stagnant loop of the river; and he asked himself how it was possible to put any sense of moral beauty into lives bounded forever by the low horizon of the factory. There is a fortuitous ugliness that has life and hope in it: the ugliness of overcrowded city streets, of the rush and drive of packed activities; but this out-spread meanness of the suburban working colony, uncircumscribed by any pressure of surrounding life, and sunk into blank acceptance of its isolation, its banishment from beauty and variety and surprise, seemed to Amherst the very negation of hope and life (*FT*, 22–23).

The doubtful plot device by which Mrs. Wharton brings Amherst and the rich owners into closer contact is the marriage of Amherst to Bessy Westmore, a spirited but mindless woman whose family owns the mill. Trying to motivate this frivolous wife to forego some of her luxuries, so that mill reforms can be accomplished, takes too much out of Amherst. Unable to achieve his goals, he becomes impatient; bored with his mill projects, she drifts away. They become estranged, and his enthusiasm for reform begins to flag. Later, after Bessy's death, Amherst does implement some of his innovations. Rough banks are leveled and sodded, trees are planted, the workers' cottages are freshly painted, the mills are enlarged, and medical facilities are improved. But one's final impression is that these improvements represent only a start: much yet remains to be done to make Hanaford Mills an adequate workplace.

III

The Fruit of the Tree is not a successful novel, despite its many favorable reviews.[9] What finally subverts it is not Mrs. Wharton's ignorance of mill technology—her errors were corrected anyway in the first book edition—but rather her failure to see her subject steadily and see it whole. The novel is, in fact, backbroken. Midway through the book—probably because she recognized that labor fiction was not her *métier*—Mrs. Wharton abandoned the theme of labor reform in favor of another: the moral implications of euthanasia. When Amherst's impulsive wife is injured by a fall from a horse, Mrs. Wharton's heroine, the nurse Justine Brent, deliberately puts Bessy out of her misery by giving her an overdose of morphine. Justine's is, ostensibly, a "moral motive"—to put to an end the agonizing pain from which Bessy, it is said, can never recover. Felt compassion, grounded on a rational motive, thus leads her to kill Amherst's wife.

Later, Amherst and Justine are drawn together, fall in love, and marry. They are "soul mates" who have, at the beginning, a perfect married life. As Justine reflects on the marital problems of Bessy and Amherst, it seems to her that

> the tragic crises in wedded life usually turned on the stupidity of one of the two concerned; and of the two victims of such a catastrophe she felt most for the one whose limitations had probably brought it about. After all, there could be no imprisonment as cruel as that of being bounded by a hard small nature. Not to be penetrable at all points to the shifting lights, the wandering music of the world—she could imagine no physical disability as cramping as that. How the little parched soul, in solitary confinement for life, must pine and dwindle in its blind cranny of self-love (*FT,* 227–228).

Thus the cramping marriage of Amherst and Bessy—and, doubtless,

---

9 For the contemporary reception of *The Fruit of the Tree,* see *Edith Wharton: The Contemporary Reviews,* eds. James W. Tuttleton, Kristin O. Lauer and Margaret P. Murray (Cambridge: Cambridge University Press, 1992), pp. 145–154.

of Edith and Teddy Wharton. But not, apparently, of Amherst and Justine, who enjoy unparalleled marital rapport.

Yet sustained happiness is not characteristic of Edith Wharton's imaginative world. And the Fates intrude in this novel in the form of Stephen Wyant, a doctor, who guesses what Justine has done in injecting Bessy with too much morphine, for—of all things—he himself is a narcotics addict. Disintegrating in this addiction, Wyant blackmails Justine. Although she tries to keep her crime a secret, Wyant eventually tells Amherst about the euthanasia. Justine had acted on principles of moral conduct which Amherst had often grandly proclaimed—*"La vraie morale se moque de la morale. . . . We perish because we follow other men's examples. . . . Socrates used to call . . . the opinions of the many by the name of Lamiae—bugbears to frighten children"* (*FT,* 429). But Amherst is in fact shaken at the revelation of Justine's mercy killing. It is one thing to endorse, on the cerebral level, euthanasia; it is another to carry it out—particularly on his wife Bessy. Justine reflects that "her fault lay in having dared to rise above conventional restrictions, her mistake in believing that her husband could rise with her. . . ." She sees that Amherst "would never be able to free himself from the traditional view of her act" (*FT,* 523–525). Indeed, he cannot.

After Justine's crime is discovered, she and Amherst separate for a year, but finally decide that in fact they need each other. Even so, the "secret inner union which had so enriched and beautified their outward lives" (*FT,* 623) has been destroyed by Justine's act and by Amherst's inability to reconcile his rational approval, in principle, of euthanasia with his moral revulsion at the mercy killing of his own wife Bessy. They can only throw themselves into the mill reforms that both are determined to effect. In assisting him, Justine thus pledges herself "to the perpetual expiation of an act for which, in the abstract, she still refused to hold herself to blame" (*FT,* 624).

IV

Calling the novel backbroken implies that it has just two themes: labor reform and euthanasia. But for Cynthia Griffin Wolff there are many themes embedded in the plot. She has asked:

> What is the "problem" of the novel? Euthanasia, the need for industrial reform, the old problem of idealized expectations coming up against the harsh realities of real-world existence, marriage, the role of women, the devastating results of failures in communication be-

tween the sexes, men's unrealistic expectations of women, the insuf-
ficiency of women's education and of the roles they are given to
enact—the list could go on and on.[10]

All of these may be aspects of Mrs. Wharton's varied story. But most
of them, it seems to me, can be subsumed under a rubric we might
call "the perils of abstract idealism." A full reading of this theme
would disclose how abstract idealism permeates several plot elements
and is played out through various characters. Despite his seeming
practicality, I am convinced that a separate paper could be written
with the title "Amherst: Or, The Perils of Abstract Idealism." But in
the space available here, I should like to concentrate on two important matters: (1) why Justine's idealism is disastrous; and (2) how a
misconceived admiration for Justine has produced a false view of
Amherst as a misogynist and of the novel as an attack on marriage.

Justine, as I have noted, pledges herself "to the perpetual expiation of an act for which, in the abstract, she still refused to hold herself to blame" (*FT,* 624). Is Justine's feeling of blamelessness justified?
The key phrase is of course *in the abstract.* But in much current criticism of the novel, this phrase is ignored. Justine is such a strong, independent, free-thinking, and self-reliant heroine that for many
readers of the novel she can do (and indeed *has done*) no wrong. The
deliberate fatal injection of morphine, for Cynthia Griffin Wolff, "is
unequivocally justified in the mind of the author and narrator." "The
text," we are told by Deborah Carlin, "presents unequivocally Justine's choice to perform euthanasia on Bessy as the morally correct
one. . . ."[11] It is even rightly pointed out that Mrs. Wharton felt, in
the case of a hopeless injury to one of her Lenox neighbors, Ethel
Cram, that the victim's sufferings might be ended "with a dose of
morphine."[12]

But such an act, Mrs. Wharton knew, could never be performed
"cleanly," that is, without affective consequences to the sensibilities of
other people. Hence the question for criticism is somewhat different:
whether the text of the novel endorses euthanasia in actuality, not in
the abstract—whether, that is, the novel approves euthanasia in the
specific circumstances in which Justine commits it. I do not believe
that it does.

---

10 Cynthia Griffin Wolff, *A Feast of Words: The Triumph of Edith Wharton* (New York:
   Oxford University Press, 1977), p. 139.
11 Wolff, p. 137; Deborah Carlin, "To Form a More Perfect Union: Gender, Tradition,
   and the Text in Wharton's *The Fruit of the Tree,*" in *Edith Wharton: New Critical Essays,*
   eds. Alfred Bendixen and Annette Zilversmit (New York: Garland Press, 1992), p. 69.
12 Lewis, p. 181.

Now, in order to exonerate Justine from the possibility that she has really done something wrong, a number of critics have recently shifted the moral issue away from her act of euthanasia to Amherst's reaction to it. Elizabeth Ammons suggests that Amherst's estrangement from Justine, after he discovers that she has killed Bessy, arises because she "did not feel bound to seek his approval [for the euthanasia] after the fact." For Ms. Ammons, there is apparently nothing wrong in Justine's killing Bessie, much less in her declining "to consider herself morally accountable to him" either before the euthanasia or after she married him.[13] The view that a spouse is not ethically accountable to the other, whether held by the husband or the wife, would seem to me to make marriage a moral impossibility. Mrs. Wharton clearly did not mean to suggest this, although some current feminist criticism insinuates as much.

In any case, to salvage Justine as a blameless heroine, this view undertakes to transform Amherst into a typical sexist pig who cannot tolerate moral autonomy in a woman. His great dismay at Justine —for actually performing a killing that they have only abstractly and theoretically discussed—automatically converts him into a hypocritical villain who is the destroyer of Justine's marriage and her affectional life. Amherst's dismay has the effect of "ruining yet another of his attempts at marriage," Deborah Carlin remarks. That is, if he has killed one woman, he's killed two—by victimizing not only Justine but Bessy before her. The argument that the center of the novel is the destruction of two wives by a misogynistic husband presupposes that Amherst *causes* Bessy's accident. And in fact Ms. Carlin transmogrifies the selfish Bessy into the long-suffering, self-sacrificing wife of Victorian sentimental fiction: Bessy "performs the only sacrifice that social and literary traditions have taught her to do; she destroys herself, though even then she still doesn't get it right."[14]

Moreover, Amherst is now to be seen as a bogus reformer since, although he "espouses a kind of socialist democracy in the work place, when it comes to his own spouses, he remains locked in a reading of a natural domination by men and a subordination of women utterly at odds with his reformist ideology."[15] Instead of labor reform or euthanasia, then, we are now advised to see the tale as

---

13 See Elizabeth Ammons, *Edith Wharton's Argument with America* (Athens: University of Georgia Press, 1980), pp. 50–51.

14 Carlin, "To Form a More Perfect Union: Gender, Tradition, and the Text in Wharton's *The Fruit of the Tree*," p. 68.

15 Carlin, "To Form a More Perfect Union: Gender, Tradition, and the Text in Wharton's *The Fruit of the Tree*," pp. 59–60. Amherst, it should be noted, is far from a socialist or social democrat in his economic thought and labor policy.

really about the victimization of women by men. Elizabeth Ammons goes even further than Ms. Carlin, finding in the novel an attack on the institution of marriage itself. When "we last see this brave New Woman," Ms. Ammons says of Justine, "she is a prisoner of a paternal, authoritarian husband"; in fact, "the book concludes by arguing that marriage to even the most enlightened man is, in the end, repressive."[16] "Once independent and self-supporting," Susan Goodman complains, "Justine is now 'an angel in the house.'"[17]

That marriage is always repressive certainly was an argument of the free-love advocates of the *fin de siècle,* but it is surprising to see the notion ascribed to Mrs. Wharton. Does *The Fruit of the Tree* really condemn marriage as such? Does Justine end up as a doormat? Does the book really attack the repression of all impulse in marriage as evil? And supposing that Justine is repressed, what is the agency of her repression? Is it Amherst? Or, when we last see her, has she repressed her own feelings—her contempt for Bessy and disgust at Amherst's idealizing memory of her—in the service of marital harmony? And if so, is any spouse, man or woman, who compromises in this way—by sidestepping a pointless conflict—a dupe and a fool? These are engaging questions which the reader will want to ponder. But two points must be stressed. First, the novel is a narrative, and is not "arguing that marriage to even the most enlightened man is, in the end, repressive." Lesbian polemics and even works of literary criticism may make such arguments, but not novels, which are works of art; and, second, Mrs. Wharton's characterization is much more complex than can be allowed by some ideological critics who wish to see the strong heroine prevail, no matter what act she may have committed, no matter what the disastrous ramifications of the act.

Justine Brent is an appealing, well-defined, fully realized woman character; but she is, I submit, far from an ideal heroine.[18] She cannot be because Mrs. Wharton's whole plot is intended to reveal the train of disasters that follow from her failure to think through the possible consequences of her act and, in particular, to anticipate, once she decides to marry Amherst, what effect a knowledge of the act might have upon him. In reality, as the title suggests, *The Fruit of the Tree* is

16 Ammons, pp. 48, 25–26.

17 Susan Goodman, *Edith Wharton's Women: Friends and Rivals* (Hanover, N.H.: University Press of New England, 1990), p. 141.

18 Only Millicent Bell seems to have noticed that, in killing the wealthy Bessy and then in marrying her husband (thereby securing in one stroke her social and economic future), Justine's nobility is tainted: "few readers, I think, feel complete confidence in Justine's disinterested 'mercy-killing' of Bessy." See *Edith Wharton and Henry James: The Story of Their Friendship* (New York: George Braziller, 1965), p. 256.

a modern instance of the fall—Justine's and Amherst's fall from purity into sin, from innocence into guilt, from ignorance into a knowledge of the moral life in all its complexity. At the heart of the book is their descent from abstract idealism into a fallen awareness of the contingency of all moral action. Yet the tendency of much criticism of *The Fruit of the Tree* is to see its moral analysis as rigidly inflexible and absolutist. H. Wayne Morgan once said once that Mrs. Wharton "committed herself to a system of absolute truth, which required an absolute code of conduct."[19]

But this, it seems to me, is a total misreading of the novelist. Edith Wharton had, in fact, immersed herself in the skeptical sciences, especially in evolutionary Darwinism, and she understood both manners and morals to be evolved products of slowly altering social and ethical conventions. It is in fact Justine who is the absolutist: she believes that if, in principle, euthanasia is right, it is always right in practice. And that, the novel shows us, is wrong.

I cannot think of a passage in Mrs. Wharton's work that expresses more vividly than the following her sense of the way in which any abstractly conceived absolute must necessarily—and *properly*—be constrained and tempered by the weight of the received moral and social tradition. "Life," Mrs. Wharton has Justine at last ruefully perceive, "is not a matter of abstract principles, but a succession of pitiful compromises with fate, of concessions to old tradition, old beliefs, old charities and frailties." That is the lesson that Justine must learn:

> that was the word of the gods to the mortal who had laid a hand on their bolts. And she had humbled herself to accept the lesson, seeing human relations at last as a tangled and deep-rooted growth, a dark forest through which the idealist cannot cut his straight path without hearing at each stroke the cry of the severed branch: *"Why woundest thou me?"* (FT, 624).

To eat the fruit of the tree is therefore to gain a knowledge of good and evil in their inextricable human entanglement. It is the knowledge of the complexity of the moral life in a world where an idealistic act, abstractly conceived and subjectively justified, may prove destructive because, whether or not it breaks the law, it may ignore a tangle of inconsistencies in the moral sense of others. The opinions of the many create not only the mores but also the morals

---

19 H. Wayne Morgan, "Edith Wharton: The Novelist of Manners and Morals," *Writers in Transition* (New York: Hill and Wang, 1963), p. 28.

of society; what society deems immoral may be a bugbear to frighten children, or it may not. (Euthanasia is not.) But the individual who violates a society's ethical judgment on such a matter does so at her own risk. The irony of the novel is that this risk is especially dangerous to the idealist who does not anticipate one recurrent fact of the moral life: that even a person of "emancipated thought," like Amherst, may remain "subject to the old conventions of feeling."

I hope that it will not be perceived as a digression if I observe that in *A Motor-Flight Through France*, Mrs. Wharton remarks that the proper way for a modern unbeliever to appreciate the Gothic cathedral is to cultivate, along with one's "enfranchised thought," an "atavism of feeling"—that is, a capacity to *feel and appreciate* the old religious conviction, the spiritual ardor, and the moral passion that produced the cathedral. Justine and Amherst are "enfranchised" in thought. But Justine does not recognize that an atavism of feeling may prevent Amherst from emotionally assenting to an act like euthanasia, which, historically, has been—and is still—condemned in Western moral thought. A wiser woman than Justine would have known that, in questions of existential value, the emotions of any particular individual may proceed toward enfranchisement at a slower pace than the cognitive faculty.

Justine is surely an admirable woman in many ways, but she is not the morally autonomous and triumphant heroine that some critics want her to be. She is bound to Amherst. They are entangled with each other—not only by marriage but by and through the deadly act that he abstractly endorsed and she committed. Like Adam and Eve, they have lost their once paradisal relationship and must live with the consequences of their actions. But both are humanized by a new and deeper understanding of the unanticipated irony of fate in human affairs. Justine is, finally, a woman chastened by her experience; she is beautiful in her submission to reality—to that which is, morally, the case; she is, at last, a woman wise in the humility that permits her to learn this hard lesson of life: that if there be virtue in an abstract moral proposition, it can only be fully known in its practical consequences, some of which may be totally unforeseen. Although Justine is one of the earliest of Mrs. Wharton's heroines to discover, as Irving Howe puts it, that "the punitive power of society" is greater than she had supposed and that a moral law "assumed to be lifeless" still retained "a certain wisdom,"[20] she is no doormat or vapid

---

20 Irving Howe, "Introduction: The Achievement of Edith Wharton," in *Edith Wharton: a Collection of Critical Essays*, pp. 16–17.

angel at the hearth. And the marital adjustments that she and Amherst finally make, far from enslaving her to him or to the institution of wedlock, define the complexity of living, both in and of itself and certainly in the estate of marriage, where silence may be wisdom rather than servitude. Amherst is not perfect, but he is, as Margaret McDowell has remarked, "one of the few strong, virile, and charitable men in Wharton's fiction," and Justine's decision to stay with him is "a wise compromise."[21] At the same time, Justine's fall into a knowledge of good and evil and the wisdom at which she finally arrives allowed Mrs. Wharton to express—in a way that the simpler Lily Bart did not—her pragmatic view of ethics as a continually shifting question involving one's own immediate relation to life.

---

21 Margaret McDowell, *Edith Wharton* (Boston: Twayne Publishers, 1991), pp. 32, 35.

American Literary Radicalism in the Twenties

Writing in the socialist journal *Dissent*, David Bromwich—a professor of English and the author of a study of William Hazlitt—reflected not long ago on the phenomenon of "Literary Radicalism in America" as a means of ascertaining the effect of American literary avant-gardes on the politics and art of this country. In the course of his essay, he took occasion to advert to *The New Criterion* and its writers as being engaged in the effort to "invent cultural conservatism in America," a task he evidently found lacking in high seriousness, if not a vain pursuit.[1]

I should not have said that *inventing* conservatism was the general aim of *The New Criterion*, which in fact offers a variety of serious reflections on the life of art and the life of the mind in America today. To invent cultural conservatism *now* would be a paradox, in fact, since cultural conservatism has been a constant fact of American life from the beginning and is reflected in our jurisprudence and law, in our politics and religion, in all the human sciences, in social and intellectual history, and in our art and criticism. Cultural conservatism is the glue that holds our society together. It connects us to the past, preserves what has proved socially and personally valuable, and makes it possible for us to contemplate the future without terror. It therefore cannot be invented, although it may be defended. In any case, the principles of cultural conservatism provide the most relevant

---

1 David Bromwich, "Literary Radicalism in America," *Dissent* (Winter 1985), p. 35. Quotations from this work will hereafter be given as "LRA," in parentheses, in the text.

perspective from which to ask the truly important questions about the condition of American aesthetic culture today, particularly questions about the value of literary radicalism.

Bromwich is clearly right to suggest that the conservative wishes "to guard the values already in place" in American society—or at least to guard *some* of them. The conservative wants to preserve enduring positive values that enhance liberty and make for decency, order, and justice in society. But the conservative is not a defender of the status quo. Why? Because a great many of the forms of contemporary American society have, in fact, become destructive of these values: the crime rate is a scandal; welfare is a mess; society is a hostage to bloated government payrolls and programs that sink us ever deeper in deficit spending; we have mortgaged our children's future with a horrendous national debt; and the government is trying to regulate virtually every aspect of our lives. These problems represent the debris of the collapsed liberal tradition; they are expressions of the dead ideas that even yet litter the intellectual landscape. What is to be done? The conservative sees the disastrous consequences of "progressive" notions, and he wants to get rid of the defunct "bright ideas" that never worked and that are now ossified and encrusted in an impracticable and defunct liberalism.

Bromwich's idea of conservative thought is indeed mechanical and wildly reductive: he defines conservatism as a set of judgments dictated by "a sequence of implicit equations." These are the equations: "taste=inherited opinions=rules=norms (=social norms)." If I understand this Bromwich equation, it is so breathtaking an oversimplification of any serious conservative notion of American culture that the mind can do nothing with it. No conservative I know is unwilling to scrutinize taste, inherited opinion, rules, or norms. Conservatism is not to be identified with a resistance to change; and the conservative study of the cultural forms by which wisdom is transmitted from the past is, in reality, quite flexible and intellectually alive, more so than Bromwich's equational reductionism, which exhibits the usual leftist stereotypical thinking.

In the long run, the conservative knows that there will always be a valuable wisdom embedded in tradition. Certainly, whatever survives the passage of time testifies in some way to a deep human need that is being fulfilled. The conservative is therefore loath to abolish what has served so long to fulfill that need and is especially skeptical of whatever novelty is proposed, the consequence of which might be incalculable or patently disastrous. But given the present "hegemony" of bankrupt liberal policies, the conservative nowadays is likely to want to knock down and dispose of the wreck and ruins of failed liberal thought in the social polity.

In any case, the burden of Bromwich's essay is somewhat different. He wants to hold out for consideration two radical avant-garde groups that affected the course of American literature and to assert—frankly without sufficient evidence—their utility and suggestiveness for the future. These two groups are: 1) Emerson and the circle connected to him at *The Dial* in the 1840s—though only Margaret Fuller is actually mentioned; and 2) "their successors," whom Bromwich lists as William James, Van Wyck Brooks, Randolph Bourne, and John Dewey—"those social critics whose work began in earnest about 1915." The intent of the Bromwich essay would appear to be expressed in his surprising statement that "The legacy of Emerson, Fuller, James, Dewey, Bourne, and Brooks is what we still have to build on" ("LRA," 40, 43).[2]

II

The politics of programmatic dissent sometimes makes for strange bedfellows. Nothing, in fact, will seem odder than this collection of disparate minds Bromwich brings into unnatural intercourse under the cover of "literary radicalism." What is, after all, the common bond between Emerson, whose essential genius was to commend individual consciousness over against society (which he called "a conspiracy against the manhood of every one of its members"),[3] and Brooks, who espoused revolutionary socialism? None that I can see. From the 1830s onward, Emerson was the chief spokesman for American individualism. "In all my lectures," he observed in 1840, "I have taught one doctrine, namely, the infinitude of the private man." In "New England Reformers," he observed that "society gains nothing whilst a man, not himself renovated, attempts to renovate things around him." Even as late as 1867, in his Phi Beta Kappa ad-

---

2 How to lay claim to Emerson as the godfather of socialism seems to have been a hot topic in the editorial offices of *Dissent* and *Raritan* in the 1980s. For what should have immediately followed Bromwich's article but Irving Howe's *The American Newness: Culture and Politics in the Age of Emerson* (Cambridge: Harvard University Press, 1986) and Richard Poirier's *The Renewal of Literature: Emersonian Reflections* (New York: Random House, 1987)? Both are even more egregious than is Bromwich in claiming spiritual descent from an Emersonian paternity. For my own irascible view of such political pretensions, see "The Consolations of Emerson," *The New Criterion*, 4 (April 1986), 68–77, and "Literary Free Play at Rutgers," *The New Criterion*, 5 (June 1987), 63–68.

3 Ralph Waldo Emerson, "Self-Reliance," in *Ralph Waldo Emerson: Essays and Lectures*, ed. Joel Porte (New York: Library of America, 1983), p. 261.

dress "Progress of Culture," he insisted—as Carlos Baker has rightly put it—on "the supreme importance of minorities of one, proving that the human intellect is the prerennial revolutionary power."[4]

Is there, moreover, any kind of link between Emerson and Randolph Bourne? Even less. Emerson is hardly mentioned in Bourne's letters. And if Emerson was the great champion of the freedom of the will, Bourne espoused an antithetical doctrine of cultural determinism of the kind argued in Edward Thorndike's *Individuality* (1911). This is the same deterministic Bourne who (in total repudiation of Emerson's social thought) commended in "The Next Revolution" the "three cardinal propositions of Marx—the economic interpretation of history, the class struggle, and the exploitation of the workers by capitalistic private ownership of the means of production."[5]

But Bromwich also makes much of Deweyan pragmatism as the intermediate link between nineteenth- and twentieth-century literary radicalism. Did either Brooks or Bourne acclaim Dewey as offering the intellectual ground on which their politics could be based? Hardly. Though Bourne studied with Dewey, he had after all no use for Dewey's instrumentalism, which he saw as a tool for justifying immoral acts like America's entry into World War I. And Brooks likewise found in pragmatism's emphasis on "social efficiency" a lack of idealistic vision. Brooks is inescapably clear, in *Letters and Leadership* (1918), that James and Dewey "failed us," and not merely failed us but "traduced us" by their devotion to the given, to the "existing fact," that is, by their acceptance of the socioeconomic status quo. For Brooks, who took his cue from Bourne, pragmatism was "the dog in the manger of the creative life."[6] These radicals, in my view, owed nothing to Emerson and were contemptuous of pragmatism. It is therefore a sign of sheer intellectual incoherence to try to merge them in a tradition that contemporary socialists "still have to build on."

If the literary radicals of the twenties rejected Emerson, can he nevertheless still be the spiritual godfather of today's *Dissent* radicals? Of course Professor Bromwich can claim any political ancestry he

---

4 See *The Journals and Miscellaneous Notebooks of Ralph Waldo Emerson,* ed. William Henry Gilman, *et al.* (Cambridge: Harvard University Press, 1960–), VII, 342; "New England Reformers," in *Ralph Waldo Emerson: Essays and Lectures,* p. 596; and Carlos Baker, *Emerson Among the Eccentrics: A Group Portrait* (New York: Viking, 1996), pp. 468.

5 Randolph Bourne, "The Next Revolution," *Columbia Monthly,* 10 (May 1913), 222.

6 Van Wyck Brooks, *America's Coming-of-Age* (Garden City, N.Y.: Doubleday, 1958), pp. 140–144. Quotations from this work will hereafter be given as *ACA,* in parentheses, in the text.

likes. But it may be helpful to ask what Emerson thought of socialist politics in his own time. Fortunately, he defined his political viewpoint with crystal clarity. Emerson found revolutionary socialism coercive and highly objectionable, and he deplored Margaret Fuller's Fourierist (not Marxist) socialist utopianism. Further, he was profoundly averse to any kind of party politics. He was especially opposed to the kind of big-government intrusion into our lives that socialism always tries to institute. In "Politics," he writes,

> the less government we have the better,—the fewer laws, and the less confided power. The antidote to this abuse of formal government is the influence of private character, the growth of the Individual; the appearance of the principal to supersede the proxy; the appearance of the wise man; of whom the existing government is, it must be owned, a shabby imitation. That which all things tend to educe; which freedom, cultivation, intercourse, revolutions, go to form and deliver, is character; that is the end of Nature, to reach unto this coronation of her king. To educate the wise man the State exists, and with the appearance of the wise man the State expires. The appearance of character makes the State unnecessary. The wise man is the State.[7]

Bromwich observes that "Since Emerson, the project of literary radicalism has never been isolable from an ambition to reform our social arrangements" ("LRA," 40). But as Emerson's remarks make plain, this social reform will arise only in consequence of the moral reform of single individuals who aspire to wisdom and character, not as a consequence of the subordination of individuals to the state. Emerson would in fact have been appalled at the veneration of the state in twentieth-century radical politics. His individualism is forever irreconcilable with statist ideologies.

The socialists in Emerson's own time tried to coopt him, just as the *Dissent* crowd is doing today. The communitarians at Brook Farm, according to Emerson, had a noble intent in longing for economic equality and in wishing to institute a Fourierist phalanx at West Roxbury, Massachusetts, in 1841. But Fourierism, "the most entertaining of French romances,"[8] was based on a misunderstanding of human reality in its social and sexual character, and its economic practice was simply another form of economic competition with the

---

7 "Politics," in *Ralph Waldo Emerson: Essays and Lectures*, p. 567.
8 Ralph Waldo Emerson, "Historic Notes of Life and Letters in New England," in *The American Transcendentalists: Their Prose and Poetry*, ed. Perry Miller (Garden City, N.Y.: Doubleday, 1957), p. 18.

surrounding farmers. In "Historic Notes of Life and Letters in New England," Emerson personally praised the reformers who tried to induce him to join their commune, but he refused. In "Fourierism and the Socialists," he explained his reasons, observing that

> in spite of the assurances of its friends that it was new and widely discriminated from all other plans for the regeneration of society, we could not exempt it from the criticism which we apply to so many projects for reform with which the brain of the age teems. Our feeling was that Fourier had skipped no fact but one, namely Life. He treats man as a plastic thing, something that may be put up or down, ripened or retarded, moulded, polished, made into solid or fluid or gas, at the will of the leader; or perhaps as a vegetable, from which, though now a poor crab, a very good peach can by manure and exposure be in time produced,—but skips the faculty of life, which spawns and scorns system and system-makers; which eludes all conditions; which makes or supplants a thousand phalanxes and New Harmonies with each pulsation.

For Emerson, in practical terms, Brook Farm failed because there was "no head," because "intellectual sans-culottism" and anarchic impulse ruled. But failure was also implicit in the plan. And what he said about the vision of the Brook Farm reformers might be said of any such socialist utopian scheme: "The mistake is that this particular order and series is to be imposed, by force or preaching and votes, on all men, and carried into rigid execution."[9]

Emerson's idea of politics, then, is indeed extreme. But his political extremism lies in Emerson's very aversion to political organizations like caucuses and parties, in his disgust at wheeling and dealing, and in his moral horror at negotiated political compromises (which, by his lights, are are *always* sordid). His politics is epistemologically grounded on the priority of the unarguable moral intuition, which is always an expression of the Divine Will. Emerson's politics will of course be rejected by the conservative, who does not have a perfectibilitarian view of human possibility or a belief in the daily and direct apprehension of divine reality through transcendental intuitions. But the conservative will, nevertheless, assent to Emerson's emphasis on the individual, his impatience with impractical utopian schemes, and his critique of statism. Socialists do not like to acknowledge his acerbic criticisms, but Emerson was deadly accurate in calling the

---

9 "Fourierism and the Socialists," in *Ralph Waldo Emerson: Essays and Lectures*, pp. 1207–1208.

Brook Farm experiment "a perpetual picnic, a French Revolution in small, an Age of Reason in a patty-pan."[10]

My point is thus a very simple one. The individualistic Emerson cannot, with any logical consistency, be made to ground the radicalism of the Brook Farm collectivists or of the later generation of Van Wyck Brooks and Randolph Bourne. The nineteenth-century Fourierists had every shot at recruiting Emerson, but they did not understand his aversion to collectivization, which was not much different from that of Hawthorne in *The Blithedale Romance*. Furthermore, Van Wyck Brooks and Randolph Bourne were hardly Emersonian: they reflect a collectivist mentality that led them to espouse a sentimental socialism that they glorified in the *New Republic*, *Seven Arts*, the *Freeman*, and in other journals of the teens and twenties. And, finally, Emerson's politics will not serve the purposes of *Dissent* and *Raritan* today. For Emerson's emphasis is always on the priority of mind, on consciousness, and on individual self-reformation as the instrument of the amelioration of social ills.

Let me go a little further with this criticism of the Bromwich connection. To present Emerson as the radical predecessor of socialist critics of the 1920s, like Bourne and Brooks, is also to ignore the whole history of developing American socialist thought in the 1880s and 1890s, evident in both party politics and in literary works by Howells, Bellamy, London, and others. These are of course lesser figures than Emerson; and there is a tendency at *Dissent* to want to coopt the best major figure of the past as the spiritual father of the current generation. But the "progressives" I have named are the real American forebears of Brooks and Bourne, Floyd Dell and John Reed, Waldo Frank and Max Eastman—even as George Ripley, C. A. Dana, Warren Burton, and William Henry Channing at Brook Farm were the American predecessors of the *fin-de-siècle* generation of socialists.[11]

In fact, none of the major artists of the American Renaissance, as F. O. Matthiessen called the period—not Emerson, Thoreau, Dick-

---

10 See Ralph Waldo Emerson, "Historic Notes of Life and Letters in New England," in *The Complete Works of Ralph Waldo Emerson*, ed. E. W. Emerson (Boston: Houghton Mifflin, 1904), X, 364.

11 Of course many Europeans—Morris, Shaw, Wells, the Fabians, and Tolstoy—also contributed to American radical thought in the twenties. Some of the American sources of twenties radicalism have usefully been analyzed in Daniel Aaron's *Men of Good Hope: A Story of American Progressives* (New York: Oxford University Press, 1961). But Aaron's discussion of Henry George, Edward Bellamy, H. D. Lloyd, Thorstein Veblen, and others is likewise vitiated by his trying to turn Emerson's perfectibilitarian spirituality into the source of leftist politics.

inson, Melville, Hawthorne, or even Whitman—will serve as an adequate foundation for the socialist reconstitution of America called for by the literary radicals who came to their majority in the 1920s.

III

Much of Van Wyck Brooks's conception of the American experience and American literature is perfectly inadequate—even, I should imagine, for literary radicals. The reason for this is plain: Brooks manipulated the facts of our literary past in order to prove one or another thesis about the inadequacy of American culture as nutrient for the writer. I am particularly speaking here of Van Wyck Brooks before 1930, not of the later author of the comprehensive "Makers and Finders" series. That impressive multivolume literary history is not marked by the socialist extravagance of Brooks's youth; it deals with our past more in historical and literary than in ideological and political terms. But in his youth Brooks's cultural disgust with America overwhelmed his perception of the literature before him. I need not go into his fantastic argument about Twain's genius being thwarted by the frontier experience, which Bernard DeVoto demolished years ago, or his dubious interpretation of Henry James's expatriation, which biographers and critics long ago dismissed. Nor, finally, can one commend his understanding of Emerson, who in fact provoked in him (in Brooks's phrase) "a persistent spleen" (*ACA*, 38).

Yet in one respect Brooks understood Emerson better than the *Dissent* group. Brooks intuited that Emerson's individualism could be translated into the laissez-faire capitalist's advocacy of commodity and economic power. Brooks conceded that "if the logical result of a thorough-going, self-reliant individualism in the world of the spirit is to become a saint, it is no less true that the logical result of a thorough-going, self-reliant individualism in the world of the flesh is to become a millionaire." Hence Emerson's views were, for Brooks, never "inconveniently inconsistent with the facts and requirements of business life" (*ACA*, 43, 45). They therefore served to support the economic status quo. Bromwich wishes to salvage Emerson for the tradition of radical left politics. But as John Gerber has rightly concluded, Emerson's economic thought undertook to "combine socialistic ends with capitalistic means" and were thus incompatible with communistic experiments.[12]

---

12 John Gerber, "Emerson and the Political Economists," *New England Quarterly*, 22 (1949), 336–357.

Brooks was highly critical of Emerson and his Transcendental circle for what might be called the absence in them of rigorous intellectual discrimination. He complained of them as "that queer miasmatical group of lunar phenomena, in which philosophy, self-culture, politics, art, social reform and religion were all mixed up and all felt to be, in some vague way, the same thing" (*ACA*, 38). This is an accurate observation with which I am in full agreement. But I wish to extend it further by suggesting that it is also true of later American avant-garde literary groups: they mix up willy-nilly politics, religion, art, self-culture, and the rest with no conception of whether the elements are compatible. Certainly this was manifestly true of the generation of Brooks and Bourne, although living in it, and aflame with their political passions and New Age enthusiasms, they were not prepared to see that such an objection might be raised against themselves. But let me extend this argument yet one step further.

To coopt Emerson and William James for the purposes of Left political radicalism is of a piece with the intellectual muddlement evident in the *Partisan Review* circle of the 1930s and 1940s, who attempted forcibly to yoke together Trotskyist politics and Eliotic artistic modernism. Although their bizarre misunderstanding of artistic modernism constitutes a minor scandal in recent American critical thought about the relation of politics and literature, Bromwich is disposed to gloss over the contradiction in the *Partisan Review* position and even to celebrate it as constituting "a new conception of intellectual freedom," as a new "style of cultural tolerance" ("LRA", 43).

Whatever may be the virtues of cultural tolerance and intellectual freedom—and they are many—they are purchased here at the cost of mental confusion and intellectual consistency. In the twenties, amongst the more lucid radicals of the time, these things were understood more clearly. V. F. Calverton acknowledged that many literary modernists were radical in literary technique while conservative in sociopolitical ideology. He took no comfort in this; nor did he see the embrace of these artists as a means of effecting the revolution.[13] Max Eastman, as editor of the *Masses*, claimed to be hospitable to intellectual diversity, but in some remote part of his mind he understood that those of his contributors who praised modernist *literary* radicalism did not understand its contradiction to a "correct" left-wing politics. Writers like Bourne and Brooks wanted to give intellectual "leadership" to the revolution; but Eastman made it perfectly

---

13 See V. F. Calverton, "American Literary Radicalism," *Modern Quarterly*, 3 (September–December 1926), 260.

plain in *The Liberator* in 1921 that writers and critics, the young intellectuals, would need "guidance and careful watching by the practical
and theoretical workers of the movement."[14] This "supervisory" point
of view came to full fruition in the thirties, when the Stalinist
theoreticians made it plain to leftist writers and intellectuals that even
the truth would have to be sacrificed for "the good of the party." This
was more than even Eastman could stomach. But looking back on
the immediate postwar years, Eastman told Ely Estorick in 1931 that
"the most unique and important feature of the old *Masses* . . . was
that while maintaining an editorial policy essentially Marxian it drew
into its pages the works of wide circles of the intelligentzia who had
revolutionary feeling, but *no understanding of such a policy and very
little conception of what it was all about*" (italics added).[15]

IV

I am not sure that Bromwich knows what it was all about. And certainly Brooks and Bourne lacked the foresight and understanding to
know what it was all about, to know what was being asked of them
by Eastman, John Reed, and the political radicals just before and
after World War I. *The Masses* and *Liberator* bosses knew what it was
all about: it was about destablizing our political and economic culture and igniting an American revolution along the Soviet line. What
it was all about the events themselves, as they unfolded in the
thirties, made plain. The Leninist-Stalinist agenda, like the Fourierist,
was to impose its regimen, "by force or preaching and votes, on all
men," to carry it "into rigid execution." Brooks, Bourne, and the
young intelligentsia hadn't the wit to see the hideous enormity of a
social engineering scheme like that of Lenin and Stalin. By and large
they merely wanted to ventilate a moral contempt for big business,
puritanism, Comstockery, Prohibition, and the older generation. The
puerility of this kind of radicalism, oedipal in its origin, was inadvertently suggested by James Oppenheim, editor of the *Seven Arts*: "socialism, sex, poetry, conversation, dawn-greeting—anything so long
as it was taboo in the Middle West."[16]

"The Apostolic 'Student Movement,' or, the Priests of Young
America" are the terms used by Daniel Aaron, in *Writers on the Left*,

---

14 Max Eastman, "Inspiration or Leadership?" *The Liberator*, 4 (August 1921), 7.
15 Eastman is quoted in V. F. Calverton, *The Liberation of American Literature* (New
York: Scribner's, 1932), p. 454.
16 James Oppenheim, "The Story of the *Seven Arts*," *American Mercury*, 20 (June 1930),
157.

to characterize the "League of Youth" clustered around Bourne and Brooks—figures like Lewis Mumford, Waldo Frank, James Oppenheim, Paul Rosenfeld, and even, to some extent, Walter Lippmann.[17] These literary radicals gave themselves, for a time, to the service of violent political revolution. Bourne advised Brooks that the liberalism of the *New Republic* (Croly, Lippmann, Dewey) was lacking in "youthful violence" and was too "priggish."[18] He wanted something more draconian and violent. In "The State," Bourne annexed Marx to Charles Beard's economic determinism (in *An Economic Interpretation of the Constitution*) in order to equate, as Lenin had done, capitalism and imperialism with war.[19] Lenin, in fact, was his chief intellectual hero. Not for nothing did the *New Masses* create, after his death in 1918, the Randolph Bourne Memorial Award. They wanted to honor a radical who, at the end, said that he felt "very much out of touch with my times, except perhaps with the Bolsheviki."[20]

How much the irresponsible young took their cue from Bourne is indicated by Lewis Mumford's formulation of their agenda in the *Forum* in 1930. He wanted, he said, "an uprising on the part of the downtrodden, who would overthrow the master class and bring about a regime of equality and brotherhood."[21] Bourne died in the influenza epidemic of 1918 and so did not live to see the fate of his ideas on America and the Soviet Union. Mumford and Brooks outlived their radicalism and became more conservative as the decades passed. But it is important to remember *les jeunes* as they were in the teens and twenties: Bourne, Brooks, Eastman, Michael Gold, and Mumford were at that time dangerous enemies of American constitutional liberty. Speaking of the clarion call to youth in *Letters and Leadership*, Bourne told Brooks that "There is a certain superb youthful arrogance in your implication that it is we and our friends who are to be masters," to be directors, that is, of America's revolutionary coming-of-age.[22] Of course they thought they were equal to the task of running the country. But had our native Lenins and Stalins succeeded, had the political *apparat* that had infiltrated big

17 Daniel Aaron, *Writers on the Left* (New York: Avon, 1961), pp. 43–44.
18 Quoted in Bruce Clayton, *Forgotten Prophet: Randolph Bourne* (Baton Rouge: Louisiana State University Press, 1984), p. 246.
19 Randolph Bourne, "The State," in *War and the Intellectuals*, ed. Carl Resek (New York: Harper and Row, 1964), pp. 65–106.
20 Quoted in Aaron, *Writers on the Left*, p. 66. The unpriggish Bolsheviki had of course already inaugurated the wholesale butchery of their political opponents.
21 Lewis Mumford, "What I Believe," *Forum*, 84 (November 1930), 263.
22 *The Letters of Randolph Bourne: A Comprehensive Edition*, ed. Eric J. Sandeen (Troy, N.Y.: Whitson, 1981), p. 410.

labor, the universities, Hollywood, and American journalism triumphed, Van Wyck Brooks and his friends would have been the first to face the firing squads.

Was Emerson their fountain of inspiration, as Bromwich proposes? Hardly. With their repudiation of the past and their emphasis on youth, Brooks and Bourne created the atmosphere in which Floyd Dell could airily dismiss the nineteenth century and most of what it meant. The literature of that period "meant, to many of us, almost nothing at all." He said that "we can now discount almost to worthlessness—for our own purposes—the greater part of what New England took the trouble to say." For the spiritual drifters and literary vagabonds of that time, for this young coterie of literary and political radicals, nineteenth-century literature was "an intrusion of the past into our lives"; it was "a nuisance": "We had our own lives to live—and all these classical utterances of the nineteenth century literature had no relation to our lives."[23] So much for the utility of Emerson and his circle at the *Dial*.

About the most that can be said for Van Wyck Brooks and the members of the Apostolic Student Movement of the period 1915–1930—and I fix the time precisely, since a number of its members outgrew their youthful radicalism—is that they were young, brash, estranged from their own culture, sentimentally utopian but without any understanding of the political consequences of their ideas. They were deluded about the Soviet Union and without any political foresight. However noble may be the goals of equality, brotherhood, and spiritually fulfilling labor, the Brooks-Bourne tradition serves mostly as a cautionary instance—like the counterculture movement of the 1960s—of the effect on youthful idealism of passionate ignorance.

V

The question of the utility, for the present, of the radicalism of the Brooks-Bourne generation must also, it seems to me, take into account their after-years. That is, their radicalism was not intellectually rigorous enough to sustain these revolutionary ideologues as they matured into a wider experience of the world. We know this from the many memoirs of the period now bequeathed to us: Malcolm Cowley's *Exile's Return*, Matthew Josephson's *Life Among the Surrealists*, Joseph Freeman's *An American Testament*, Harold Loeb's *The*

---

23 Quoted in James Burkhart Gilbert, *Writers and Partisans: A History of Literary Radicalism in America* (New York: John Wiley, 1968), p. 19; Floyd Dell, *Intellectual Vagabondage* (1926; reprinted Chicago: Ivan R. Dee, 1990), pp. 105–106.

Way It Was, and Brooks's *Days of the Phoenix*. Of these retrospectives, Gorham Munson's *The Awakening Twenties* is a useful account of the writers, artists, publishers and editors whom he personally knew (Hart Crane, Carl Van Vechten, John Reed, Floyd Dell, Alfred Stieglitz, Waldo Frank, Bourne and Brooks, Robert Frost, William Carlos Williams, Jane Heap, Mable Dodge, Margaret Anderson, Herbert Croly, Eugene O'Neill, Man Ray, George Bellows, Emma Goldman, William Sommer, and Marsden Hartley). But it is also a clear account of how the young who wanted to realize Pound's call, in "Patria Mia" (1913), for an "American Risorgimento" (or "political awakening" in which the arts would lead the way) were seduced by left-wing subversives.

In his essay on "Advance-Guard Writing in America: 1900–1950," Paul Goodman has argued that "An artist does not know that he is advance-guard, he must be told so or learn it from the reaction of the audience." [24] But as we have seen, most of these figures claimed themselves to be an avant-garde almost before they had written a line. If they called themselves *les jeunes,* it was, thanks to Bourne and Brooks, without a trace of irony. Munson describes himself and his friends as flushed with the need to rebel and find themselves. For them, every manifestation of the new art was a revival of the national spirit, an occasion for enthusiasm. Their lives were marked by intellectual and artistic ferment of an intense order. But what was it grounded on and what were its fruits?

With respect to politics, the Munson circle was predisposed by both Bourne and Brooks toward a perpetual cultural revolution that would somehow lead to state socialism. How the political revolution was to be mounted was not yet clear to these callow youth. But arousing class hatred—through an "us vs. them" hostile psychology—was essential to laying the groundwork for the barricades. Bourne, a member of the Intercollegiate Socialist Society at Columbia (a left-wing group founded by Jack London and Upton Sinclair, who had advocated revolution since the turn of the century), was one of the chief propagandists. In a complaint that was to be picked up and parroted by a leftist now all the rage in the academy, Walter Benjamin, Randolph Bourne electrified *les jeunes* with arguments such as the following, which is drawn from "For Radicals": In the United States, Bourne wrote,

---

24 Paul Goodman, "Advance-Guard Writing in America: 1900–1950," in *Creator Spirit Come! The Literary Essays of Paul Goodman*, ed. Taylor Stoehr (New York: Free Life Editions, 1977), p. 144.

the very food we eat, the clothes we wear, the simplest necessities of life . . . have their roots somewhere, somehow, in exploitation and injustice. It is a cardinal necessity of the social system under which we live that this should be so, where the bulk of the work of the world is done, not for human use and happiness, but primarily and directly for the profits of masters and owners.[25]

Munson thrilled to Bourne's invocation of the Wobblies as the true "revolutionary Socialists" and warmed to ecstasy at the coming revolution. Bourne's youthful Marxism has been falsely underplayed as "schoolboy rhetoric."[26] But people like Munson, despite their being *adults*, were electrified by the daring of such pronouncements.

One can see the enthusiasm of *les jeunes* in Munson's enchantment with Waldo Frank's *Our America* (1919), which chanted the socialist denunciation of the United States. "Our America," for Frank, was "the America of cultural and social radicals, 'the men who listen to Stieglitz, and have not quite joined him in their mind with the example of Bill Haywood.'" For *les jeunes*, the America of the Founding Fathers was "Their America."[27] "Our America" was the socialist paradise about to happen. This was heady stuff to young Munson, and it led him to write *Waldo Frank: A Study* (1923), in which Frank's "genius" and the new political faith were stoutly proclaimed.[28]

But Munson finally could not accommodate his literary interests to the violent political radicalism of his contemporaries. In particular, he could not reconcile his growing belief in Jeffersonianism ("that government is best which governs least") with the statism of Marx, Shaw, Wells, Gold, Frank, and the rest. Thereupon ensued what Munson called his period of "philosophic anarchism," which was stimulated by the contributors to the *Freeman*. An amalgam of vague notions proclaimed by Albert Jay Nock, Francis Neilson, Emma Goldman, and Margaret Anderson, this anarchism of Munson's led him to abandon electoral politics "on principle," to attack the liberalism of the *Nation* and the *New Republic*, which he had formerly espoused, and to call the state "fundamentally anti-social." The task at

---

25 Bourne, "For Radicals," in *Youth and Life* (1913; reprinted New York: Burt Franklin, 1971), p. 303.

26 Bruce Clayton, *Forgotten Prophet: Randolph Bourne*, p. 77.

27 Quoted in Gorham Munson, *The Awakening Twenties: A Memoir-History of a Literary Period* (Baton Rouge: Louisiana State University Press, 1985), p. 67. Quotations from this work will hereafter be given as *AT*, in parentheses, in the text.

28 Lewis Mumford said that "Frank felt himself in his own words a Jew without Judaism and an American without America." He joined the socialist movement, by his own admission, in search of some kind of community. See *Memoirs of Waldo Frank*, ed. Alan Trachtenberg (Amherst: University of Massachusetts Press, 1973), pp. xxvi, 196.

hand, said the *Freeman*, was to improve the state "off the face of the earth, not by blowing up office-holders, as Mr. [A. Mitchell] Palmer appears to suppose, but by the historical processes of strengthening, consolidating and enlightening economic organization" (*AT*, 93–94). When we recollect that the enlightenment of the economic organization proposed by these anarchists rested upon the ideas of Henry George (the unearned increment, the single tax), the absurdity of their economic position becomes manifest. Munson himself eventually came to realize the untenability of his situation:

> Having been in rapid succession a liberal, a socialist, a supporter of the Soviets, I had called myself for a couple of years a philosophical anarchist. . . . Anarchism was an emotional choice; I waived the question of practicality. The vision of Kropotkin would prove practical in the washing, I told myself. . . . Looking back, it seems I had an ambition without a clear goal and a vague sense of dissatisfaction with current American writing without a fixed viewpoint to give meaning to my dissatisfaction (*AT*, 159–160).

This is a remarkable admission. It defines the twenties as a time of diversely energetic enterprises, in art and social thought, yet one lacking in principle, lacking a clear understanding of what America was all about, of what philosophically and historically was meant by the notion of the individual and the state, and of what the role of literature and criticism might be within the state. Being young geniuses together (that is, waiving all questions of practicality) produced a twenties version of what Lionel Abel has called the intellectual follies. Although Munson tried to remain as impersonal as possible, truth broke in with all her matter-of-fact in this extraordinary assessment of the time:

> But taking a retrospective view of those days . . . , I will venture the remark that if the word for the Yellow Nineties is petty infantilism, the word for the Twenties is arrogant juvenility. Perhaps that is why I cannot, in the manner of several chroniclers of the early jazz age, review my immersion in it with romantic regret over time's passing. The period was something to be outgrown (*AT*, 169).

One appreciates the candor and self-criticism of this remark. It is an older and wiser man's reflection on the excesses and confusions of the generation of his youth. It witnesses to a truth that has been obscured by the self-serving memoirs of its survivors who romanticized their intellectual, artistic, and political muddlement under the banner of compassionate liberal values.

Perhaps the central issue here is thought, reflection on principles, and the consequence of abandoning reason to feeling. For Bourne, "too much rationality makes a man mercenary and calculating." Bourne, like Frank, preferred the monitions of the heart as "usually better than the logic of the head, and the consistency of sympathy is superior as a rule for life to the consistency of the intellect."[29] This represents a perilous anti-intellectualism for youth who aspire to cultural leadership and is implicitly dismissive of historical understanding. Jefferson, Madison, Hamilton, Franklin, and many others had already worked out the logic of our constitutional democracy and had established the essential arguments for our system of political, economic, and civil rights. They had also already considered and rejected alternatives that seemed novel in the twenties to *les jeunes*. The formulation of the framers was not yet perfect, as they themselves understood, but it was open to rational change, based on an electoral consensus and judicial understanding. Especially they understood what Emerson was later to call, in "Politics," the "law for man" and the "law for property," each of which will always assert its claim, both together making up our life in society.

But *les jeunes* were impatient with rationality and accumulated experience; they were deficient in historical understanding and insufficiently educated in political theory. Their critique of property rights in the name of economic redistribution, based on admirable enough humanitarian feeling, produced in the twenties both a longing to overthrow the system—through labor violence, if need be, as Big Bill Haywood proposed—and the reactionary excesses of state authority in the form of Attorney General A. Mitchell Palmer's raids on suspected subversives. Between perpetual revolution and reactionary repression the American people were somehow supposed to make a choice. It is not a matter of luck that neither type of extremism succeeded in carrying the day. Both the constitutional safeguards to American liberty and legal provisions for social order restrained—despite much testing and some failures—the kind of violence that Haywood propounded and the repressive intolerance that marked the embattled authorities.

VI

When politics fails, what is left? For those without religious belief, not much. We see an unmistakable emptiness in the behavior and

---

29 Randolph Bourne, "The Experimental Life," *Youth and Life*, pp. 238, 244.

writing of those whose work came to be identified with the Jazz Age, the Lost Generation, and the Waste Land cult. There was, of course, an immediate excitation in Freudianism, Jungianism, Constructivism, Futurism, Imagism, Vorticism, Cubism, Skyscraperism, and Dadaism. But these had no substance and, like politics, failed to save the soul. Certainly for Munson, these movements were expressions of an energy without a clear objective, a manifestation of the frenetic confusion of the time. As an older man, Munson could not rediscover what he once found in the second-rate Waldo Frank, and he came to be certain that Irving Babbitt's New Humanism offered more than its critics even allow to this day. An instance of the speed with which Munson outgrew the jejune romanticism of the twenties appears in his *Robert Frost: A Study in Sensibility and Good Sense* (1927), which found Frost's "conservatism" and "classicism" an antidote to the political and intellectual anarchy of the times.

"Anarchy" may seem an exaggerated term, but Malcolm Cowley in his Dadaist phase is clearly illustrative of it. We came to think of Cowley, in the last thirty years of his life, as the grandfatherly custodian of true literary values. But in the twenties, in his Dadaist phase, Cowley exhibited an irrationalism so inane that it was matched only by the stunts of the sixties "Beat" crowd. If Bourne was merely suspicious of reason, Cowley, like Louis Aragon and André Breton, repudiated rationality itself in favor of nonsense manifestos and "significant gestures" of violence intended as a "shock treatment for a crazed humanity." Cowley punched the proprietor of the Rotonde cafe in Paris because his Dadaist principles apparently "required" him to do so. But a more significant gesture of revolt against reason was the episode, at Cowley's home in Giverny, marked by a book-burning and micturating party. There Cowley burned a number of books (including a set of Racine, on whom he was writing his thesis) in a gesture of revolt against rationality and "book fetishism." Accounts of this episode vary, but Cowley was described by Harold Loeb as roaring "Too much *merde*, too much junk. Words aren't enough," while "the soft night smelled of urine and burning paper." Ah, *les jeunes*. Horace Gregory was later to ask: "What group of young Americans today would set fire to books written by their betters in an open fireplace?" (*AT*, 182–183). Gregory could hardly have guessed that within a few years, in the 1960s, whole libraries would be trashed by radical youth, and some—like my own at New York University—would be put to the torch.

It is very likely that Cowley, Loeb, and others at the book-burning party were drunk. And Cowley tried to minimize the incident as involving only some wretched French reviews and old textbooks. But in fact this Dadaist repudiation of the literary tradition played out at Giverny—with Cowley speechifying, commending his books to the flames, and peeing on them—is not different from the self-important posturing of the young artists in that satirical scene in Chapter 41 of Somerset Maugham's *Of Human Bondage* (1915). There Maugham, in describing the young literary radicals of the *fin de siècle* in Paris, breathtakingly anticipates Brooks, Bourne, Cowley, and *les jeunes* of the New York literary scene in the twenties:

> "Great art can't exist without a moral element."
>
> "Oh God!" cried Lawson furiously. "I knew it was that. He wants morality." He joined his hands and held them towards heaven in supplication. "Oh, Christopher Columbus, Christopher Columbus, what did you do when you discovered America?"
>
> "Ruskin says . . . "
>
> "Gentlemen," he said in a stern voice, and his huge nose positively wrinkled with passion, "a name has been mentioned which I never thought to hear again in decent society. Freedom of speech is all very well, but we must observe the limits of common propriety. You may talk of Bouguereau if you will; there is a cheerful disgustingness in the sound which excites laughter; but let us not sully our chaste lips with the names of J. Ruskin, G. F. Watts, or E. B. Jones."
>
> "Who was Ruskin anyway?" asked Flanagan.
>
> "He was one of the great Victorians. He was a master of English style."
>
> "Ruskin's style—a thing of shreds and purple patches," said Lawson. "Besides, damn the Great Victorians. Whenever I open a paper and see Death of a Great Victorian, I thank Heaven there's one more of them gone. Their only talent was longevity, and no artist should be allowed to live after he's forty; by then a man has done his best work, all he does after that is repetition. Don't you think it was the greatest luck in the world for them that Keats, Shelley, Bonington, and Byron died early? What a genius we should think Swinburne if he had perished on the day the first series of *Poems and Ballads* was published!"
>
> The suggestion pleased, for no one at the table was more than twenty-four, and they threw themselves upon it with gusto. They were unanimous for once. They elaborated. Someone proposed a vast bonfire made out of the works of the Forty Academicians into which the Great Victorians might be hurled on their fortieth birthday. The idea was received with acclamation. Carlyle and Ruskin,

Tennyson, Browning, G. F. Watts, E. B. Jones, Dickens, Thackeray, they were hurried into the flames; Mr. Gladstone, John Bright, and Cobden; there was a moment's discussion about George Meredith, but Matthew Arnold and Emerson were given up cheerfully. At last came Walter Pater.

"Not Walter Pater," murmured Philip.

Lawson stared at him for a moment with his green eyes and then nodded.

"You're quite right. . . ."[30]

In the case of Maugham's youth, an exception for Pater was made in the name of aestheticism. But whatever the Victorian past might have meant in terms of sound social values and high moral ideals, these—insofar as they were embodied in the work of the great Victorians—counted for naught. All young artists of course try to distinguish themselves on the ground of the "purity" of their art. Yet one invariably finds in such instances of youthful artistic radicalism little understanding of the relation between the aesthetic and the moral, social, or historical; in fact, there is an evident inclination to deny the relationship. And the result is what Gertrude Himmelfarb has recently called "the de-moralization of society."

VII

In "The Idea of Order at Key West," Wallace Stevens meditated on the creative process as a "rage for order," with the implication that art is constructive and constitutive of reality. And so it is. Art orders reality by organizing perception and understanding. Painting and music, literature and architecture, these and the other arts, together with those social institutions that, by their very survival, testify to their necessity for us as social beings—these make up the indispensable elements of civilization that the conservative would guard; they are values already in place, but continually in question, and the destruction of them would be an impoverishment of our lives.

But another argument could be and has been made that art is a rage for disorder,[31] for the destruction of form, with the implication that the such "beautiful murderings of reality" (to use E. E. Cummings's description of Picasso's art) are necessary to destroy our

---

30 Somerset Maugham, *Of Human Bondage* (New York: Modern Library, 1942), pp. 228–229.

31 See Morse Peckham's valuable *Man's Rage for Chaos: Biology, Behavior, and the Arts* (Philadelphia: Chilton Books, 1965), especially pp. 308–315.

encrusted perceptual habits, our tendency to passive, thoughtless, surrender to the culturally given.[32] There is merit in this view. Whenever original genius reconstitutes our perception of reality in beautiful forms we are individually enriched; and culture in its historical configuration becomes a more valuable gift to the young coming into it. But the burden (on the young) of the culturally given can never justify their periodic wish to destroy it; nor does the conservative want them to be able to. Hence the satire, in *The Gods Arrive* (1932), on the Parisian radicals' wish to "break the old moulds" and "demolish the old landmarks": "Who ever consulted you and me when the Pyramids were built—or Versailles? Why should we be saddled with all that old dead masonry? Ruins are what we want—more ruins!"[33] This is merely a fictive way of saying what the *Masses* had already announced:

> The broad purpose of the Masses is a social one: to everlastingly attack old systems, old morals, old prejudices—the whole weight of outworn thought that dead men have saddled upon us—and to set up new ones in their places. . . . We intend to be arrogant, impertinent, in bad taste, but not vulgar. We will be bound by no one creed or theory of social reform, but will express them all, providing they be radical.[34]

Of course in France *les jeunes* are especially adept at such rhetorical overkill—as when Aragon, Breton, Artaud, Paul Eluard, and twenty-four others proclaimed the following, in an "Open Letter to M. Paul Claudel, French Ambassador to Japan" (1925): "Creation matters little to us. We profoundly hope that revolutions, wars, and colonial insurrections will annihilate this Western civilization whose vermin you defend even in the Orient." The destruction of Western civilization, they announced, would give them the greatest intellectual satisfaction.[35] This is Gallic *No, in Thunder*—a cultural alienation and a self-loathing so self-destructive that would bring down the temple of civilization *on everyone*. (It also reflects the influence on the always appalling French avant-garde of the unpriggish, homicidal Bolsheviki.) But whether French, English, or American in origin, the idea that "Hey, ho, Western Civ's gotta go" arises out of infantile cultural disappointment, desire unfulfilled, out of the discrepancy

---

32 Quoted in Barry A. Marks, *E. E. Cummings* (New York: Twayne, 1964), p. 96.
33 Edith Wharton, *The Gods Arrive* (New York: D. Appleton, 1932), p. 128.
34 Quoted in Daniel Aaron, *Writers on the Left*, p. 39.
35 Quoted, in Mark Polizzotti, *Revolution of the Mind: The Life of André Breton* (New York: Farrar, Straus, and Giroux, 1995), p. 237.

between a daydream of possible social perfection and the hard, intractable order of reality—the intractable order of life, which, as Emerson observed, cares little for systems and system-makers, whether they be utopian social engineers or makers of aesthetic systems.

VIII

What should be the relationship between the modern artist and his culture? William Phillips has proposed that the avant-garde artist should be a "suspended man" who "keeps the balance of opposing forces," who is situated "between tradition and revolt, nationalism and internationalism, the aesthetic and the civic, and between belonging and alienation."[36] There is something appealing about this formulation. But this was not a position allowed to the avant-garde artist by the critics of the radical left, who demanded political alienation. Even literary radicals like Brooks and V. L. Parrington posed literary issues in terms of sociological categories, as in fact mutually exclusive extremes: liberals and reactionaries; highbrows and lowbrows; and, more recently, palefaces and redskins. The center ground in the twenties was the joke of middlebrowism, with all the negative implications of a bourgeois conservatism ascribed to it. This middle ground was thus no ground at all for the writers of what Chase called "the insurgent movement in this country which defended 'modernism'—that is, the aesthetic experimentalism and social protest of the period between 1912 and 1950" ("AG," 367).

The reduction, by Brooks and others, of America's rich cultural complexity and diversity to such oversimplified sociological categories thus left many artists in the 1920s with nowhere to stand. Fortunately, the best artists stood for art. How did the radical left receive them? A good test case is the reception of *The Waste Land* and *Ulysses*, both published in 1922, both cornerstones of the modernist avant-garde. As literary editor of the *Freeman*, Van Wyck Brooks had nothing worthwhile to say about them. To have acknowledged their distinction as artists would have trapped him in a political contradiction that he—unlike the later *Partisan Review* group—could not tolerate.

But if Chase did not accurately perceive the dilemma of the experimental artist who was being told that socialist alienation was his

---

36 Phillips is quoted in Richard Chase, "The Fate of the Avant Garde," *Partisan Review*, 24 (Summer 1957), 374. Quotations from this essay will hereafter be given as "AG," in parentheses, in the text.

only response to American life, he did grasp the way in which the irreconcilable motives of insurgency in art and politics disoriented Brooks, once he came to understand them:

> Brooks abdicated from modern culture about 1925, drawing back in horror from the genie whose bottle his early polemics had helped to unstopper. For behold! among the great writers who really spoke for the present and the future were Eliot, Joyce, Proust, Gide, Hemingway, and Pound, and they all seemed to Brooks culturally dangerous—they were, he said, undemocratic, highbrow, coterie writers ("AG," 371).

Of course it is nonsense to think that Eliot, Joyce, Proust, and Gide would have been bottled up, and uncreative, had not Brooks's polemics unstoppered them. Brooks's influence was localized in America and important only to writers of the second order. The conclusion is thus inescapable that the really great artistic modernists of the teens and twenties managed to realize their genius by ignoring, or resolutely rejecting, the alienated insurgent politics demanded of them by the literary sociologists of the left. In declining what the age demanded, they sometimes appeared to be more undemocratic than in fact they were—the Pound of the thirties always, of course, excepted.

IX

But what of avant-garde writers who could not find themselves, or find that ideal middle ground within American culture that Phillips hypothesized? The effect on a great many writers was indeed poignant. For some, early promise was never quite fulfilled; and some were destroyed or even destroyed themselves. Van Wyck Brooks, F. Scott Fitzgerald, and T. S. Eliot had nervous breakdowns. Edna St. Vincent Millay, Ring Lardner, and Fitzgerald became alcoholics. And Jack London, Vachel Lindsay, and Sara Teasdale killed themselves.

In respect to the most important spiritual questions of life, the fate of both Hart Crane and Gorham Munson is exemplary. Close friends during Crane's best years (1919–1925), they were both wracked by the cultural incoherence and pervasive cynicism of the time. Munson felt appalled at Crane's collapse into alcoholism, compulsive homosexuality, artistic paralysis, and eventual suicide. He presents Crane to us as an instance of the cost to genius of the intellectual deracination and spiritual alienation so pervasive in the twenties. Munson himself, as we have seen, had not fared too well in the period up to about 1924, for the demand upon him, as well as upon the others, to be insurgent in sociopolitical thought as well as in art immersed him in such a welter of competing political, social, and literary movements that—without a principle with which to question the concept of insurgency itself—he was at sea. In a negative reaction to Brooks's reduction of literature to an instrument of class analysis and social change, Munson eventually came to call for a deeper aesthetic understanding which would see the work of art in its own right, and not as a datum of "sociological criticism." In his *Dial* essay of January 1925, "Van Wyck Brooks," Munson's search for a ground upon which the work of art could regain an intrinsic aesthetic autonomy begins to be apparent. This search became more obvious in his book on Frost, which commended such principles as restraint, order, and the "law of decorum or measure or proportion." Such views smacked of the New Humanism, which had tried to re-introduce the faculty of reason into these issues; but with this move-ment, headed by Irving Babbitt, the radical insurgency of *les jeunes* could have no traffic.[37]

If we ask how Munson escaped the chaotic rootlessness of his generation, the answer does not lie in art or its social function. Mun-son took the route of New Age spiritualism. Introduced to P. D. Ouspensky's *Tertium Organum* by Hart Crane and thence to the bizarre mysticism of G. I. Gurdjieff and his English apostle A. R. Orage, Munson surrendered himself to the esoteric regimen by which, his guru said, one could ascend to the highest level of cosmic consciousness. This does not get us much beyond Whitman and his disciple Richard Maurice Bucke (and is of a piece with it). Gurdjieff claimed to have rediscovered the technique by which the ancient Egyptians, Buddhists, Pythagoreans, and Gnostics attained unto "The Fourth Way." In New York salons and at the Chateau du Prieuré, where Gurdjieff had founded his Institute for the Har-monious Development of Man, Munson and his wife submitted themselves to the discipline, which involved sacred gymnastics or ex-otic dancing, the repression or denial of the ego, and humiliating manual labor (like breaking up stones on the guru's estate), all in-tended to produce the new illumination.

Gurdjieff was a quack and a charlatan or a spiritual genius, depending on one's point of view. For Waldo Frank, who went to Prieuré seeking the Light, Gurdjieff was a devil; Munson thought

---

37 See Kenneth White's review of Gorham Munson, *The Dilemma of the Liberated: An Interpretation of Twentieth-Century Humanism* (New York: Coward, McCann, 1931), in *The Forum*, 86 (January 1931), viii.

otherwise. What is evident here is that in the intellectual, social, and moral disorder of the twenties, rootless artists and intellectuals were predisposed to search for absolutist remedies that conferred, at least for a while, some meaning on life. When political radicalism failed, some of *les jeunes* found it in Theosophy, Anthroposophy, Coué-ism, or Moral Rearmament, in the Society for Psychical Research, Freudianism, in Aimee Semple McPhersonism, in the esoteric doctrines of highly touted swamis, and in the California nut cults that Nathanael West satirized in *Miss Lonelyhearts*.

Something of the ridiculous side of twenties spiritualism is inadvertently revealed in Munson's fond descriptions of the meetings of the Orage group in New York City—at Muriel Draper's, Margaret Anderson's, and Rosetta O'Neill's—where Gurdjieff's mysticism was commended to what Munson calls the intelligentsia, "the public that in 1924 read the *Dial* and the *New Republic* and *Vanity Fair*, listened to Stravinsky and Schoenberg, looked at Picasso and Matisse, discussed psychoanalysis and the progressive education of John Dewey, and inclined toward socialism" (*AT*, 256).[38] The list of those who came to Orage's presentations—some to scoff, some to pray—is impressive: Brooks, Padraic Colum, Edna Kenton, Mable Dodge Luhan, Boardman Robinson, T. S. Matthews, Herbert Croly, Melville Cane, Jean Toomer, Hart Crane, Margaret Naumberg (Mrs. Waldo Frank), and Helen Westley. Toomer, like Katherine Mansfield, seems to have been a total convert, but Crane was turned off by the New Age nonsense and had nothing but contempt for those who had

> rushed into the portals of the famous Gurdjieff institute and have put themselves through all sorts of Hindu antics, songs, dances, incantations, psychic sessions, etc., so that now, presumably, the left lobes of their brains and their right lobes respectively function (M[unson]'s favorite word) in perfect unison.[39]

Waldo Frank, whose "mysticism" created great anxiety in the party theoreticians, attended weekly sessions "at the house of Herbert Croly, who had been baptised in the Positivist Church." But Frank grew disillusioned: he found Gurdjieffism to be a method for evad-

---

38 If these were the pastimes of the intelligentsia, they sound suspiciously like the pretentious Chicago soirées that beguiled the gullible Carol Kennicott in Sinclair Lewis's *Main Street* (1920). The provincial Lewis was taken in and actually identified such big-city amusements with culture, but as Mencken remarked, it was in fact bogus, an ersatz culture.

39 *The Letters of Hart Crane*, ed. Brom Weber (Berkeley: University of California Press, 1965), p. 298.

ing human community.[40] What seems evident is that these people needed some kind of foundation in a belief-system deeper than that provided by their skeptical culture and its New Age nut cult sects.

Munson hoped that Crane was on his way to a true understanding of Ouspensky's view that "Art in its highest manifestation is a path to cosmic consciousness." But when Orage came to America to elaborate on Ouspenskian-Gurdjieffian mysticism, Crane became disillusioned. He was unwilling to submit himself to the discipline of the "C" influence, which (it is said) is "exercised only by direct contact of master with disciple." Crane recoiled from Gurdjieff, "as though shocked by a high-voltage current," as Munson put it, in consequence of which his "magnetic center" dissolved, he became creatively paralyzed, failed to finish *The Bridge*, and presumably was fated for suicide (*AT*, 197, 207, 215). One would have to be a mystic oneself to accept this reading of Crane's tragic decline, which in fact expressed poignant emotional instability. But he was simply one of many who, in that chaotic time, lacked the support that a coherent culture with an orthodox religious tradition and a grounded, objective ethical value system may provide.

X

What necessary effect, if any, does an imperative of political insurgency have upon a literary avant-garde moved by idealistic social longings? In the case of *les jeunes* in the twenties, we can see that the legacy of Bourne and Brooks was a legacy of cultural criticism on a wobbly base, with the effect that, along with other forces, it served to unsettle their politics, to subvert the principles of constitutional democracy as envisioned by the Founding Fathers, and to render somehow plausible the chilling Communist Party agenda of the 1930s.

In this respect the radical left in the 1920s and 1930s did great damage to American culture, and its effects are still to be felt now at the end of this century. If some of the young in the twenties escaped into the past or into spiritualism and sacred gymnastics, something of the same moral history can be seen in the insurgent youth of the 1960s who were swept up into New Left radicalism, who fomented social disorder, got a good look into the abyss, and then became disillusioned. Some withdrew to Tibet, submitted to one or another

---

40 See *Memoirs of Waldo Frank*, p. 196, and Frank's The *Rediscovery of Man* (New York: George Braziller, 1958), pp. 424–427.

popular guru, deified one or another rock 'n roll star, wrote *Wichita Vortex Sutras*, or took up the saffron robes and tambourines of the Hari Krishnas. Such modes of escape from one's own cultural alienation at times of social disorder are a constant fact of American experience.

Most of us, however, are fated to live in the real world, the world of work and love, of getting and spending, of thinking and feeling, and of integrating our experience into a sense of the continuity of our culture, aware of the finitude of our private being. In such a world the vitality of established religion is central, and the character of art and the critical tradition it generates must invariably engage the mind. In respect to criticism, we note that Clayton called Bourne a "forgotten prophet." Perhaps he was also right in saying: "Only historians and a few older professors of English [like Bromwich?] take Brooks seriously today."[41] Clearly the best artists of the period from 1915–1930 were averse to the sociological reductionism of critics like Brooks and Bourne. Eliot, Pound, Hemingway, Faulkner, Frost, and Stevens created works of art that still claim our attention because they are inextricably rooted in the writers' creative genius, aesthetic individualism, and aversion to the view of art as the instrument of socialist revolution.

We need the kind of imaginative experimentalism, or literary radicalism, their work represents. For the reconstitution of aesthetic forms is by no means in conflict with the conservation of worthwhile values in American culture. Much aesthetic experimentalism will lead down a blind alley. But we can never predict what elements of form, sedimented in our culture or lost to feeling in a neglected work from the past, will somehow be revitalized and renovated in a new work of genius. Culture is immediately enriched by the recognition of such works. Unseen intellectual relations are discovered, human perception is clarified, taste is corrected, and standards of judgment are perfected. And the relation of these matters to the regulative and normative conditions of our public being, as a democratic society under the rule of a law hospitable to genius, is made plain to consciousness. When we think about *The Waste Land, The Cantos, The Sound and the Fury*, and like works, they raise issues about taste and judgment, politics and culture, tradition and the individual talent, in a way that the works of Floyd Dell and Waldo Frank, of Max Eastman and Upton Sinclair, of Sinclair Lewis and Mike Gold—the fading voices of leftist radicalism—can never do.

---

41 Quoted in Bruce Clayton, *Forgotten Prophet: Randolph Bourne*, p. 260.

Seeing Slightly Red: Fitzgerald's "May Day"

"May Day," a tale rich in social resonance, is an authentic Fitzgerald story. It flutters like a warning flag; it signals the locus of serious tensions and divisions in American society. It gazes with both bemusement and fascinated horror at the malaise of the time. It embodies the social sickness of the era in images of ennui, emotional deadness, complaisant self-indulgence, and in visions of the violence of accidental death, suicide, and anarchic riot. Yet the story vibrates just as resonantly with those very personal urgencies and intensities that always signal Fitzgerald's most autobiographical fiction. If, as John P. Marquand once claimed, a writer has only one story to tell and repeats it with variations throughout his career, "May Day" is a particularly apt, early formulation of "the Fitzgerald story." It combines with uncommon adroitness the social and the psychological, the public and private tensions of Fitzgerald the man and the historical moment, the year 1919. Very nearly all of the themes of the major and more mature stories are here, masterfully disposed, as Sergio Perosa has remarked, with "an economy of means that makes it possible for a vast frame of events to find its focus."[1]

As a very personal narrative, expressing Fitzgerald's analysis of his own emotional states, we may note the relation of his personal life to the facts of its composition. The tale was written in the early months of 1920 and published in July of that year in H. L. Mencken's *Smart*

---

[1] Sergio Perosa, *The Art of F. Scott Fitzgerald*, trans. Charles Metz and Sergio Perosa (Ann Arbor: University of Michigan Press, 1965), p. 33.

Set.[2] Between Fitzgerald's departure from Princeton in 1917 and the composition of the story, he had gone through his army experience at Camp Sheridan in Alabama; he had met, fallen in love with, proposed to, and been rejected by Zelda Sayre, who thought him too poor to provide the style of life they both wanted; he had rewritten, revised, and sold his first novel, *This Side of Paradise*; he had discovered Dreiser, Mencken, and Frank Norris; and he had shuttled back and forth between Montgomery and New Orleans, Princeton and New York in an effort, finally successful, to induce Zelda to marry him.[3] These experiences find their fictional transformation in "May Day."

Getting the "top girl" is of course a recurrent, even obsessive aspect of the one story that Fitzgerald had to tell; and in the relationship of the struggling artist Gordon Sterrett and Edith Bradin, the "World's Worst Butterfly," aspects of the emotional history of Scott and Zelda in the immediate postwar years are intricately elaborated. As Fitzgerald later remarked in "My Lost City" in 1932, with reference to the four miserable months he spent living in the Bronx just before the publication of "May Day," "I was so entangled in life that a period of mellow monasticism in Washington Square was not to be dreamed of . . . and in a haze of anxiety and unhappiness I passed the four most impressionable months of my life."[4] Something of Sterrett's sensibility—as one rejected in love, failed in his art, and estranged from his wealthy former classmates—is also suggested in Fitzgerald's remark in "The Crack-Up" that New York City during those four months

> had all the iridescence of the beginning of the world. The returning troops marched up Fifth Avenue and girls were instinctively drawn East and North toward them—this was the greatest nation and there was gala in the air. As I hovered ghost-like in the Plaza Red Room of

2 Robert Sklar, *F. Scott Fitzgerald: The Last Laocoön* (New York: Oxford University Press, 1967), p. 71.

3 Parts of the story appear to have been written in New Orleans during January 1920, while Fitzgerald was living on Prytania Street. Twice during that month he went up from New Orleans to Montgomery to allay Zelda's anxiety about his marginal income and about their future together. Later that spring, back in Princeton, he wrote to Maxwell Perkins from the Cottage Club that he could not work there, "so have just about decided to quit work and become an ash-man. Still working on that Smart Set novellette ['May Day']." *Dear Scott/Dear Max: The Fitzgerald-Perkins Correspondence,* eds. John Kuehl and Jackson R. Bryer (New York: Scribner's, 1971), p. 29. Very probably the tale was finished late that spring, while Fitzgerald was living in the Bronx and working for a Manhattan advertising agency.

4 F. Scott Fitzgerald, *The Crack-Up,* ed. Edmund Wilson (New York: New Directions, 1956), p. 25.

a Saturday afternoon, or went to lush and liquid garden parties in the East Sixties or tippled with Princetonians in the Biltmore Bar I was haunted always by my other life—my drab room in the Bronx, my square foot of the subway, my fixation upon the day's letter from Alabama—would it come and what would it say?—my shabby suits, my poverty, and love. While my friends were launching decently into life I had muscled my inadequate bark into midstream. . . . I was a failure—mediocre at advertising work and unable to get started as a writer. Hating the city, I got roaring, weeping drunk on my last penny and went home.[5]

Fitzgerald's attitude toward money—mingled envy and hatred of the rich man who might exercise a *droit de seigneur* and take away his girl—finds expression in Gordon Sterrett's ambivalence toward Phil Dean, whose Biltmore Hotel room is littered with silk shirts and expensive ties, while Gordon in a "faint gray" shirt frayed at the cuffs contemplates his own "faded and thumb-creased" necktie.[6] The scene at Brooks Brothers (here called Rivers Brothers), where Phil picks out a dozen neckties and laments the unavailability of the "Welsh Margotson" and the "Covington" collars while Gordon suffers a growing panic over whether he will get a $300 loan, brings into sharp focus the emotional estrangement between the casual and careless rich man and the impoverished would-be artist.

Both Phil Dean and the top girl, Edith Bradin, emotionally withdraw from Sterrett because the stink of failure is on him. "'I'm a failure,'" he tells Edith. "'I'm poor as hell'" (*S*, 104). This equation of poverty and failure is endemic in all of Fitzgerald's most personal prose. As Gordon remarks, "'I'm on my own now, you know, and Phil, I can't stand being poor.'" To Phil, Gordon seems to be "sort of bankrupt—morally as well as financially," with the effect that an aura of evil surrounds him. For Gordon, that "air of worry and poverty and sleepless nights" makes the two kinds of bankruptcy, moral and economic, "'go together'" (*S*, 87).

Implicit in the fate of Gordon Sterrett, however, are two other considerations which bear remark. Sterrett is sometimes seen as an artist figure victimized by philistine American culture, which is said to destroy the man of imagination and talent. Sterrett pleads, "'I've got talent, Phil; I can draw—but I just don't know how. I ought to

---

5 Fitzgerald, *The Crack-Up*, pp. 25–26.
6 See *The Stories of F. Scott Fitzgerald*, ed. Malcolm Cowley (New York: Scribner's, 1951), p. 84. Hereafter, citations from this collection of short stories will be given as *S*, in parentheses, in the text.

go to art school and I can't afford it.'" He claims to be able to "'draw like a streak'" but "'half the time I haven't had the money to buy decent drawing materials—and I can't draw when I'm tired and discouraged and all in'" (*S*, 87–88). But Sterrett hardly serves as a club to beat philistine America. He is too self-indulgent and full of whining self-pity, as was his author some time later, to merit much sympathy. His making "'a hell of a mess of everything'" (*S*, 85) in the three months since his discharge seems less the consequence of the "dirty war" than of the continuous immediate postwar fun and games: "'everybody began to come back from France in droves—and all I did was to welcome the newly arrived and go to parties with 'em. That's the way it started, Phil, just from being glad to see everybody and having them glad to see me'" (*S*, 86). If it is true that Sterrett is "Fitzgerald's exaggeratedly condemnatory portrait of himself," and if Gordon's suicide reflects "Fitzgerald's moments of acute despair over his financial situation,"[7] Robert Sklar is undoubtedly right in remarking that "there is no evidence in the story that Gordon Sterrett is the victim of anything more than natural weakness; and his poverty is not a cause of his degeneration, but its result."[8]

Nor are we made to feel much sympathy for Sterrett in his relationship with Jewel Hudson. In the early part of the story, she is projected as a low, sexually corrupted woman who covets Gordon's money and social status. "'She used to be 'pure,' I guess, up to a year ago,'" he tells Phil. "'Lived here in New York—poor family. Her people are dead now and she lives with an old aunt'" (*S*, 86). As such, she might seem an effective foil to the top girl, the "pure woman" Edith Bradin, who sees "a quality of weakness in Gordon that she wanted to take care of," who thinks of herself as "made for love," and who in fact wants to get married. But like most of the fictional top girls, Edith is emotionally insincere and inaccessible, thoroughly trivial, and totally shallow. She mistreats Peter Himmel "because he had not succeeded in kissing her" (*S*, 100); fakes a friendliness with various shadowy men on the dance floor; and, after "falling in love with her recollection of Gordon Sterrett" (*S*, 98), cuts the real Gordon dead at the Delmonico dance. Jewel Hudson may be overrouged and pulpy of lip, but marriage to her seems hardly a cause for suicide. And Fitzgerald is careful to establish the authenticity of her feelings for Gordon: "'Haven't I just been saying that it [the money] doesn't matter? I wanted to see *you*, Gordon. . .'" (*S*, 56).

---

7 Arthur Mizener, *The Far Side of Paradise: A Biography of F. Scott Fitzgerald* (Boston: Houghton Mifflin, 1965), p. 88.
8 Sklar, p. 77.

In several ways, then, the disintegration and suicide of Gordon Sterrett are less the consequence of philistine America or a gold-digging woman than the effect of a self-induced paralysis of the moral will. In the portrait of this psychic condition, Fitzgerald was immeasurably affected by two new overwhelming influences—Frank Norris and H. L. Mencken. In a letter dated February 3, 1920, Fitzgerald told Maxwell Perkins:

> I've fallen lately under the influence of an author who's quite changed my point of view. He's a chestnut to you, no doubt, but I've just discovered him—Frank Norris. I think McTeague & Vandover are both excellent. I told you last November that I'd read *Salt* by his brother Charles and was quite enthusiastic about it. Odd! There are things in "Paradise" that might have been written by Norris—those drunken scenes, for instance—in fact all the realism. I wish I'd stuck to it throughout! Another of my discoveries is H. L. Mencken, who is certainly a factor in present day literature. In fact I'm not so cocksure about things as I was last summer—this fellow Conrad seems to be pretty good after all.[9]

Norris, like many of his favorite authors, was a postcollege discovery of Fitzgerald. At Princeton, he later complained, none of his English professors ever revealed that books like Norris's had been or were being written. The effect was a sanitized literature: "The realism which now walks Fifth Avenue was then hiding in Tenth Street basements." But since then, "Brigadier General Mencken has marshalled the critics in an acquiescent column of squads for the campaign against Philistia."[10] To Fitzgerald's proposal that a special edition of Norris's fiction be published, Mencken replied, "it goes without saying that I'll be glad to help it along."[11] From *McTeague: A Story of San Francisco,* Fitzgerald may indeed have been inspired in "May Day" "to try a more expansive social setting, to widen his range of characters—in short to tell rather than to just imply the story of a place and time," as Sklar observes. And it seems inescapably true that the degeneration of Gordon Sterrett is derived from *Vandover and the Brute,* which also portrays "an upper-class pseudo-artist who drank, let his talent go, lost his money, and got in trouble with a girl." Sterrett's death, as Sklar rightly remarks, is "simply the last step of an al-

---

9 *Dear Scott/Dear Max,* p. 28.
10 F. Scott Fitzgerald, review of *Brass* by Charles Norris, *Bookman,* 54 (November 1921), 253.
11 John Kuehl, "Scott Fitzgerald's Reading," in *Profile of F. Scott Fitzgerald,* ed. Matthew J. Bruccoli (Columbus: Charles E. Merrill, 1971), p. 50.

ready determined solution to a naturalistic equation. . . ."[12]

Yet Norris's influence is also to be seen in the characterization of the soldiers Gus Rose and Carrol Key, who are called "human beings" but who are described as ugly, ill-nourished, and "devoid of all except the very lowest form of intelligence" (*S,* 91). Both incarnate the view, derived from Norris's *McTeague,* that certain individuals are biologically degenerate, or virtually subhuman, owing to hereditary atavisms induced by generations of ancestral alcoholism, syphilis, or other diseases. Indeed, if Key's name hints that "in his veins, however thinly diluted by generations of degeneration, ran blood of some potentiality," Key's face offers no "suggestion of either ancestral worth or native resourcefulness." Rose, the Jew with "rat eyes" and a "much-broken hooked nose," is a creature of the "world of snarl and snap" (*S,* 92). As animal-like incarnations of Norris's brand of naturalism, both are instruments and victims of the social disorder which erupts on May Day in the tale, Key plunging accidentally to his death from the office window of *The Trumpet* and Rose arrested and jailed for assault and battery upon Henry Bradin.

Mencken's influence is immediately to be seen in two aspects of the story: the theme of character in decay, and the satiric treatment of socialism as a political ideology. The second of these themes will be discussed later on. Here it is sufficient to say that Mencken served as a powerful impetus to Fitzgerald's natural tendency to see something romantic in the touch of disaster befalling the decadent protagonist. Throughout his whole career Fitzgerald was fascinated with the deterioration of a man going gallantly to the devil. If, as Fitzgerald put it in "The Note-Books," "the very elements of disintegration seemed . . . romantic,"[13] Mencken's championing of realism served to put the theme in a new perspective. In both "May Day" and *The Beautiful and Damned* we are given realistic portrayals of character in decline; in fact, it is well to remember that "May Day" was a discarded beginning to *The Beautiful and Damned.*

With remarkable prescience, Fitzgerald foresaw in 1920 the implications of the riotous events of May 1, 1919, as inaugurating a new historical era, the Jazz Age. He later told Max Perkins that "if Mark Sullivan is going on you might tell him I claim credit for naming it [the Jazz Age] & that it extended from the suppression of the riots on May Day 1919 to the crash of the Stock Market in 1929—almost exactly one decade."[14] In "Echoes of the Jazz Age" (1931), he observed

---

12 Sklar, pp. 73–74.
13 Fitzgerald, *The Crack-Up,* p. 206.
14 *Dear Scott/Dear Max,* p. 171.

that the Jazz Age began with the police riding down "the demobil-
ized country boys gaping at the orators in Madison Square"—the sort
of action

> bound to alienate the more intelligent young men from the prevail-
> ing order. We didn't remember anything about the Bill of Rights
> until Mencken began plugging it, but we did know that such tyranny
> belonged in the jittery little countries of South Europe. If goose-
> livered businessmen had this effect on the government, then maybe
> we had gone to war for J. P. Morgan's loans after all. . . . It was
> characteristic of the Jazz Age that it had no interest in politics at all.[15]

Yet more than gaping motivated the police charge on the mob of
servicemen listening to the orators, and "May Day" is not lacking in a
political point of view. The facts are these. On May 1, 1919, in several
American cities, including New York, mobs of soldiers and sailors attacked political groups celebrating May Day, the traditional socialist
holiday.[16] Several factors made the 1919 holiday especially violent. The
Socialists and trade-unionists were protesting the imprisonment of
Eugene V. Debs, "Big Bill" Haywood, and Thomas J. Mooney for
their political opinions. In the week before May Day, more than
thirty homemade bombs had been discovered in the United States
Post Office, some of them addressed to Mayor John F. Hylan of New
York City, Judge D. C. Westenhaver, who had sentenced Debs, and
Judge Kenesaw Mountain Landis, who had sentenced Haywood.

The soldiers and sailors who provoked the riots were animated by
a hatred of the Socialists' pacifist views during World War I, which
they equated with pro-Germanism, and by hatred of the Bolsheviks,
who had mounted the revolution in Russia in 1917, only two years
before. On this May 1, the eve of what has come to be called Attorney General Mitchell Palmer's "Red Decade," a mob of about four
hundred servicemen invaded *The Call*, a Socialist daily with offices on
Pearl Street. They also broke up a reception of the board of directors
at the new office of *The Call* at 112 Fourth Avenue. The *New York*

---

15 Fitzgerald, *The Crack-Up*, pp. 13–14.
16 Even though "May Day" takes its name from the labor and socialist holiday, its other
   implications should not be discounted. The association of the day with various fertility
   festivals, indicated by dancing about the May Pole and crowning the May Queen, may
   have an ironic bearing on the relationships of Edith Bradin and Jewel Hudson to
   Gordon Sterrett. That Edith might be so regarded as the May Queen is intimated,
   perhaps, in the suggestive remarks of the soldiers who invade *The Trumpet* office. In
   addition, the call "May Day" is a wireless or radio distress signal, especially for aircraft
   and ships at sea—falsely derived, it would seem, from the French *m'aidez*, "help me."
   As such, the urgency of the call in the presence of disaster is particularly appropriate to
   the story.

Times reported that "one of the Call stockholders, who was threatened by soldiers, ran to the rear of the building and jumped from a window twenty-five feet above the ground."[17] Another mob of soldiers and sailors, repulsed at the Madison Square Garden concert arranged by the Amalgamated Clothing Workers Union, marched down to the People's House at 7 East 15th Street and forced the Socialists to raise an American flag in front of the building. Another mob entered the Russian Workers' House at 133 East 15th Street, "trashed" all of the printed propaganda they could find, and forced those present to sing "The Star-Spangled Banner." Other Socialist groups were attacked at Webster Hall and at open-air rallies in Harlem, where Communist resolutions were proclaimed calling for "the repeal of the espionage law, withdrawal of American troops from Russia, and the lifting of the postal ban on radical publications."[18]

There seems every likelihood that these were not spontaneous demonstrations but were secretly financed and well-organized attacks. In the repulsed assault on the Madison Square Garden concert, the soldiers—who claimed to be in search of "the German meeting"—arrived in a large white sightseeing bus and formed a phalanx when the bugle calls "Assembly" and "To Arms" were sounded. Sidney Hillman, the president of the Amalgamated Clothing Workers Union, later absolved these "duped" servicemen of the attack and blamed "the Junker element," which he said was "attempting to destroy the labor movement."[19]

The tension between capital and labor in the story is neither merely historical nor incidental. And Fitzgerald's sympathy with the Socialists is not shallow. At Princeton, Fitzgerald had been deeply influenced by Shaw, Wells, and the English Fabians. With his traumatic resentment of the very rich, he found a natural sympathy with the views of literary figures like Upton Sinclair, whose *The Jungle* had ended in a call for socialism. Sinclair Lewis, who had been with Upton Sinclair at Helicon Hall, a communitarian society, had also boldly proclaimed "The Passing of Capitalism" in *The Bookman* in 1914. Sherwood Anderson's "Why I Am a Socialist" is another of those formulations by literary figures who had a pronounced sympathy with the socialist political position.

In the decade between 1926 and 1936, Fitzgerald later confessed,

---

17 "Soldiers and Sailors Break Up Meetings," *New York Times,* May 2, 1919, p. 3; reprinted in *Fitzgerald and the Jazz Age,* eds. Malcolm and Robert Cowley (New York: Charles Scribner's, 1966), pp. 57–59.
18 "Soldiers and Sailors Break Up Meetings," p. 3.
19 "Soldiers and Sailors Break Up Meetings," p. 3.

"my political conscience had scarcely existed . . . save as an element of irony in my stuff."[20] But this fact should not make us disregard the explicit "political content" of the fiction before 1926 or after 1936; nor should we be insensitive to its implicit ideology during that decade. A work contemporaneous with "May Day"—*This Side of Paradise* —ends with Amory Blaine's defense of socialism to the capitalist father of one of his former Princeton classmates. "'This is the first time in my life I've argued Socialism,'" Amory declares. "'It's the only panacea I know. I'm restless. I'm sick of a system where the richest man gets the most beautiful girl if he wants her, where the artist without an income has to sell his talents to a button manufacturer.'" And he tells Jesse Ferrenby's father that he has "'every reason to throw my mind and pen in with the radicals.'"[21] Upton Sinclair, Fitzgerald told Perkins in 1922, had led him to conclude that "freedom has produced the greatest tyranny under the sun" in America. "I'm still a socialist," he wrote; but he said that he dreaded that "things will grow worse and worse the more the people nominally rule. The strong are too strong for us and the weak too weak."[22]

The Great Gatsby is pervaded with, if not revolutionary fervor, at least deep-seated resentment of the careless and irresponsible affluent class produced by capitalism. And it is well to remember that *Tender Is the Night,* in its outline form, identifies Dick Diver as a Communist who will at the end of the novel send his son to Russia for the right kind of education. Between 1932 and 1934, in fact, Fitzgerald even "let 'La Paix' [his home] be used for meetings organized by local Communists."[23] He had great trouble, he told Ceci Taylor at this time, in reconciling his "double allegiance to the class I am part of, and the Great Change I believe in" (*L,* 437), and he broke with the Communists in 1934 only because of their meddlesomeness in his art and their reprehensible position on the Negro question. Yet toward the end of his life he reaffirmed to his daughter Scottie that he did not believe that "the system that produced Barbara Hutton [a millionaire playgirl] could survive more than ten years, any more than the French monarchy could survive 1789" (*L,* 51). He said that "most questions in life" had an "economic basis (at least according to us Marxians)" (*L,* 62), and he reminded Scottie that if she read "the ter-

20 F. Scott Fitzgerald, *The Crack-Up,* p. 79.
21 F. Scott Fitzgerald, *This Side of Paradise* (New York: Scribner's, 1920), pp. 277–278.
22 *The Letters of F. Scott Fitzgerald,* ed. Andrew Turnbull (New York: Dell, 1966), p. 173. Hereafter, citations from this text will be given as *L,* in parentheses, in the text.
23 Henry Dan Piper, *F. Scott Fitzgerald: A Critical Portrait* (New York: Holt, Rinehart and Winston, 1965), pp. 175–176.

rible chapter in *Das Kapital* on 'The Working Day'" she would never be "quite the same" (*L*, 120). Finally, to Perkins just before his death, Fitzgerald observed that Spengler and Marx were "the only modern philosophers that still manage to make sense in this horrible mess" (*L*, 317).

I have gone somewhat afield from "May Day" in order to accent what I believe to be a lifelong sympathy with the ideology of socialism. It is doubtless true that Fitzgerald was an individualist, hustling with the best of the entrepreneurs to make a dollar—in his case from fiction. And it is unarguable that his views were sketchy and based more on feeling than on dialectical materialism. But his socialist sympathies color his fiction and should not be lightly regarded by those who would grasp the ideological subtext of his work.

In "May Day," however, the treatment of socialism is a rather confused and ambivalent affair. On the one hand, we are made to sympathize with the Socialists as idealistic victims of the mindless mobs which rove the streets. The man on Sixth Avenue who is beaten up for haranguing the crowd on J. P. Morgan's and John D. Rockefeller's war beautifully adumbrates the fate of Henry Bradin, who is assaulted in his office by Rose, Key, and the mob. The mindless chant, "Kill the Bolsheviki—We're Americuns," is artfully satirized as the raving of those who have already been shown to be less than fully human.

Yet the Socialists presented here are not wholly noble political standard-bearers of the brotherhood of man. Something of Fitzgerald's own American nativism is suggested in the language describing the street-corner orator as a "gesticulating little Jew with long black whiskers" (*S*, 93); *The Trumpet* office worker Bartholomew, described as giving "the impression of a Middle-Western farmer on a Sunday afternoon," is called "loosely fat" (*S*, 112). And before we ever meet him, Henry Bradin is described by Gordon Sterrett as "sort of a socialistic nut" (*S*, 90). We later learn that he has left a Cornell instructorship in economics to come to New York in order, in Fitzgerald's words, "to pour the latest cures for incurable evils into the columns of a radical weekly newspaper" (*S*, 100). A member of the upper class, given to radical chic, Bradin is described as dissociated from the working class he presumes to help. Twice he is described as having "far-away eyes" that seem "always fixed just over the head of the person to whom he was talking" (*S*, 111); and when the soldiers break into the newspaper office and he declaims his propaganda with his "far-away eyes fixed over the heads of the crowd" (*S*, 115), it is no wonder that they break his leg. As a visionary idealist, he cannot establish any human connection with those for whom socialism was supposed to be the only panacea. Small wonder that Sterrett's activism is wholly ineffectual.

Why should Fitzgerald here have satirized those with whom he would normally have sympathized? He may of course have wished to explore what Henry James had called "the possible other case"; that is, he may have wished to lay bare another dimension of his political subject, the artist's natural wish to deepen the complexity of his material. And it is true that Fitzgerald always projects something of a double point of view toward the moral character of the social classes produced by capitalism. But the peculiar quality of his treatment of the Socialists is in part to be explained, I think, by the sudden influence of Mencken, who warped him out of his natural orbit. Mencken's various essays in the *Smart Set* and elsewhere shocked Fitzgerald into perceiving, among other things, the impractical dreaminess of many of the liberals and the mindlessness of the populace. Fitzgerald's image of "the people," the bedrock on which liberal society was to be based, is faithful to Mencken's notion of the "lower orders" as "inert, timid, inhospitable to ideas, hostile to changes, faithful to a few maudlin superstitions." [24] Mencken's *A Book of Prefaces* (1917) and like works are filled with witty and withering satire on the "American booboisie," the "democratic fustian," and the "truculent and mindless plutocracy." Like many of the avant-garde young of the time, Fitzgerald was under the spell of Mencken's freewheeling satirical style and became something of a debunker himself, both of liberal socialist theoreticians and of the people themselves.

Mencken's influence extends even into the texture of the style of "May Day." The prologue, which has the flavor of Stephen Crane's ironic phrasing, broadens revealingly into the coarser satiric style of the Baltimore sage. It describes a set of armistice attitudes keyed to peace and prosperity, to victory and consumer goods. But even the Menckenesque, dead-giveaway phrasing of the prologue [25] should not obscure for us its function. In its avoidance of the specific indices of time and place, Fitzgerald's generalized introduction—like the image of Columbus discussed below—is meant to offer a context applicable to nearly every American postwar experience, against which will be

24 H. L. Mencken, "The National Letters," in *Prejudices: Second Series* (1920); reprinted in *The Vintage Mencken*, ed. Alistair Cooke (New York: Vintage, 1955), p. 100.
25 I have in mind the hyperbole, the high-flown rhetoric, and the archaisms put to the service of satiric deflation in a sentence like ". . . all exulted because the young men returning were pure and brave, sound of tooth and pink of cheek, and the young women of the land were virgins and comely both of face and figure" (*S*, 83).

measured the experience of specific soldiers (like Sterrett, Key, and Rose) who returned from World War I, and those young women (like Edith and Jewel) who awaited them. Fitzgerald's prologue emphasizes the concurrence of the "many adventures that happened in the great city," and he remarks that "of these, several—or perhaps one—are here set down" (*S*, 83).

There is no doubt that Fitzgerald saw the diverse simultaneous experiences of his several characters as composing a single story. The tale has eleven parts, very nearly each one explicitly specified as to time and place, with the effect that the simultaneity of the actions and the interconnectedness of the characters and the settings fuse the parts into a single experience. Clearly this was Fitzgerald's intention, for as he later remarked in his Preface to *Tales of the Jazz Age*, although the events in life "were unrelated," he had tried, "unsuccessfully I fear, to weave them into a pattern."[26] His modesty is engaging here, but in this instance he may have builded better than he knew, Perosa rightly remarking that "there are no loose ends, no incongruous parts in the story. . . ." [27] The focus of these diverse experiences, the pattern, comes down to Fitzgerald's attempt to characterize the American social order, at a particular moment in time, as a complex interaction of economics (wealth and poverty), social dislocation (caused by the war), and collapsed personal values (leading to hedonism and mindless violence). Throughout, Fitzgerald interconnected the several parts through a network of interlacing adumbrations and recurrences so artfully disposed that they unify the work. They all bear upon the principal image of the dawn sun striking the statue of Columbus, which elevates to the dignity of an artistic theme the notion of the decline of potentiality implied in the discovery of the New World:

> A fresh argument ensued at the cashier's desk, where Peter attempted to buy another dish of hash to take with him and throw at policemen.
>
> But the commotion upon his exit proper was dwarfed by another phenomenon which drew admiring glances and a prolonged involuntary "Oh-h-h!" from every person in the restaurant.
>
> The great plate-glass front had turned to a deep creamy blue, the color of a Maxfield Parrish moonlight—a blue that seemed to press

---

26 F. Scott Fitzgerald, *Tales of the Jazz Age* (New York: Scribner's, 1922), p. viii.

27 Perosa, p. 33. For an excellent discussion of the story's theme and structure, see John Kuehl's *F. Scott Fitzgerald: A Study of the Short Fiction* (Boston: Twayne Publishers, 1991), pp. 39–45.

close upon the pane as if to crowd its way into the restaurant. Dawn had come up in Columbus Circle, magical, breathless dawn, silhouetting the great statue of the immortal Christopher, and mingling in a curious and uncanny manner with the fading yellow electric light inside (*S,* 120).

Sklar has remarked that this dawn passage at Columbus Circle is charged with an irony that undercuts its putative transcendental significance. He calls attention to "an advertisement for 'Edison Mazda' light bulbs painted by the artist Maxfield Parrish, which appeared in *Ladies' Home Journal* for January, 1918. In the painting dawn is rising over a mountain lake. A lightly-clad, golden-haired beauty of nature sits on a rock in the center foreground, watching with sublime awe as golden dawn strikes the mountainside, driving back the 'deep, creamy blue' of a Maxfield Parrish moonlight, quite as Fitzgerald has described it." Sklar does not venture to say that Fitzgerald knew of this advertisement, but it leads him to argue that "such 'magical, breathless' dawns are false and sentimental dawns, and that if nature produces dawns equally as beautiful as a commercial artist can, they are equally to be distrusted." For him, "this passage is not an evocation of romantic wonder, but a heavily ironic deflation of it."[28]

We owe Sklar a debt in calling our attention to this advertisement, but the inference he draws from it, in interpreting the scene, is almost exactly wrong. It is entirely possible that Fitzgerald did see the advertisement. Maxfield Parrish was a well-known illustrator, no mere hack commercial artist, as Sklar's remark implies. (He was well known to a number of novelists of the period, whose works he illustrated—for instance, Edith Wharton's *Italian Villas and Their Gardens.*) If Fitzgerald did see the advertisement, it probably struck him just as did the dust jacket of *The Great Gatsby,* with its picture of the eyes of Dr. T. J. Eckleburg—a pictorial image to be put to the service of a deeper symbolism in the story. Certainly no one would want to err by reading into "May Day" a sophisticated prototype of Fitzgerald's mature symbolic technique. Yet, like *The Great Gatsby,* where the Dutch sailors gaze in breathless romantic wonder at the "green breast" of the New World, this dawn image of romantic possibility is suffused with the style of lyrical enchantment utterly free, as I read it, of ironic deflation. Moreover, like the green breast of the New World, this image of romantic possibility is shown as tawdrily betrayed in the actual condition of society represented by the rich

---

28 Sklar, p. 78. This advertisement is reproduced in *The Ladies' Home Journal Treasury,* ed. John Mason Brown (New York: Simon and Schuster, 1956), p. 30.

and poor, the privileged and the dispossessed, as well as by the merchants whose life-denying materialism is suggested by their stores, which, covered at night by "great iron masks," are "shadowy tombs of the late day's splendor" (*S,* 111). Surely the tale's pattern of light imagery (darkness, yellow and kaleidoscopic artificial lights, and dawn sun) supports Edwin Fussell's claim that the image of Christopher Columbus, the "Christ-bearer," offers Fitzgerald the means of expressing "the behavior and attitudes of the Lost Generation with a symbol of romantic wonder extensive enough to comprehend all American experience, as far back as 1492. . . . What Fitzgerald is almost certainly trying to say with this image is: we are at the end of Columbus's dream, and this is our brave new world."[29]

Of the radical disparity between the ineffable romantic promise implied by Columbus's discovery and the tawdry actualities of the Jazz Age, two episodes are particularly striking. The first is the orchestra at the Gamma Psi dance, which is "headed by a famous flute-player, distinguished throughout New York for his feat of standing on his head and shimmying with his shoulders while he played the latest jazz on his flute" (*S,* 107). For pure inanity, Fitzgerald could hardly have improved on this choice example of contemporary idiocy—except in the case of Mr. In and Mr. Out. This transient pair is ironically introduced as having no identity in the social order:

> You will search for them in vain through the social register or the births, marriages, and deaths or the grocer's credit list. Oblivion has swallowed them and the testimony that they ever existed at all is vague and shadowy, and inadmissible in a court of law. Yet I have it upon the best authority that for a brief space Mr. In and Mr. Out lived, breathed, answered to their names and radiated vivid personalities of their own (*S,* 120–121).[30]

Their drunken search for more liquor, the satire on Yale and Sheffield students, and their vaudeville clowning convey more than just Princeton undergraduate hijinks. A deeper meaning is suggested in the pattern of physical movement, both circular and vertical, that pervades the story. Toward the end of the tale, when Mr. In and Mr. Out observe Rose being arrested by the police in the lobby of the

---

29 See Edwin Fussell, "Fitzgerald's Brave New World," *English Literary History,* 19 (December 1952), 291–306, reprinted in *F. Scott Fitzgerald: A Collection of Critical Essays,* ed. Arthur Mizener (Englewood Cliffs, N.J.: Prentice-Hall, 1963), p. 46.
30 While their identities are obscure in the tale, Phil Dean and Peter Himmel were in fact suggested by a Fitzgerald prank with his Princeton classmate Porter Gillespie. Mizener remarks that after the interfraternity dance at Delmonico's in May 1919, Fitzgerald went to the Child's restaurant on 59th Street and proceeded to mix up "hash, dropped

Biltmore Hotel as they are entering the elevator, Fitzgerald writes:

> the stout person made a sort of lightning-like spring toward the short, dark soldier, and then the lobby closed around the little group and blotted them from the sight of Mr. In and Mr. Out.
>
> But to Mr. In and Mr. Out this event was merely a particolored iridescent segment of a whirring, spinning world.
>
> They heard loud voices; they saw the stout man spring; the picture suddenly blurred.
>
> Then they were in an elevator bound skyward.
>
> "What floor, please?" said the elevator man.
>
> "Any floor," said Mr. In.
>
> "Top floor," said Mr. Out.
>
> "This is the top floor," said the elevator man.
>
> "Have another floor put on," said Mr. Out.
>
> "Higher," said Mr. In.
>
> "Heaven," said Mr. Out (*S*, 126).

This passage has been called "a parody of the Ascension" which serves comically to express "the materialistic hedonism, along with its traditional counterpart, a vulgar idealism, which Fitzgerald is already identifying as his culture's fatal flaw."[31] But this movement upward should also be seen in the light of the aimless circular drift of several of the characters (for example, the dancers on the dance floor) and of the mob (which circles about the city). It should also be seen as the countersymbol of the descent of both Carrol Key and Gordon Sterrett.

In Key's case it is a literal fall from an upper-story window at *The Trumpet* that causes his death: "He had fallen thirty-five feet and split his skull like a cracked cocoanut" (*S*, 118). This death is anticipated in the violence offered to the street-corner orator and is alluded to several times in the Mr. In and Mr. Out episode (although it is clear that Phil Dean and Peter Himmel could not have known about Key's fall). The idea of the waiters objecting to their having champagne for

---

eggs, and catsup in his companion's derby. When he was interrupted he insisted on climbing on a table and making a speech, and after he had been dragged from the table and out of Child's he wanted to explain to everybody that the façade of the buildings around Columbus Circle does not really curve; it only seemed to because he was drunk. Later he and a college friend, Porter Gillespie, returned to the party at Delmonico's and played their game of Mr. In and Mr. Out. Well into the next morning they breakfasted on shredded wheat and champagne, carrying the empty bottles carefully out of the hotel and smashing them on the curb for the benefit of the churchgoers along Fifth Avenue." See Mizener, *The Far Side of Paradise*, pp. 88–89.

31 Fussell, "Fitzgerald's Brave New World," p. 45.

breakfast seems "mortifying" to the pair, and "they collapsed into laughter, howled, swayed, rocked back and forth in their chairs, repeating the word 'mortifying' over and over to each other—each repetition seeming to make it only more brilliantly absurd" (*S,* 124). Later, "either of them had only to mention the word 'mortifying' to send them both into riotous gasps." The play on the words *mortifying* and *riotous* has a double function: it directs the reader backward and forward along the narrative line. Key's death calls into focus the riotous violence that smolders in the hearts of the economically dispossessed. His death is compounded in irony by the fact that Key and the mob offer violence to the very ideologists who are committed to alleviating their lot in life but have that violence turned against them by the counterviolence of the Socialists and the police.

Descent and mortification of another kind are figured in the social decline of Gordon Sterrett, which also ends in death. Sterrett is no different from the rest of the Yale boys, except that once the prop of money is removed, his feeble moral will and incapacity for resolute action make him a prey to depression and whining self-indulgence. Marriage to a social inferior as an adequate cause for suicide is an outdated theme and is not, as I suggested earlier, the central point of Sterrett's death. What is at issue here is the terrifying fluidity of the American social organization, which, with its emphasis on wealth, carries morally weak individuals up and down with irrational power.

The twin aspects of this theme of social mobility—first, character in decay (or a man going to the devil) figured as social descent; and second, the upward aspiration of the *nouveau riche* outsider—are also a constant in the one story Fitzgerald had to tell. The personal urgency of this theme, however, found a powerful expression in Fitzgerald's latest discovery, H. L. Mencken. In *The American Credo,* Mencken had pointed to this terrible fluidity in remarking that "such a thing as a secure position is practically unknown among us. There is no American who cannot hope to lift himself another notch or two, if he is to keep on fighting for whatever position he has; no wall of caste is there to protect him if he slips. One observes every day the movement of individuals, families, whole groups, in both directions." And he concluded that "it is this constant possibility of rising, this constant risk of falling, that gives a barbaric picturesqueness to the panorama of what is called fashionable society in America."[32]

Lacking "interior security," however, Fitzgerald could not take a

---

32 H. L. Mencken and George Jean Nathan, *The American Credo* (New York: Alfred A. Knopf, 1920), pp. 30, 32.

satirist's mere amusement in the picturesqueness of that panorama. He wanted to be one of the beautiful, moving upward, rather than one of the damned. But living in the Bronx in early 1920, struggling with his failure in love and literature, and meditating on the strengths and weaknesses of his own character, he inclined toward the view—ambivalently expressed in "May Day"—that perhaps only a socialism adequately grounded on the redistribution of wealth could create a more stable social order. Mencken's forceful debunking of visionary egalitarianism briefly deflected Fitzgerald from his own point of view, for in the end his sympathy for socialism was sentimental. Nevertheless, this sympathy was sufficiently constant in his thought to constitute one of the emotional subtexts of his greatest work. In the 1930s it brought him to the point of saying that "to bring on the revolution it may be necessary to work inside the Communist party." [33] Fortunately, that double point of view, that attraction-repulsion, that ambivalence about "the panorama of what is called fashionable society in America," prevented him from taking an ideologist's narrowly didactic approach to his materials. "May Day" may not be his best work, but it richly demonstrates how Fitzgerald could tap and organize his own inner conflicts in order to produce a vision of the troubled complexity of American social interrelationships.

---

33 Fitzgerald, *The Crack-Up,* p. 126.

A Note on
Dos Passos

Kudos to The Library of America for bringing back into print (in a compact, well-edited, and handsomely produced volume) a major American fictional achievement—the trilogy *U.S.A.* by John Dos Passos (1896–1970). [1] Composed of *The 42nd Parallel* (1930), *1919* (1932), and *The Big Money* (1936), this trilogy enjoyed great critical esteem during the writer's youth. Since his death, however, the author and his books have suffered an unjustified neglect. This publication should serve to remedy it.

As a writer, Dos Passos wanted to be "the architect of history." *U.S.A.* he intended as a fictional account of the changing character of American social conditions between about 1900 and 1930. Writing the novel was rebuilding the past in condensed and dramatic form. Like his earlier novel *Manhattan Transfer* (1925), the narrative line of *U.S.A.* was decentralized; that is, it was a story without a single protagonist. Instead of a single hero, Dos Passos offered interwoven portraits of twelve major fictional personae (plus a host of minor characters) whose lives were presented as representative of American national experience as it altered under the impact of industrialization, World War I, the Red Scare, the Jazz Age, the Sacco-Vanzetti case, and the depression. Amongst the major characters in the trilogy are Mary French, who starts out a secretary and ends up working for the Sacco-Vanzetti defense team; Mac, an Irish-American printer who turns Communist and then drifts down into Mexico; J. Ward Moorehouse, the executive who invents public relations and becomes

---

1 John Dos Passos, *U.S.A.*, eds. Daniel Aaron and Townsend Ludington (New York: The Library of America, 1996).

a spin-doctor for "the establishment"; Dick Savage, a would-be poet gone sour in a philistine America; Joe Williams, a merchant seaman whose life is an empty waste; Charley Anderson, a World War I pilot and mechanic turned executive whose very life is destroyed in the corporation rat race; Ben Compton, the revolutionist who gives his life for the cause, only to be expelled from the Communist Party for deviationism (or independent thinking), and so forth. The American Dream, for Dos Passos, was a story of such failures, and the trilogy ends during the depression with Vag, a hobo on the road, hitchhiking to who knows where.

Given his historical objective, "Dos" wanted the book to mirror what were then commonly called the "objective conditions" of American life. Anyone who has read around in the magazines and newspapers of the 1930s will immediately recognize the term "objective conditions" as a left-wing synonym for "capitalist exploitation." And, indeed, the young Dos Passos was so slavishly Marxist in his reading of social conditions that his fiction was usually considered proletarian literature. Even so, Dos Passos was not a proletarian by birth. He had, in fact, grown up as the natural child of a wealthy American businessman of Portuguese descent who—because he was married to a woman not the boy's mother—did not recognize John until the boy was sixteen. Still, the father gave the boy a great many privileges like international travel and private schooling at Choate and Harvard. These advantages, however, only seemed to confirm the boy in his rebellion against capitalism and the class to which his father belonged.

The political rebellion of Flaming Youth, as *les jeunes* were called in the 1920s, was in part a generational phenomenon and is evident in the superficial socialism of many other young writers of the time —Scott Fitzgerald, Sinclair Lewis, Edmund Wilson, and Theodore Dreiser among them. Still, Dos Passos was for a time vehement about his left-wing faith. During the Great War he drove ambulances for the Red Cross and afterward, when America entered the war, he enlisted in the army. His experiences in France confirmed him in his belief that the war had been provoked by a capitalist conspiracy. He felt that Harvard unfitted men for life in the modern world, and he remarked to Arthur K. McComb in 1917 that "Until Widener [Library] is blown up and A. Lawrence Lowell [the Harvard president] assassinated and the Business School destroyed and its site sowed with salt—no good will come out of Cambridge." He told one of his friends, "My only hope is in revolution—in wholesale assassination of all statesmen, capitalists, war-mongers, jingoists, inventors, scientists. . . . My only refuge from the deepest depression is in dreams of vengeful guillotines."

Luckily, his dreams remained unrealized. After the Great War he was constantly on the road, writing novels, plays, political reportage, and travelogues. He was especially popular with the editors of left-wing magazines like the *Liberator*. For a time he was even a contributing editor to the Communist *Daily Worker* and the *New Masses*. Like other "socially conscious" writers, he toured the Soviet Union and liked what he saw; he covered strikes in America and didn't like what he saw. The execution of Sacco and Vanzetti, left-wing anarchists who in a robbery had murdered a factory paymaster and guard, Dos Passos called "judicial murder" and twice got himself arrested in protest against it. In 1932 he voted for Foster and Ford, the Communist ticket.

In order to suggest the "objective conditions" of American life, Dos Passos engaged in a number of stylistic innovations that mercifully lift *U.S.A.* above the level of hack propaganda and prove him to be one of the most creative fiction writers of his time. These innovations included some sixty-eight intercalated passages called "Newsreels," each of which presents a string of newspaper headlines, overheard conversations, political speeches, advertising jingles, radio broadcasts, and popular songs. As the trilogy moves forward, decade by decade, these of course change with the times and create a sense of the chaotic fluidity of American popular culture as it rushes headlong into a meaningless future.

A second novelistic innovation was a series of interspersed biographical vignettes of public men and women whose lives were coterminous with and ominously revelatory of the changing times. Politicians like Woodrow Wilson and Theodore Roosevelt, capitalists like Andrew Carnegie and J. P. Morgan, efficiency experts like F. W. Taylor, and journalists like William Randolph Hearst are caricatured in *U.S.A.* with rhetorical verve and a savage economy. And it is these "establishment" figures who suggest an entrenched power structure preventing the evolution of a wholesome American culture. Meanwhile, the sentimental favorites of Dos Possos are here exalted—left-wing political figures like Eugene V. Debs and Big Bill Haywood, whose defeat or imprisonment presumably accounted for the decline of America into a moral wasteland.

Less objective was a third major stylistic innovation—the fifty-one "Camera Eye" passages that are devoted, à la Joyce, to the development of the artist who sees and records the objective conditions of American life—as, for example, in a novel like *U.S.A.* The fleeting glimpses of John Dos Passos that we catch in these passages suggest that he was not willing to surrender to the canons of Socialist Realism, which demanded naturalistic portraits of "the grim horrors of life under capitalism." Even so, the burden of all these stylistic innovations was the failure of America to become the utopia of social and economic equality that only communism could supposedly realize.

To be perfectly frank, the dustbin of history is full of thirties American proletarian fiction that was awful then, is awful now, and needs no revival. And so overdetermined is the leftwing ideology of *U.S.A.* that it would be easy to dismiss this trilogy as mere propaganda. But the manifest self-contradictions of the Dos Passos work and the sheer art of his prose make the trilogy still engaging more than a half-century after its publication. For all his Marxist bias, Dos Passos was too keen an observer and too fine a novelist not to see the essential vacuity of Soviet communism. *U.S.A.* is therefore shot through with evidence that Dos Passos could not stomach the coercive and repressive diktats of the literary commissars. (At a *New Masses* organizational meeting, according to Malcolm Cowley, Dos Passos once derisively announced: "Intellectual workers of the world unite, you have nothing to lose but your brains." The party-line Communists knew him for the bourgeois liberal that he was and ostracized him accordingly.)

Dos Passos's insistence on the writer's right to see with his own eyes and judge with his own intelligence—evident everywhere in *U.S.A.,* despite the periodic ideological sludge—finally led him, toward the end of the depression, to break with the left. Though he found big business still unfair to organized labor, he came to prefer the defects of American capitalism to the coercion of Earl Browder, Mike Gold, and the other American Communists who had tried to dictate what he should write about. Of course, in spurning the left Dos Passos incurred the wrath of the party hacks (and their liberal fellow travelers in the reviewing media), and his reputation has never completely recovered.

What is finally most intriguing about Dos Passos is not his flirtation with the left. After all, many American writers were likewise seduced during the depression by an *apparat* preying upon their utopian dreams. What redeemed him was his finally waking up to the evils of Stalinism and the left. In grasping the threat they represented to democracy everywhere, he became increasingly passionate in the defense of republican American political traditions. His growing detestation of Stalinism and its leftist derivatives was quite vocal. By the mid-1950s he had embraced a conservative Republican vision of America for which Senator Barry Goldwater was then the principal spokesman.

Such works as Dos Passos's *The Head and Heart of Thomas Jefferson* (1954), *The Theme Is Freedom* (1956), and *The Men Who Made the Nation* (1957) all reflect an older, wiser, more mature and historically well-informed student of democratic political principles. And his mélange of history, fiction, and biography in *Midcentury* (1961) was an attempt, though not so successful as *U.S.A.*, to define from a conservative perspective the more recent conditions of American life. Although, for his volte-face, the left and the liberal media never forgave him, he is well worth a rereading today. Besides the intrinsic merit of his fiction, Dos Passos is worth knowing for another reason: his literary and political odyssey expresses in a particularly pure way the fate of a great many early-twentieth-century American artists and intellectuals who innocently and naively accepted but then recoiled in horror from the lethal embrace of communism.

The Short Stories
of Sinclair Lewis

Although Sinclair Lewis's reputation as an author has declined since his death, it was his distinction to be the first American writer to win the Nobel Prize for literature. This award, conferred on him in Stockholm in 1930, honored a career highlighted by such fictional successes as *Main Street*, *Babbitt*, *Arrowsmith*, *Elmer Gantry*, and *Dodsworth*. Few American writers had ever produced so many remarkable novels, and novels provocative of so many extreme critical reactions, and all in a single decade, the 1920s.

Main Street (1920), Lewis's first triumph and a remarkable best-seller, was a hilarious satire of American small-town bourgeois philistinism and anti-intellectualism. Debunking the myth that although "cities were evil and even in the farmland there were occasional men of wrath, our villages were approximately paradise," *Main Street* was an overnight sensation. The novel dealt with the quality of village life in America just at the time when it was drying up, as economic and cultural energies, as well as young people, were gravitating toward the cities. The heroine, Carol Kennicott, is a young woman brought into the village of Gopher Prairie through marriage. Although she tries valiantly to elevate the town's social tone, refine its artistic style, raise its educational level, and invest it with life and vitality, she is a total failure. In indicting village life, Lewis complained of its

> unimaginatively standardized background, a sluggishness of speech and manners, a rigid ruling of the spirit by the desire to appear respectable. It is . . . the contentment of the quiet dead, who are scornful of the living for their restless walking. It is negation

canonized as the one positive virtue. It is the prohibition of happiness. It is slavery self-sought and self-defended. It is dullness made God.

The reaction to *Main Street* was a critical firestorm. A thinly veiled picture of life in Sauk Centre, Minnesota, where Lewis had been born, the novel outraged his own family and the townsfolk, who ostracized him. Carping small-town Jaycees and village boosters praised their wholesome lives and cited statistics on how many player pianos had been sold in small towns across America. Yet scores of women readers wrote Lewis to thank him for having portrayed in Carol their desperate lives. Sales of the novel soared. *Main Street* was parodied or answered in *Jane Street*, *Ptomaine Street*, and Meredith Nicholson's *The Man in the Street*. Lewis kept the furor going by contributing an introduction to Frazier Hunt's *Sycamore Bend*, a defense of the small town by one of his friends. In that introduction he reversed his satire and turned it on urban readers who pitied the villagers for "not knowing gunmen, burlesque girls, boot-leggers, and gum-chewing stenographers of the cities." *Main Street* was such a remarkable literary phenomenon that it was nominated by the committee of judges for the 1920 Pulitzer Prize, but the trustees of Columbia, who give the prize, overruled the jury and awarded it instead to Edith Wharton for *The Age of Innocence*. Their reason: *Main Street* did not fulfill the terms of the award—namely, to "present the wholesome atmosphere of American life, and the highest standard of American manners and manhood."

Lewis's next novel, *Babbitt* (1922), though offending tired businessmen everywhere, was likewise a popular success for its free-swinging attack on the commercial "religion of business" then so commonly acclaimed in the popular media. The protagonist George Babbitt, a middle-aged, middle-class, paunchy real estate man, is a satiric composite of all the Regular Guys in the Chamber of Commerce, Lions, Rotary, Elks, Kiwanis, and other social clubs. And Zenith, a symbol of mid-sized cities everywhere in America, is burlesqued for its class-conscious, status-oriented, upwardly mobile, racially prejudiced, and materialistic conformists who engage in "orgies of commercial righteousness" as they hustle for profits.

Less satirical was *Arrowsmith* (1925), his next novel, a celebration of the scientist-physician who devotes himself to the noble end of saving human lives. In the portrait of Martin Arrowsmith, Lewis may have indeed intended to depict the highest standards in American manhood. At least the Columbia trustees apparently thought so, for the novel won the Pulitzer Prize in 1926. But in hurt vanity and protesting that the first prize had been "stolen" from him, Lewis created another public uproar that year by declining the award. *Elmer Gantry* (1927) also created a tumult, this time with ministers and pious churchgoers, by presenting a charismatic preacher as a fraud, a hypocrite, and a lecher. By the time of *Dodsworth* (1929), which explored the battle of the sexes through an international theme—in which the contrast between Europe and America is usually to Europe's advantage—Lewis had managed to stir up about as much controversy over his themes and techniques as any American novelist ever has.

By 1930, then, Lewis was internationally known for burlesques and satires on nearly every phase of American life: provincial hicks, bogus artistic types, lazy expatriates, bohemian frauds, mendacious admen, backslapping and devious salesmen, crass movie producers, ignoramus college professors, psychiatrists, spiritualists and New Thought devotees, castrating females, corrupt evangelists, Prohibitionists, snobs, fools, and pretentious intellectuals and artists. It is no wonder that a common American view was that the Nobel Prize committee had given him the award because of Lewis's scathing satires on America's people, her values, and her institutions. As Lewis Mumford wryly remarked, Sinclair Lewis had

> created a picture of America that corresponds in a remarkable degree with the naïve caricature of America that all but the most enlightened and perceptive Europeans carry in their heads. In crowning Mr. Lewis's work the Swedish Academy has, in the form of a compliment, conveyed a subtle disparagement of the country they honored.

Sherwood Anderson put it more jingoistically: Lewis got the prize "because his sharp criticism of American life catered to the dislike, distrust, and envy which most Europeans feel toward the United States." In fact, however, the America that emerges out of Sinclair Lewis's fiction is largely a country of his own invention.

Born in 1885 in Sauk Centre, Minnesota, Harry Sinclair Lewis was the third son of Dr. Edwin J. and Emma Kermott Lewis. A small village with little claim to culture, Sauk Centre was nevertheless a complete world of social types for the future fiction writer. Lewis grew up to be a tall, shy, skinny, awkward boy, doomed with an impossibly bad facial complexion. (Budd Schulberg called it "one of the ugliest faces I had ever seen," and Frederick Manfred described it as "a face to haunt one in dreams.") Lewis compensated for his loneliness by nothing else than continuous boyhood reading—largely romances of fantasy and escape. After a teenage job at the *Sauk Centre Herald* and the *Avalanche*, in 1903 Lewis went off to Yale, where he apprenticed himself to the *Yale Literary Magazine* and the New Haven papers.

Yale was a traumatic experience for the lonely provincial boy. In New Haven he found a great deal of genuine learning, but he was estranged by Yale's pedantry and by its social and intellectual pretensions. As a provincial Midwesterner without intellectual distinction or any of the social graces, Lewis felt himself to be always an outsider. His professor, William Lyon Phelps, noted in his autobiography that Lewis was not disliked in college but was regarded with amiable tolerance as a freak. And another teacher, Chauncey Brewster Tinker, later remarked that "The conventions and restrictions of good society—especially of collegiate society—were offensive to him. His abiding temptation was to undermine them and blow them at the moon."

Something of Lewis's disappointment with Yale is poignantly mirrored in "Young Man Axelbrod," first published in June 1917 in the *Century* magazine. There the Midwestern dreamer who seeks after truth and beauty is ridiculed by his townsfolk as a crank and a crackpot. Knute Axelbrod, as a young Scandinavian, came to the New World to fulfill a dream, to find in America "the world's nursery for justice, for broad, fair towns, and eager talk." Yet after a lifetime of hard farm labor, Axelbrod is left unsatisfied, and he is overcome by the dream of making "a great pilgrimage to the Mount of Muses; for he really supposed college to be that sort of place." In spite of the town view that he is a crazy old man, he strikes off for Yale in the East, only to discover there that the callow undergraduates and pedantic professors likewise consider him cracked. It cannot be imagined that Axelbrod is equal to the Ivy League; but his dream reflects a noble idealism and marks his spirit as that of perennial youth. Lewis's sense of not belonging at Yale, of being regarded as a freak, is very strong in this tale. Only in Young Axelbrod's night out with Washburn, when they go to Hartford to hear Ysafe play, visit the exotic Jewish ghetto in search of rich food, and talk till dawn about art and life in Washburn's rooms, only then does Axelbrod finally experience what he had hoped to find in the East: "This is what I come to college for—this one night. I will go away before I spoil it." And he returns to the town of Joralemon with a single memento, Washburn's volume of Musset's poetry.

This volume of French poetry, which Axelbrod cannot read, together with Washburn's crystal, silver plate, Persian rugs, and handsomely bound volumes, are, it must be said, inadequate indices of genuine high culture and learning. For Lewis never knew how to represent the real thing and always sentimentally fixed upon material objects to imply elegance and culture. What Axelbrod essentially gains from his moment of initiation is not learning and high culture but rather an experience of acceptance, of friendship, of fellow feeling, from a young man for whom this style of life—a European style, incidentally, rather than an American one—is natural and un-forced. It is a shared moment of reverence for the elements of a cul-ture higher than the author, or Axelbrod, or the Midwestern town could claim. In any case, the theme in "Young Man Axelbrod" is the same as that in *Main Street, Babbitt,* and many other Lewis works: the fate of the protagonist who, as Mark Schorer has said, finds him-self "in a stultifying environment, tries to reform and then break out of that environment, succeeds for a time, and then makes a necessary compromise with it."

After graduation in 1908, Lewis traveled about the country, hold-ing down odd jobs, until he settled in New York in 1910 and took work in the publishing business. During the next decade he pub-lished six unsuccessful novels which are worth mentioning only as apprentice work. *Hike and the Aeroplane* (1912), *Our Mr. Wrenn* (1914), *The Trail of the Hawk* (1915), *The Job* (1917), *The Innocents* (1917), and *Free Air* (1917) did not satisfy Lewis, nor did they impress his family, for they always thought he ought to have been a profes-sional man like his father. In fact, Lewis later confessed that "I never quite get over the feeling that writing isn't much of a profession, compared with being a doctor, that it's not quite manly to be sitting on the seat of your pants all the time." Still, he persisted in his chosen vocation: editing, writing short stories, working on novels, hoping for a big breakthrough.

In 1914 this socially awkward young man who aspired to the high culture of the East achieved the remarkable feat of marrying one of the most elegant young women he had ever met, Grace Hegger. This "lady from the Upper West Side," who had escaped "the trap of shabby gentility" by taking up a career at *Vogue,* had stylish clothes, an English accent, and aristocratic ways—including a French maid, because, as she later confessed in *With Love from Gracie: Sinclair Lewis, 1912–1925* (1951), it pleased her to "give orders in French before guests." Their whole high style of life was rather "furrin" to Lewis, but there was no doubt that Gracie had class. But consorting with the Eastern "quality" naturally enough produced a reaction. The biographical record is full of anecdotes about Lewis's talent for violating the dictates of decorum. He often failed to show up at dinner parties (including his own), or, when he did, he would scandalize the hostess by singing dirty songs or daring guests to take off their shoes. Once he got out on a window ledge two stories above ground and crawled about like a human fly. That he was drunk most of the time suggests that Lewis's impossible shyness and social discomfort led him to act out in the most self-destructive ways. As he later admitted, he "detested polite dinner parties," couldn't stand the "amiable purring of nice matrons," and was "a barbarian in the arts of the table."

Needless to say, his first marriage was full of irremediable conflicts. By 1928 he and Gracie had divorced, whereupon he immediately married Dorothy Thompson, a journalist playmate with fewer social pretensions. Throughout the 1920s, the decade of his great success, Lewis traveled widely, collecting material for *Babbitt, Arrowsmith*, and the other novels. But city life and continual traveling produced in him a longing for the country, and he and Dorothy bought a farm in Vermont. There Lewis fulfilled a dream, temporarily, that Sidney Dow in the story "Land" (*Saturday Evening Post*, 1931) is never able to realize. Always moody, bibulous, and egotistical, Lewis was divorced from Dorothy Thompson in 1942.

Lewis's reputation declined sharply after 1930, but he continued to write, producing a series of novels which include *Ann Vickers* (1933), *Work of Art* (1934), *It Can't Happen Here* (1935), *The Prodigal Parents* (1938), *Bethel Merriday* (1940), *Gideon Planish* (1943), *Cass Timberlane* (1945), *Kingsblood Royal* (1947), and *The God-Seeker* (1949). During these years Lewis also cultivated his interest in the theater as an actor, producer, and director of a good many plays, and he taught creative writing classes at Wisconsin and Minnesota. Aside from the Pulitzer and Nobel prizes, he was also elected to the National Institute of Arts and Letters and was given an honorary degree by Yale in 1936. He died in 1951 in Rome of a heart ailment and was buried in Sauk Centre, which has now embraced him as the man who put the town on the map. His last novel, *World So Wide*, was posthumously published in 1951.

While Lewis is unquestionably best known as a novelist, between 1904 and 1947 he published approximately 117 short stories, culling the best himself for the 1935 *Selected Short Stories of Sinclair Lewis*. During this forty-four-year span as a story writer, Lewis had the good fortune to write at a time when the magazine business was at its peak. The large number of weekly and monthly periodicals publishing short stories made it possible for him to travel abroad and live very well at home while at the same time he worked on the novels.

By Lewis's time the short story had attained the brilliance we associate with the names of Irving, Hawthorne, Poe, James, Crane, Anderson, Hemingway, and Faulkner, and to these American masters we must of course add the names of Chekhov, Joyce, and other European writers of distinction. Yet Lewis learned little from these masters of the art of the short story, and he had no interest in little magazines, like the *transatlantic review* or *The Little Review*, where some of the most interesting and experimental short fiction was often published. In fact, Lewis told Gracie that "he hated these sophomoric little magazines" and did not intend to publish in them. As William Peden has noted in *The American Short Story*, "In one major line of its early development, the short story became a piece of literary merchandise written to conform to the unsophisticated tastes of a rapidly expanding middle-class audience." To this line of development Lewis's stories belong, for he preferred to adapt his work to the editorial demands of the large, mass-market slick magazines that paid and paid well. Lewis's tales thus form a part of the popular tradition of commercial short fiction associated with the names of writers like O. Henry, Jack London, and Richard Harding Davis—writers for whom the *Saturday Evening Post*, *Redbook*, *Cosmopolitan*, and the *Pictorial Review* were favorite outlets. Lewis, as D. J. Dooley has remarked in *The Art of Sinclair Lewis*, "never practiced the short story as an art form—it was a frankly commercial product."

Lewis's short stories fall into several recognizable categories: tales of romantic fantasy or escape, melodramas of heroic or mock-heroic adventure, boy-meets-girl stories, satires of pretension and folly, and tales of isolation and loneliness. Often played are variations on a theme more fully developed in the novels. In style and form the tales change very little between the earliest stories and the last. Even so, Lewis was an excellent storyteller with an enviable command of narrative development. His tales have a remarkable vividness produced by colorful and concrete detail, rapidly paced action, and a gallery of characters and a medley of dialects that are *sui generis*. What other writer has come up with character names like Rippleton Holabird, Myron and Ora Weagle, Omar Gribble, Sara Hetwiggin Butts, Jared Sassburger, Grover Butterbaugh, and Opal Emerson Mudge? And these characters do not merely talk, as has been frequently noted, but rather whinny, boom, chirp, bumble, warble, carol, gurgle, and yammer in Lewis's inimitable slang.

The elements of style so famously evident in the novels are apparent in his stories as well: the bizarre blend of realism and bald romanticism; the stylized diction that sounds so much like, but was not, vernacular American speech; the exaggeration of that speech through mimicry and slang; the flat characters; the improbable plots somehow sustained despite the dizzying divagation into farce and burlesque; the O'Henry-like trick endings; the wild exaggeration and hyperbole; the staccato effect produced by Lewis's gusto and nervous energy; and the sacrifice of any plot or character or consistency of theme for the sake of a belly laugh. In this last respect, though Lewis has often been called the American Dickens, he is really the child of Mark Twain—as "Let's Play King," with its uproarious amalgam of *Huck Finn* and *The Prince and the Pauper*, makes clear. When he read over the tales chosen for *Selected Short Stories of Sinclair Lewis* in 1935, Lewis remarked that "One of the things interesting to the author, though perhaps to no one else, in rereading these stories, is the discovery that he, who has been labeled a 'satirist' and a 'realist,' is actually a romantic medievalist of the most incurable sort."

We can see the romantic medievalism clearly enough in the "boy-meets-girl, boy-rescues-girl" theme in "Speed," originally published in *Redbook* in 1919, where the Knight who rescues the lady is a cross-country automobile racer; or in "Moths in the Arc Light" (*Saturday Evening Post*, 1919), where a couple's romantic fantasies sustain their long-distance relationship. In "The Ghost Patrol," which appeared in *Redbook* in 1917, the rescuer is a cop on the beat who is not content to stay in retirement. Lewis had an ardent longing to believe in acts of nobility and heroism, as we see in "The Kidnaped Memorial" (*Pictorial Review*, 1919), where the decent and generous Mr. Gale, a Confederate veteran, shames a Northern community into honoring its G.A.R. dead.

More realistic in tone is "The Willow Walk," a 1918 *Saturday Evening Post* tale. This story is a marvel of suspense as we watch the bank teller Jasper Holt—in a doppelgänger transformation worthy of a Poe or a Dostoevsky—become his invented alter ego. In the most comprehensive study ever made of Lewis's tales, Tobin Simon has argued in his doctoral dissertation, "The Short Stories of Sinclair Lewis" (New York University, 1972), that "The Willow Walk" is probably Lewis's "finest" story: "Carefully and poignantly Lewis has probed the theme of identity, and in Jasper Holt one reads the inevitable fate of men who in putting on faces to meet faces cannot find the face they once claimed as theirs."

In "The Cat of the Stars," first published in the *Saturday Evening Post* in 1919, Lewis offers the *reductio ad absurdum* of astrological determinism, in showing how little Willis Stodeport brings down a kingdom merely by petting a cat. Lewis's satiric vein also surfaces in

"Things" (published in 1919 in the *Saturday Evening Post*) and "The Hack Driver" (*Nation*, 1923), where the ordeal of polite society and the evil effects of material possessions are ridiculed. If we can locate Lewis's deepest social values anywhere in his wide-ranging, self-contradictory satire, it is in the Thoreauvian desire for freedom from polite society and from the aspiration for material possessions that leads him improbably to observe in "The Hack Driver" that

> we retain a decent simplicity, no matter how much we are tied to Things, to houses and motors and expensive wives. . . . [The] apparently civilized man is at heart nothing but a hobo who prefers flannel shirts and bristly cheeks and cussing and dirty tin plates to all the trim, hygienic, forward-looking life our women-folks make us put on for them.

In "Letter from the Queen," published in *Cosmopolitan* in 1929, we have a splendid instance of Lewis's satire on ignoramus college professors; and the 1930 tale, "Go East, Young Man" (*Cosmopolitan*), should be read alongside *Main Street* and *Babbitt* as an instance of how Lewis could switch sides, idealize the Midwestern small-town life and a business career, and satirize the phony pretensions of artistic life in the East and in Paris.

Despite the stylistic zest that carries his stories along, they embarrassed Lewis into virtual silence. Gracie said that Lewis "was the first to declare that he was not a great story writer." At times Lewis regarded his stories as merely a means to pay the bills. Although he had been writing them for more than a decade, he confessed to Joseph Hergesheimer in 1916 that "I am not a short story writer, but a novelist . . . and I turn to short stories with difficulty—as yet." What bothered him about "this short story game" was its "formula, pat philosophy, rot! Man, if you and I don't make it good among these stubfooted plaster gods, go farther than any of them," he told Hergesheimer, "then may God take us and boil us in olive oil taken from the claret-spotted table of a Hobohemian restaurant in Greenwich Village." As the formulaic construction, the pat philosophy, the obligatory love angle, and the optimistic ending turned stale, Lewis came to regard story writing as involving "slick, nimble tricks," a kind of "fictional vaudeville" that, as he warned his Minnesota students, "will ruin you." He advised Charles Breasted not "to waste your energies on short stories and stuff for ephemeral publications. Write *books*!" During the public furor over *Main Street*, Lewis even conveyed a fear to his publisher, Alfred Harcourt, that a volume of short stories might kill interest in the novel:

I am, frankly, having a hell of a time in trying at once to turn myself back into the successful S.E.P. [*Saturday Evening Post*] writer I was a year ago—and yet to do for them nothing but stories so honest that they will in no way get me back into magazine trickiness nor injure the M. St. furore [sic]. . . . I don't believe I shall ever again be the facile Post trickster I by God was—for which, doubtless, we shall in the long run be glad.

This kind of candor led George Jean Nathan to observe in his *Intimate Notebooks* that, "always forthright and completely honest with himself," Lewis "made no bones of what he was doing, but frankly announced to anyone who would listen that he was, to use his own locution, turning out a swell piece of cheese to grab off some easy gravy."

Lewis's deepest theorizing about the craft of fiction was no more profound than that "the art of writing is the art of applying the seat of your pants to the seat of your chair." And he loved to repeat the maxim that "a mighty important thing for all authors to cultivate is this thing [H. L.] Mencken refers to as 'Sitzfleisch.'" Lewis felt that "almost all rules about 'how to write' are nonsense" because they are based "upon what some writer did in the past, upon something which may have been very useful for him but may not suit anybody else." He despised the self-consciousness of some of his contemporaries and insisted on the utter naturalness of the creative process. The writer writes "as Tilden plays tennis or as Dempsey fights, which is to say, he throws himself into it with never a moment of the diletante's [sic] sitting back and watching himself perform." "Brother Lewis," he said of himself on another occasion, is "essentially a story teller—just as naïve, excited, unself-conscious as the Arab story-tellers beside the caravan fires seven hundred years ago, or as O. Henry in a hotel room on Twenty-third Street furiously turning out tales for dinner and red-ink money."

Even so, Lewis had to live with himself as a short story writer, and that meant coping with the conventions dictated by popular magazine editors. To write the kind of stories he wanted to write and still to satisfy editors like George Horace Lorimer at the *Saturday Evening Post*, Lewis played variations on the themes they liked and recombined and altered, ever so slightly, the old familiar formulas. Gracie defended his stories in saying that "swiftly though he wrote there was no 'dashing off a story': his revisions were always painstaking." And when the critic Carl Van Doren described his tales as "brisk and amusing chatter," Lewis vigorously defended himself by saying that

> even in my magazine stories . . . I have steadily sought to work out a
> means of doing as honest work as the powerful negations of the
> magazine editors would permit. Out of perhaps fifty stories in Satur-
> day Evening Post, Century, Harper's and so on, I doubt if more than
> ten could with the slightest justice be classified as "brisk and amusing
> chatter."

In this respect Lewis was quite right, but his academic critics have
rarely agreed. In fact, tested against the great masters of the form,
Lewis has even been denied the status of an artist. Mark Schorer,
whose *Sinclair Lewis: An American Life* (1961) is the definitive biography, has remarked that "perhaps it is futile to approach any Lewis
novel as a work of art." And Sheldon Grebstein has remarked in
Sinclair Lewis that, of the thirteen stories collected here,

> all but a few range from the canned, slick, or unforgivably sentimen-
> tal to the merely contrived. Such a collection forces conclusions hos-
> tile to Lewis. If we presume that these stories are Lewis's best or
> representative of his best short fiction, then his best was inferior. It is
> also impossible to trace any consistent values or standards in the
> stories; rather, they contain some direct contradictions.

Certainly they are not stories of the greatest aesthetic distinction,
worthy to be classed with the best of Chekhov, Joyce, Faulkner,
Hemingway, and Henry James. Lewis himself, in 1935, also had some
doubts about them because they were "so optimistic, so laudatory";
somehow they seemed tonally off-key during the depression. But he
speculated whether "this American optimism, this hope and courage"
were not "authentic parts of American life"—as indeed they are. But
most literary critics in our century have preferred stories of "the
power of blackness," tales that convey a bleak existential condition,
that—in Melville's phrase, say "NO, in Thunder!" In this respect,
American critics have been largely at odds with a fundamental aspect
of the American spirit.

Of Lewis's critics, only Stuart P. Sherman appears fully to have
appreciated Lewis's grasp of American life, for, in *The Significance of
Sinclair Lewis* (1922), he was led to call him "one of the foremost
short story writers of this century." The century was still young in
1922, and Sherman's judgment was made before Lewis had gone on
to write scores of not very remarkable commercial tales. But at his
best Lewis's short stories, like his novels, accomplish the remarkable
feat described by E. M. Forster: "What Mr. Lewis has done for my-

self and thousands of others is to lodge a piece of a continent in our *imagination*." However we may respond to his stories, there can be no doubt that Lewis created a distinct fictional style, an authentic signature, a genuine idiom. And Dorothy Thompson was quite right in observing that Lewis is "an ineradicable part of American cultural history" and that "no one seeking to recapture and record the habits, frames of mind, social movements, speech, aspirations, admirations, radicalisms, reactions, crusades, and Gargantuan absurdities of the American *demos* . . . will be able to do without him."

Conrad Aiken's "Mr. Arcularis"

Once asked about his credo, Conrad Aiken replied: "How extraordinarily little I know about myself."[1] His answer implied curiosity not only about the complexities of his own being but also about the mystery of life as a whole. This curiosity was also responsible for Aiken's extraordinary interest in Freudian psychology as an instrument capable of revealing the deeply hidden, mysterious, secret self. "Almost alone in his generation," the psychiatrist Henry A. Murray has written,

> Aiken proved equal to the peril. He allowed the Freudian dragon to swallow him, and then, after a sufficient sojourn in its maw, cut his way out to a new freedom. When he emerged he was stocked with the lore of psychoanalysis but neither subjugated nor impeded by it. Aiken and Freud were, in a profound sense, fellow-spirits. . . ."[2]

One of Freud's principal theories—that the creation of a work of art is a revelation of the artist's hidden self, a day-dream release of hidden desires and repressed erotic elements—has had its obvious ef-

---

1 Quoted by Rufus A. Blanshard, "Metamorphosis of a Dream," *Sewanee Review*, 64 (1957), 694.

2 "Poet of Creative Dissolution," *Wake*, 11 (1952), 102. Aiken's preoccupation with psychoanalysis is evinced not only by his omnivorous reading of Freud, Adler, Pfister, Ferenczi, Rank, Wittels, Jung, and others but also by his personal friendship with some practicing psychoanalysts like Murray, Dr. G. B. Wilbur, the physiologist Dr. Grayson McCouch, and Dr. John Taylor. Aiken's *Among the Lost People* (New York: Scribner's, 1934), in which "Mr. Arcularis" was reprinted, was in fact dedicated to Dr. McCouch. Although Aiken never organized his work according to a Freudian formula, he has, in a sense, as Jay Martin has rightly observed, "always written for their inspection, according to approved psychoanalytic principles." Martin, *Conrad Aiken: A Life of His Art* (Princeton: Princeton University Press, 1962), p. 26.

fect on Aiken's poetry and prose. Aiken also extrapolated from the work of Freud a theory of literary criticism. Because historical, biographical, and aesthetic criticism cannot explain the *cause* of a work of art, the critic may therefore need to employ the techniques of the psychologist, the anthropologist, or the biologist—as "Mr. Arcularis" requires one, I believe, to do. Of the origins of art, Aiken has said:

> It has been urged that in the day-dream, or art, we do not really seek to escape from ourselves, but, precisely, to find ourselves. But what part of ourselves is it that we find? Is it not exactly that part of us which has been wounded and would be made whole: that part of us which desires wings and has none, longs for immortality and knows that it must die, craves unlimited power and has instead "common sense" and the small bitter "actual"; that part of us, in short, which is imprisoned and would escape! . . . There can be little question about it, and it is precisely of the associations connected with these major psychic frustrations that we have evolved the universal language of healing which we call art. Let us not hastily condemn this view simply because it savors of the often-flouted "new" psychology. Freud is not, by two thousand two hundred years, the first to see art as primarily a process of wish-fulfillment. Let us recall Aristotle's theory of catharsis, and rub our eyes. The difference between catharsis and wish-fulfillment is slight to the point of disappearance.[3]

If for Aiken, then, art is the therapy by which the psychic wound is healed, it is not surprising that a theme of greatest frequency in his fiction is the inward-turning eye, the deep descent into the mysteries of one's own psyche, toward that "frontier within man's consciousness where the individual, like a diver, plunges into his own depths to sound them, and in so doing believes himself effectually to have sounded the world."[4] Aiken's "Mr. Arcularis" is one such plunge, an exploration of the frontier of consciousness-nonconsciousness. Since Aiken was so steeped in Freud, in order to understand the story properly the literary critic may find it useful to think in the categories of the psychologist.

This short story is a narrative of an ether-dream experienced by Mr. Arcularis as he lies on an operating table in a hospital. Under the anesthetic, Mr. Arcularis dreams that the operation, which he is undergoing, is a completed success, that he leaves the hospital and takes

---

3 Conrad Aiken, "A Basis for Criticism," *A Reviewer's ABC* (New York: Meridian Books, 1958), pp. 61–62.
4 Aiken's description of the spiritual history of Emerson. See *A Reviewer's ABC*, p. 88.

passage aboard a ship for a long voyage of convalescence. Aboard the ship he meets Clarice Dean, a younger woman, is mysteriously drawn to her, but suffers a feeling of doom surrounding the voyage. With unaccountable anxiety, Mr. Arcularis discovers that there is a corpse aboard—in a coffin in the hold. On the first and second nights of the voyage, Mr. Arcularis also dreams that he soars up through space, at incredible speed, each time a little farther from the ship, traversing an orbit that circumnavigates the moon, the North Star, Polaris, Betelgeuse—toward Arcturus, the last signpost of finity. When he awakes from these two dreams, he finds himself near the hold of the ship, having walked in his sleep in search of the coffin, which he fears will be empty. On the third night he again has the nightmare, and awakes, presumably to find the coffin empty and ready for his occupancy.

The story has its origin in a generalization of Aiken's personal credo—that we know extraordinarily little about ourselves. In the story Mr. Arcularis's recurrent sleepwalking nightmare leads him to remark "how extraordinarily little we know about the workings of our own minds and souls" and to ask, "After all, what *do* we know?" To this Miss Dean responds: "Nothing—nothing—nothing— nothing." And Mr. Arcularis emphasizes "*Absolutely* nothing."[5]

"Mr. Arcularis" thus takes us inside the mind of a man on the operating table at the point of death, anesthetized by ether, in order to show us the workings of our own minds and souls: to show us how latent thoughts in the subconscious mind, counterpointed by preoperative anxieties of death, are distorted in the manifest dream-content by the activities of the dream work—condensation, displacement, visual representations in plastic images, secondary elaboration, and dream symbolism. To understand the meaning of Mr. Arcularis's subconscious thought, the literary critic must, like the psychoanalyst, demolish the manifest content of the dream and pierce through to what lies beneath. The mode of representing this process is the stream-of-consciousness—a beautiful and rare example of the unity of subject matter (the activity of the subconscious mind) and narrative point of view; only in the final three paragraphs of the story is

---

5 "Mr. Arcularis," in *The Collected Short Stories of Conrad Aiken* (Cleveland and New York: World Publishing Co., 1960), p. 43. This story was first published in *Harper's Magazine* (162 [March 1931], 397–408), not in *The Criterion*, as Frederick J. Hoffman suggests in his *Conrad Aiken* (New York: Twayne, 1962), p. 42. It was later reprinted in *The Criterion* (11 [April 1932], 399–418), as well as in *Among the Lost People* (New York: Scribner's, 1934), *The Short Stories of Conrad Aiken* (New York: Scribner's, 1950), and *The Collected Short Stories of Conrad Aiken*. Quotations from this last-named volume will hereafter be given as *CSS*, in parentheses, in the text.

Aiken obliged to move outside the subconscious mind of Mr. Arcularis to verify our growing awareness that Mr. Arcularis is dying on the operating table. The drama enacted upon that table, in the mind and soul of Mr. Arcularis, is the struggle between life and death, between Eros, the life instincts, and Thanatos, the death instinct.

II

Aiken's deep interest in the distortions in the subconscious mind that may be produced by ether-dreams is recorded in a *New Republic* essay about three of his own dreams while he was under the anesthetic ether on the operating table. His description of the characteristics and content of these ether-dreams, vivid enough in themselves, are worth the closest attention because of the light they shed on the meaning of "Mr. Arcularis."

> It [the ether-dream] is, to the ordinary dream, what the epic is to the short story. It is gigantic; it is grandiose; it transcends the limits of time and space; it is cosmic; and when it is at its best, it gives the dreamer an annihilating sense of understanding, a divine comprehensiveness of foreknowledge and memory. There is always one moment, in the ether-dream, when everything, the whole universe, becomes blindingly clear and simple. The sensation is, perhaps, a sensation of light—which makes one wonder whether the dream occurs usually as one is first returning to consciousness, first relaxing one's eyelids. And there is usually, also, a rather terrifying use of repetition. The pattern of the dream unfolds, and then returns upon itself and unfolds again. The movement, the drama, of the dream is as likely as not cyclic, and one draws from it an appalling sense of the everlasting determinism of things.[6]

In the first of his ether-dreams, which contains an image out of Lewis Carroll's *Alice in Wonderland,* Aiken saw the world as a chessboard in which the moves were "as pre-ordained as the moves of knights and bishops" ("GD," 146). (Thus, aboard ship, the chess game indicates to Mr. Arcularis the rigorous determinism of life.) In the second ether-dream Aiken witnessed himself on an endless voyage with Columbus. In mid-Atlantic he fell overboard, settled in spirals to the bottom, and was transmogrified into an oyster shell. Looking up he saw three keels and said to himself, "'Good Lord, I

---

6 Conrad Aiken, "Gigantic Dreams," *New Republic,* 55 (June 27, 1928), 146. Quotations from this essay will hereafter be given as "GD," in parentheses, in the text.

won't be there when they discover America!' For I knew vaguely," Aiken continued, "that America had been already discovered four hundred years ago; but I also knew that it was not *yet* discovered. I had stepped clear out of time and space; my consciousness was both before and after the event; I had become God. I felt a kind of pity and contempt for poor Columbus, who knew so little; and for myself also I felt pity, because I knew so much" ("GD," 147). Thus the Kantian postulate that time is a necessary mode of thought is short-circuited in the dream. This effect in dreams was brilliantly discussed by Freud in *Beyond the Pleasure Principle,* where he contended that "unconscious mental processes are in themselves 'timeless.' That is to say to begin with: they are not arranged chronologically, time alters nothing in them, nor can the idea of time be applied to them."[7] This work, as we shall later see, has a most significant bearing on the meaning of "Mr. Arcularis."

In the third dream, Aiken saw himself witnessing the creation of the world. At first he dreamed of Chaos. Gradually he perceived the emergence of order, of the evolution of the solar system, and then of life. As he witnessed the evolution of man's consciousness, he was aware that

> Phases of consciousness succeeded each other like so many flashes. I was aware, somehow, that we had reached the fifth or sixth century B.C. And at this point the dream hit upon a device for the demarcation of one phase of sophistication from another, the progress from consciousness to consciousness of consciousness, and then to consciousness of consciousness of consciousness, and so on, which showed an extraordinary ingenuity. To begin with, some perfectly simple remark was made: I forget what it was, but it was something as obvious as "Here we are, then." An age then passing in a flash, and a second stage of sophistication being reached, the remark was repeated, but this time with a double quotation: "'Here we are, then'" ("GD," 147).

This statement, according to Aiken, was made several times, producing a "visual image of quotation marks, quotation marks at either end of a simple statement, building themselves out at either

---

7 Sigmund Freud, *Beyond the Pleasure Principle,* trans. C. J. M. Hubback (London: Hogarth Press, 1922), p. 32. *Beyond the Pleasure Principle* was first published in German under the title *Jenseits des Lustprinzips* (1920); the second and third editions appeared in 1922 and 1923. In 1925 it was included in Freud's *Gesammelte Schriften* (VI). But it is unlikely that Aiken's limited skill in German was of use to him for any of these volumes. Jay Martin suggests (p. 65) that Aiken knew *Beyond the Pleasure Principle* by 1922; if so, he must have used Hubback's translation.

end of the statement into infinity. The simple statement became, with each addition, more appallingly and unfathomably complicated; it had become, in fact, the world itself: it had become *everything that was knowable.*" Then, unaccountably, Aiken continues, the full burden of consciousness narrowed in and focused on Aiken himself as he lay on the operating table—it reached its *reductio ad absurdum* in himself. Then the process began again:

> the dream became cyclic, and I beheld, innumerable times, the evolution of the world to its final flowering—magnificent egotism, profound solipsism!—in my own consciousness. Everything had become intelligible: the world no longer had any secrets from me. I now knew the world for what it was—a mere senseless nightmare of fatalistic and orderly but meaningless change; a mechanical ring from which no one was ever destined to escape ("GD," 147).

The description of what happened in Aiken's three ether-dreams provides an enlightening corollary to the ether-dream of Mr. Arcularis, who transcends both space in a fixed, recurrent, and repetitive cosmic orbit, as well as time, as he regresses, psychotemporally, into his childhood and beyond, as he lies dying upon the operating table. He perceives with clarity life's meaning and is annihilated at last in the full comprehension of the burden of his own consciousness. The principles by which the distortion of the latent dream-thought of Mr. Arcularis's ether-dream may be explained are those discussed by Freud as mechanisms of the dream-work, and they suggest how fully Aiken had immersed himself in psychoanalytic theory. In this tale the dream-censor distorts the latent dream-thoughts by *displacement,* the process by which latent dream-elements are replaced with something remote from them, perhaps something in the nature of an allusion, or by which the psychic accent is transferred from an important element to an unimportant element in the dream; by *condensation,* in which elements in the latent dream-thoughts are omitted from the manifest dream-content, appear in it only in fragments, or are blended in it into a single whole; by the transformation of latent thoughts into *visual images* or *plastic word-representations*; and by *secondary elaboration,* the mechanism by which incoherence and chaos in the latent dream-elements are reduced to a coherent unity. Together with these mechanisms, which disguise and distort the real meaning of the latent dream-thoughts of the subconscious, there must also be added the mechanism of *dream symbolism,* the constant relationship between a dream-element and its translation. How these principles operate in the story deserve close scrutiny.

III

One of the most important dream symbols in the story is the symbolic voyage of Mr. Arcularis. Clearly it is the voyage to death he is making. Freud is quite explicit in stating that "departing on a journey is one of the commonest and best authenticated symbols of death."[8] Long before the final three paragraphs in which we discover that he has died on the operating table, Aiken provides indications that Mr. Arcularis is dying. As Harry drives him past the Harvard Club bar, on their way to the ship, Mr. Arcularis quotes a fragment of "Crossing the Bar"—Tennyson's representation of his own death as a voyage out to sea. When Harry asks where the line comes from, Mr. Arcularis identifies it as from the *Odyssey*—the Homeric epic of the wandering voyage of Ulysses. Harry's comment, "'We're here because we're here because we're here,'" to which Mr. Arcularis responds, "'Because we're here'" (*CSS*, 36), is a hitherto unnoticed allusion to an anonymous World War I song entitled "Here We Are," to be sung, I have been told, to the tune of "Auld Lang Syne":

> We're here because we're here,
> Because we're here, because we're here;
> Oh, here we are, and here we are,
> And here we are again.[9]

This apparently aimless response, however, is in reality an echo of the "simple statement" of Aiken's third ether-dream—"Here we are, then"—a statement which in *that* dream became the world and all knowable reality. In this context the allusion suggests a displacement of the rational and fatalistic determinism from which Mr. Arcularis wishes to but cannot escape—all that can be known about reality.

Moreover, the ship on which he sails out on the voyage to death is a dream symbol of Mr. Arcularis's body. The pulsations of the motors of the ship are geared to the pulsations of his own cardiac rhythm, so that at times Mr. Arcularis cannot tell whether he feels the vibrations of the engines or his own heart. Later, as he approaches death on the operating table, the ship is barely moving, and the rhythm of the engines is "slower, more subdued and remote" (*CSS*,

---

8 *The Complete Psychological Works of Sigmund Freud*, trans. James Strachey (London: Hogarth Press, 1953), V, 385.

9 See Burton Stevenson, ed., *The Home Book of Quotations* (New York: Dodd, Mead, 1952), p. 2295:10. I am indebted to Weldon Thornton of the University of North Carolina for the identification of this song. F. L. Gwynn, in his study of the allusions in this story (see footnote 18), omits both this and the *Macbeth* allusion cited later in the essay.

52). The fog and mist that obscure his sight are suggestive of waves of "nonconsciousness" as, approaching annihilation, his life wavers on the table. Another clear indication that Mr. Arcularis is dying is that he becomes cold—the warmth of vitality is slowly fading from him. This coldness is explained to him, however, as the result of the ship's proximity to icebergs. Mr. Arcularis—his subconscious objectifying his body as the ship—muses upon all the ships that have sunk after collisions with icebergs. He is prepared for an imminent catastrophe, such as his own shipwreck, for the coffin in the hold inauspiciously augurs bad weather on the voyage. The sense of doom surrounding the voyage reflects his preoperative anxiety that he will not survive the operation. He remembers the *Titanic* and the *Empress of Ireland,* shipwrecks that foreshadow his own imminent death. The finale of the *Cavalleria Rusticana,* which he had heard from the street just before leaving the hospital and which the ship's band plays, is displaced in his subconscious by "Nearer My God to Thee," which, ironically, was played by the orchestra of the *Titanic* after it collided with the iceberg.

His dream-censor exploiting the mechanisms of displacement and dream symbolism, Mr. Arcularis moves through four stages of psychotemporal regression (comparable at many points to, and clearly based upon, Aiken's three ether-dreams). These stages of psychotemporal regression mark out the phases of the struggle between Eros, the principle of life, and Thanatos, the principle of death. The first stage of regression takes Mr. Arcularis back to his childhood; the second withdraws him further to the mother's womb; the third takes him further back to a prehistoric stage of phylogenetic evolutionary development; and the fourth takes him back to the genesis of all things, the moment of creation—and beyond it to Chaos, to the swirling bright and white light of nothingness, annihilation. Each of these stages helps us understand how Aiken employed his own experience under ether and his knowledge of Freud's commentary on dreams and the death instinct to enrich and deepen the significance of the voyage to death of Mr. Arcularis and of the workings of the mind and soul.

IV

1. *The Return to Childhood*: The most bewildering problem for Mr. Arcularis is the identity of Miss Clarice Dean, who accompanies him on the mysterious voyage. Throughout the early part of the story he tries vainly to recollect where he has seen her before, who she is. It

grows upon him that she reminds him of the freckle-faced young girl at the hospital, an assistant at the operation who had been especially kind to him. But this association is not totally satisfactory, for the freckle-faced girl reminds him of something else long ago. "The little freckle-faced girl at the hospital was merely, as it were, the stepping-stone, the sign-post, or, as in algebra, the 'equals' sign. But what was it they both 'equalled'?" (*CSS*, 43–44). Mr. Arcularis associates them both with jackstones and his Aunt Julia's rose garden at sunset, yet he feels a ridiculousness in this identification. "It couldn't be simply that they reminded him of his childhood! And yet why not?" (*CSS*, 44). This is the first stage in the psychotemporal regression of Mr. Arcularis: Clarice Dean, the hospital assistant, and his Aunt Julia are blended together, by the mechanism of condensation, into a composite figure suggesting some repressed memory of his early childhood—undoubtedly a memory of his mother.

The imminence of death reveals to Mr. Arcularis the beauty of life as only a child perceives it. He sees with joy the June spring in Boston—the streetcars, the green leaves, the drops of sparkling rainwater. Moreover, his father appears in the condensed figure of the doctor at the hospital, who reappears to him in his ether-dream as the doctor aboard the ship who prescribes a simple bromide as a remedy for the horrible sleepwalking dream. Of the doctor Mr. Arcularis says to himself, "'But why was it that doctors were all alike? and all, for that matter, like his father, or that fellow at the hospital?'" (*CSS*, 46). In such a way do people from his childhood appear in composite forms in the regressive ether-dream.

In his attempt to recollect what these childhood memories "equal," the sense of time becomes distorted in the mind of Mr. Arcularis. Once he thinks that time has ceased. Later his sense of time vanishes completely, and he thinks that he has perhaps been on the ship for aeons. This confusion of the sense of time implies not only the irrelevance of time in dreams but also the timelessness of death, eternity as the timeless absolute. In addition, it also suggests that Mr. Arcularis has nearly completed the great circle of life and, at the point of death, is psychotemporally regressing by degrees to his childhood and birth. His feeling on leaving the hospital is, "'Why should he feel sad about it and want to cry like a baby'" when "'new life would be opening before him?'" (*CSS*, 33–34). He associates his experiences with events of his childhood, but he cannot rationally define the relationship between these associations. The return to his childhood, however, is only one arc in the regressive circular orbit of Mr. Arcularis.

2. *The Return to the Womb*: Gradually it grows upon Mr. Arcularis that his obsession with his childhood has significance. Miss Dean tells him not to worry about the nightmare search for the coffin because, as she says, "'We aren't children any longer!'" and he replies, "'Aren't we? I wonder!'" (*CSS*, 47). When he has the nightmare on the second night, he is horrified to wake up at the bottom of the stairway, as *he* emphasizes it, "'*crawling on my hands and knees*'" (*CSS*, 51). On the third night Miss Dean says, "'Be a good boy and take your bromide,'" and he replies, "'Yes, mother, I'll take my medicine'" (*CSS*, 52). These facts suggest that Mr. Arcularis's voyage to death is, like Aiken's third ether-dream, psychotemporally regressive; it is an example, as Aiken put it in his novel *Great Circle*, of "the end that is still conscious of its beginnings. Birth that remembers death."[10] The great circle, the naked orbit, fixed and determined in its terrifying logical curve, is then a return not only to childhood but also to his genesis, to the mother's womb. In this respect one is reminded of Dylan Thomas's "I dreamed my genesis in a sweat of sleep."

This suggestion of the return to the womb is supported by Mr. Arcularis's conversation with Clarice Dean about the ship stewards who are "dead souls." He asks, "'How could they be stewards otherwise? And they think they've seen and known everything. They suffer terribly from the *déjà vu*'"—that is, the sense of having already been at some strange place, seen or experienced something before in the unremembered past. Mr. Arcularis's certainty about them ("'I'm sure of it. I'm enough of a dead soul myself to know the signs!'" [p. 38]) is not merely a subtle hint that he is dying but also an indication that his voyage is wombward as well. Freud's comment on this psychological phenomenon of the *déjà vu* supports this interpretation. "But '*déjà vu*' has a special significance in dreams. In this case the locality is always the genitals of the mother; of no other place can it be asserted with such certainty that one has been here before."[11] That Mr. Arcularis's dream search for the coffin implies his subconscious search for the mother's womb is also suggested by his free association at the point of death with the word "coffer." The world "coffer" suggests not only coffin but also "box," which in German (*Büchse*) and in English is a slang term for the female genitals. Although this word association may seem arbitrary and therefore suspect, no less an authority than Freud himself may again be cited in its support. His analysis in *The Interpretation of Dreams* of the association of these

---

10 Conrad Aiken, *Great Circle* (New York: Scribner's, 1933), p. 334.

11 *The Interpretation of Dreams*, in *The Basic Writings of Sigmund Freud*, trans. A. A. Brill (New York: Modern Library, 1938), p. 394.

words with the female genitals is carefully explained and expanded there to include even *Schachtel, Loge, and Kasten.*[12] Moreover, other obvious word plays and associations appear in "Mr. Arcularis," for example, the pun on Absolute/Obsolete in Absolete/Obsolute. Both Frederick J. Hoffman and Jay Martin, moreover, have shown that Aiken had read Freud's *The Interpretation of Dreams* in 1915 and was thoroughly familiar with the work of Freud and his colleagues.[13] It is not too much to say, then, that Mr. Arcularis's free association at the point of death is suggestive of his psychotemporal return to the womb.

But the identification of Miss Dean and the freckle-faced girl with Mr. Arcularis's mother and the suggestion, therefore, of a regression to the womb are, as such, too narrow to explain several indications in the story that she is in some sense also a projection of his own alienated psyche. In one passage he wonders: "'I wish I could remember who you are.'" And she replies, "'And you—who are you?'" —to which he answers, "'Myself.'" Thereupon she says, "'Then perhaps *I* am yourself.'" Taken aback, he responds, "'Don't be metaphysical!'" And she concludes, "'But I *am* metaphysical'" (*CSS,* 48). Later this hint is developed further in Mr. Arcularis's meditation about Clarice Dean:

> He broke off his sentence and looked hard at her—how lovely she was, and how desirable! No such woman had ever before come into his life; there had been no one with whom he had at once felt so profound a sympathy and understanding. It was a miracle, simply—a miracle. . . . He had only to look at her, and to feel, gazing into those extraordinary eyes, that she knew him, had always known him. It was as if, indeed, she might be his own soul (*CSS,* 49).

Only with her can he share the horror of his recurrent nightmares; only she communes with him. Only she expresses the wish that she could go with him on his dream orbit around the stars toward infinity. On the last night, just before Mr. Arcularis retires for the night, and for the third and last sleepwalking search which will lead him to the coffin in the hold, and for the third and last dream-within-a-dream which will take him out beyond the stars on the voyage to infinity, Mr. Arcularis and Clarice (whose names rhyme with each other and with "Polaris") embrace. In some sense or other they experience

---

12 Freud, *The Interpretation of Dreams,* p. 231. See also Freud, "Symbolism in Dreams," *A General Introduction to Psychoanalysis,* trans. Joan Riviere (Garden City, N.Y.: Garden City Books, 1953), p. 163.
13 See Hoffman, p. 26, and Martin, pp. 25–27.

an infinite union, are in fact each other.

> It was then that they first embraced—then, at the edge of the infinite, at the last signpost of the finite. They clung together desperately, forlornly, weeping as they kissed each other, staring hard one moment and closing their eyes the next. Passionately, passionately, she kissed him, as if she were indeed trying to give him her warmth, her life (*CSS*, 51).

The absolution expressed in this passage, the healing of what Aiken has called "the deep psychic wound," can be explained, I believe, by examination of a literary allusion to Plato dropped earlier in the story. It clarifies Clarice Dean's role in the tale and perhaps something about the nature of Mr. Arcularis's wound which would be made whole.

As he passed the Harvard Club on his ride to the ship, Mr. Arcularis thought, "'There it was, with the great flag blowing in the wind, the Harvard seal now concealed by the swift folds and now revealed, and there were the windows in the library, where he had spent so many delightful hours reading—Plato, and Kipling, and the Lord knows what . . .'" (*CSS*, 36). F. L. Gwynn[14] is right, I believe, in citing Kipling's interest in dreams and in the transmigration of souls in "The Bridge-Builders," "The Brushtown Boy," "Wireless," and "The Finest Story in the World." But his explanation of why Mr. Arcularis thinks of Plato (that Plato is distant in time and substance from Kipling, is concerned with the soul in *Phaedo* and the *Republic*, and is the originator of the motif of the Absolute and the Infinite) is not altogether satisfactory. One possible suggestion may come from a dialogue Gwynn overlooks—Plato's *Symposium*. The dialogue deals principally with the praise of love. Yet it is Plato's analysis of the origins of the sexes, put into the mouth of Aristophanes, that accounts for Mr. Arcularis's memory of Plato and for Clarice Dean's multiple role in the story.

As Aristophanes presents it, the sexes were originally three in number: man, woman, and the union of the two—called "androgynes." Because the powerful androgynes assaulted the gods, Zeus humbled them by dividing them in two. As a result, each one, separated, spent his lifetime searching for his "other half," possessed by the ancient implanted desire to reunite "our original nature, making one of two, and healing the state of man. Each of us when

---

14 F. L. Gwynn, "The Functional Allusions in Conrad Aiken's 'Mr. Arcularis,'" *Twentieth-Century Literature*, 2 (April 1956), 22.

separated, having one side only, like a flat fish, is but the indenture of a man, and he is always looking for his other half." When one meets his other half, "the actual half of himself," Plato remarks, "the pair are lost in amazement of love and friendship and intimacy,"—their desire not "the desire of lovers' intercourse, but of something else which the soul of either evidently desires and cannot tell, and of which she has only a dark and doubtful presentiment."[15]

The union with Clarice Dean, it seems to me, symbolizes not only a return to childhood and beyond to his mother's womb but also a reunification with a part of himself. Their ecstatic union, or reunion, in the final passages of the story indicates that at long last Mr. Arcularis is coming to perfect union with himself, in other words, that he has, for the first time, possessed his own soul ("It was as if, indeed, she might be his own soul"). The temporal moment of this regression is thus the point at which his soul had entered into his body. But unconscious repressions displace the recollection of his own birth and interfere with his instinctive yearning for fulfillment and completeness, of which he has only "a dark and doubtful presentiment." This interpretation of the story is thus consistent with Freud's contention that the dream is on the whole "an act of regression to the earliest relationships of the dreamer, a resuscitation of his childhood, of the impulses which were then dominant and the modes of expression which were then available."[16]

This repression of the trauma of birth is illuminated in a second allusion, from *Macbeth,* which deepens and intensifies the significance of an unaccountable feeling of guilt which seems to oppress Mr. Arcularis. As Mr. Arcularis stands with Clarice, "They leaned, shoulders touching, on the deck-rail, and looked at the sea, which was multitudinously incarnadined" (*CSS,* 47). This line seems clearly to me an allusion to *Macbeth* (II, ii, 60–63), where Macbeth agonizes because he cannot wash away the blood of murdered Duncan:

"Will all great Neptune's ocean wash the blood
Clean from my hand? No, this my hand will rather
The multitudinous seas incarnadine,
Making the green one red."

If the allusion suggests that Mr. Arcularis is torn by guilt, the origin of his guilt is obscure unless we assume a general oedipal connection. Clearly enough, the inability of Mr. Arcularis to identify Miss Dean

---

15 *The Works of Plato,* ed. Irwin Edman (New York: Modern Library, 1930), pp. 355–356.
16 *The Basic Writings of Sigmund Freud* (New York: Modern Library, 1938), p. 497.

until the point of death is the effect of the repression of an infantile psychological trauma. The parson aboard ship senses that Mr. Arcularis's sleepwalking nightmare arises from a sense of guilt: "'You feel guilty about something. I won't be so rude as to inquire what it is. But if you could rid yourself of the sense of guilt—'" (*CSS,* 47).

The nature of Mr. Arcularis's guilt, never specified in the story, deserves some elaboration. Aiken's *play version* of the story, published in 1957 (twenty-six years later than the publication of the story), explicitly defines the origin of Mr. Arcularis's guilt: as a child he had witnessed his mother's illicit love affair with her husband's brother. But the source of guilt explicit in the play cannot help us to interpret the story. In the first place, there is no direct evidence in the story that Mr. Arcularis witnessed the infidelity of his mother. Aiken, in fact, invented the play's mother-uncle motif to repair the damage done to the story by Diana Hamilton, whose previous play version included an invented wife for Mr. Arcularis. This interpolation was so obviously unsatisfactory to the psychology of his character that Aiken repaired it by borrowing a mother-uncle-affair motif from the middle section of his novel *Great Circle.* Thus the play version is so different from the story and so late an invention that only a rash critic would attempt to gloss the tale from the play. The conclusions of the two versions, story and play, are, as Rufus Blanshard suggests, "*separately* right as resolutions," but they are not, as he claims, "so akin as to gloss one another."[17] Perhaps an interpretation more consistent with the psychological context out of which this story issues is that Mr. Arcularis is repressing the trauma of birth; the red ocean might therefore suggest not guilt but the breaking of waters, or the escape of the amniotic fluid and blood at birth. Birth and the sea are identified so commonly in the literature of psychology that perhaps we need not press the issue further. Mr. Arcularis's psychotemporal return to the womb, the second stage of his regression toward death, is in itself merely an attempt to return to a condition of security prior to the birth trauma, a motive determined by the pleasure principle. But this regressive voyage reaches back beyond the memory of ejection from his prenatal home.

3. *The Return Through the Phylogenetic Development*: In his discussion of regression in dreams to the state of childhood, Freud remarks: "Behind this childhood of the individual we are then promised an insight into the phylogenetic childhood, into the evolution of the human race, of which the development of the individual is

---

17 Blanshard, "Metamorphosis of a Dream," p. 699.

only an abridged repetition influenced by the fortuitous circumstances of life."[18] Aiken has shown us this phylogenetic development
in the rehearsal of his own ether-dream; it is also present in "Mr. Arcularis." This *devolutionary* return to the past—what Frost called our
"backward motion toward the source" ("West-Running Brook")—is
indicated in Mr. Arcularis's reference to the prehistoric time when his
operation might have been performed: "'Centuries ago. When I was
a tadpole and you were a fish'" (*CSS,* 49). This line alludes to a poem
by Langdon Smith called "Evolution" (1895). It seems pertinent to
the relationship Aiken wishes to define between Mr. Arcularis and
Clarice, who is projected as a manifestation of his soul.

> When you were a tadpole and I was a fish,
> In the Paleozoic time,
> And side by side on the ebbing tide,
> We sprawled through the ooze and slime, . . .
> My heart was rife with the joy of life,
> For I loved you even then.

This evolutionary period before human life is the third stage in Mr.
Arcularis's psychotemporal regression. That the history of the human
race is contained in the development of the embryo ("ontogeny
recapitulates phylogeny") is a theory perhaps no longer seriously
believed by biologists. Nevertheless, the process of Mr. Arcularis's
regression toward annihilation is based upon this concept and, I
believe, upon Freud's discussion of it.

    4. *The Return to the Creation of the Universe*: The fourth stage in
Mr. Arcularis's voyage to infinity takes him beyond childhood, beyond the womb, even back beyond the prehistoric evolutionary
development of the race. It takes him backward to the moment of the
creation of the universe, to the frontier of Time and Eternity, Creation and Chaos, Being and Nothingness or Annihilation. Just as
Aiken witnessed in his third ether-dream the creation of the universe,
order evolving from chaos, so Mr. Arcularis's subconscious mind
regresses psychotemporally toward the moment of creation and,
when he arrives at it, he is annihilated. The coincidence of Mr. Arcularis's death at the moment when he had crossed beyond finity into
infinity is not accidental; figured lineally it is the "great circle," "the
end that is still conscious of its beginnings," "birth that remembers
death."

---

18 *The Basic Writings of Sigmund Freud,* p. 497.

V

Why, after all, it may be asked, should Aiken have dramatized these four stages in Mr. Arcularis's passage to death, his annihilation? The question itself, or one similar to it, was also asked by Aiken in his interesting little piece "State of Mind." There a man who wished to annihilate himself asked: "How could one project, in satisfactory form, this desire for annihilation? Not in suicide, but in imagination?" [19] "Mr. Arcularis" is, in fact, this imaginative projection of the desire of a man for annihilation. The desire, however, is not a simple longing. It is an *instinct* for annihilation. In *Beyond the Pleasure Principle*, Freud proposed a theory of instinct beyond the pleasure principle which would account for the regressive phenomenon of death. He argued that "in the traumatic neuroses the dream life has this peculiarity: it continually takes the patient back to the situation of his disaster, from which he awakens in renewed terror." [20] Mr. Arcularis's search for the coffin is a search for the scene of his disaster—ejection from the prenatal security of the womb. It is thus an expression of what Freud called the compulsion "to *repeat* as a current experience what is repressed, instead of, as the physician would prefer to see him do, *recollecting* it as a fragment of the past." It is this "repetition-compulsion" which defines the "regressive character of instinct." Beyond the pleasure principle is "*a tendency innate in living organic matter impelling it toward the reinstatement of an earlier condition. . . .*" Mr. Arcularis's attempt to return to the prenatal unity and security of the womb is thus a manifestation of the pleasure principle. Beyond it is the inward struggle of Eros and Thanatos, the sexual instincts of life combating the death instinct. The identity of Clarice Dean thus becomes clearer: symbolically a part of himself, she also personifies Eros (the life or sexual instincts which minister to and preserve the existence of the organism). She yearns to stay with him, to give him her warmth and vitality. But beyond Eros, beyond the sexual instincts, is Thanatos, an instinct more primitive and powerful, which inevitably leads to death. Freud's proposition was that "'*The goal of all life is death*,' and casting back, '*The inanimate was there before the animate*.'" It is worth pointing out that Aristophanes' speech in the *Symposium* about the quest of the androgynes for reunion, exactly fulfills one condition of Freud's theory of the death instinct: he derives the instinct "from the *necessity for the reinstatement of an earlier situation*." Though admittedly Plato's account is a myth, Freud him-

19 Conrad Aiken, "State of Mind," *New Republic*, 51 (July 6, 1927), 175.
20 Freud, *Beyond the Pleasure Principle*, p. 9.

self argued that "Plato would not have adopted any such story . . . had he not himself felt the truth contained in it to be illuminating."[21]

Mr. Arcularis's search for the coffin reflects the organism's compulsion to return to an earlier inanimate state—"a state never hitherto reached," yet the "final goal of all organic striving," the "ancient starting point, which the living being left long ago, and to which it harks back again by all the circuitous paths of development."[22] Mr. Arcularis reaches that goal at precisely the moment when he finds the coffin, when he passes the frontier of Time and enters Eternity, when he passes the last signpost heading toward Infinity. At that point he is immersed in the bright white swirling light of annihilation.

---

21 Freud, *Beyond the Pleasure Principle*, pp. 18, 44, 76, 47, 74–75. Freud's hypothesis of a death instinct (Thanatos) compelling the return of the organism to a prior condition of inanimation was complemented some years ago by Koshland's biochemical theory of a "death hormone," which brings about the "aging process" and death. The theory of the death hormone was based on the concept of natural selection: that the organism may synthesize a hormone deleterious to its own health in order to cooperate with and effect the larger aims of natural selection. Koshland's theory was that the organism synthesizes a hormone to inhibit the general function of enzymes, which operate on a time-controlled basis. Thus the "death hormone" explains why, at certain stages in the development of the organism, all enzymic functions are inhibited—causing symptoms of age such as dessication and decreasing metabolic rates. On the surface Koshland's theory appears compatible with Freud's speculative thesis about the death instinct, which proposed an extension of the concept of the libido into the individual cells. See D. E. Koshland, Jr., "The Research Frontier," *Saturday Review*, 46 (June 1, 1963), 46, and *Horizons in Biochemistry*, eds. Michael Kasha and B. Pullman (New York: Academic Press, 1962) for descriptions of how the theoretical "death hormone" is said to operate.

22 Freud, *Beyond the Pleasure Principle*, p. 47.

"Combat in the Erogenous Zone": Women in the American Novel Between the Two World Wars

The major claim made on behalf of American women between the two world wars was, not surprisingly, that of freedom. In fiction this claim took the form of an assertion of woman's need for liberation from domestic and sexual bondage in order to achieve full emotional and intellectual development. During the period the critics of our culture debated whether woman's place was in the home as wife and mother, whether she should move out into the "man's" business world, or whether a combination of homemaking and career was possible or desirable. The issue had been given more or less continuous public attention since Margaret Fuller's *Woman in the Nineteenth Century* (1845) and the feminist convention at Seneca Falls in 1848. Though the bloomer-clad suffragists were scorned and ridiculed throughout the nineteenth century (the neurotic fringes notably satirized in Henry James's *The Bostonians* [1886]), the problems of American women came to be increasingly and sympathetically explored in our public discourse, and in 1920 the Nineteenth Amendment, giving women the right to vote, was finally passed. Elizabeth Cady Stanton, the staunch Genteel Era feminist, had cautioned in *Revolution* that suffrage was a "superficial and fragmentary" aspect of the total woman question and that "the ballot touches only those interests either of men or women, which take their roots in political questions." And she warned that "woman's chief discontent is not with her political, but with her social, and particularly her marital, bondage."[1] Despite her warning, the finally achieved right of suffrage seemed to liberate women from the legal suppression they had hitherto suffered, and a new optimism attended the woman question at the outset of the Jazz Age.

Even before World War I, as William H. Chafe has shown in *The American Woman: Her Changing Social, Economic, and Political Role, 1920–1970,*[2] many women had entered the permanent labor force, and the availability of new job opportunities and a more tolerant attitude toward working careers made women in the twenties somewhat more economically independent than they had ever been. Increasing social approval of college education for women, moreover, offered to liberate them intellectually from a conception of themselves as fitted only to be wives and mothers. Though the forces of Victorian conservatism were still strong—Mother's Day was first celebrated in 1907 —the tide of Progressive politics, symbolized by the passage of the Nineteenth Amendment, promised to sweep aside all obstacles to woman's fulfillment.

Sinclair Lewis's *The Job* (1917) was one of the more interesting early treatments of a liberated woman's struggle to fulfill herself through a career. After much personal unhappiness, Lewis's Una Golden fights her way to the top of the business world, her achievement illustrating the claim—most vigorously argued in Charlotte Perkins Gilman's *Women and Economics* (1898)—that women could find emotional fulfillment and liberation from economic dependency in the labor force. "Even the girls who knew that they were going to be married pretended to be considering important business positions," Lewis observed in *Main Street* (1920). But his heroine Carol Kennicott "was a woman with a working brain and no work." When Carol expresses the wish to do something with her life, her boyfriend gives "the immemorial male reply to the restless woman": "What's better than making a comfy home and bringing up some cute kids and knowing nice homey people?" For Lewis the woman's plight was only part of his general complaint against capitalist society, and he affirmed the cooptation of the suffragist/feminist cause into a vaguely revolutionary socialism. Thus Carol argues:

1 "The Ballot—Bread, Virtue, Power," *Revolution,* January 8, 1868, quoted in William L. O'Neill's *Everyone Was Brave* (Chicago: Quadrangle Books, 1969), p. 19.

2 New York: Oxford University Press, 1972, pp. 48–65.

"We're all in it, ten million women. . . . What is it we want—and need? . . . I believe all of us want the same things—we're all together, the industrial workers and the women and the farmers and the Negro race and the Asiatic colonies, and even a few of the Respectables. It's all the same revolt, in all the classes that have waited and taken advice. I think perhaps we want a more conscious life. We're tired of drudging and sleeping and dying. We're tired of seeing just a few people able to be individualists. We're tired of always deferring hope till the next generation. We're tired of hearing the politicians and priests and cautious reformers (and husbands!) coax us, 'Be calm! Be patient! Wait! We have the plans for a Utopia already made; just give us a bit more time and we'll produce it; trust us; we're wiser than you.' For ten thousand years they've said that. We want our Utopia now. . . ."

But social change came slowly in small-town America (as elsewhere); and at the end of the novel Carol has deferred her hope to her daughter's generation. She does not change the institutions of a conservative capitalistic society, but she does apparently save her soul by refusing to concede that "dish-washing is enough to satisfy all women!"[3]

That the wife and mother's role *could* be a sufficient source of fulfillment was argued by Elizabeth Cook in "The Kitchen Sink Complex"[4] and by Rose Wilder Lane in "Woman's Place Is in the Home."[5] Both of these essays, published in the thirties in the *Ladies' Home Journal,* are representative of the continuing defense in women's magazines of the view that women would find greater happiness in the home than at the office. Much of the popular fiction of the time sustained this view by implying that the career girl betrayed the charm of her sex and her true purpose in life. For "the peace of the home," as S. M. Hutchinson's novel *This Freedom* (1922) put it, "rests ultimately on the kitchen."[6] In "Sex and Achievement," Margaret Mead defined the poignancy of the choice confronting women by observing that a woman could either acknowledge herself "as a woman and therefore less of an achieving individual, or an achieving individual and therefore less of a woman." If she chose to be a womanly woman, she had a greater chance to be a "loved object, the

---

3 Sinclair Lewis, *Main Street* (New York: Harcourt Brace, 1920), pp. 201–202.

4 Elizabeth Cook, "The Kitchen Sink Complex," *Ladies' Home Journal,* 48 (September 1931), 12.

5 See Rose Wilder Lane, "Woman's Place Is in the Home," *Ladies' Home Journal,* 53 (October 1936), 18.

6 Quoted in Chafe, *The American Woman,* p. 99.

kind of girl whom men will woo and boast of, toast and marry." But if she chose the life of self-assertion and achievement, she stood to forfeit, "as a woman, her chance for the kind of love she wants."[7] In Booth Tarkington's *Alice Adams* (1921), the heroine's enrollment in a business college, at the end of the novel, is the seal of her failure as a womanly woman. (Very few of the novelists of the twenties who pointed to careers as a way out of the domestic trap were prepared to see what became increasingly evident, especially during the depression—namely, that the work of a stenographer, salesgirl, or even business executive could be as alienating, in the Marxist sense, as domesticity. Lewis eventually conceded the possibility in *Ann Vickers* [1933].)[8]

Looking back, one must concur with Chafe's view, in *The American Woman,* that few of the political and social reforms in behalf of women in the twenties and thirties had much real effect on their situation. The availability of the vote took the steam out of feminism, and when male politicians recognized that women as a sex constituted no real political constituency (and thus no real threat), legislation in their behalf quickly declined. (The Equal Rights Amendment, first proposed in 1923, was quietly entombed in committee, where it languished for more than forty years, and at this writing it still has not been ratified by a sufficient number of state legislatures.) At work women found themselves ill paid, relegated to jobs deemed inferior to those of men, and underpaid even when doing identical work. But toward the end of the twenties, "feminism," as Dorothy Dunbar Bromley noted, had become "a term of opprobrium" for young women that signified "either the old school . . . who wore flat heels and had very little feminine charm, or the current species who antagonize men with their constant clamor about maiden names."[9]

Nevertheless, feminism was one of the forces that served to create a great deal of *felt* freedom among women in the twenties. And that felt freedom manifested itself most clearly in the relationship of the sexes. Edith Wharton's *The Age of Innocence* (1920) is a convenient point of departure in discussing "the sexual revolution" of the postwar period because this novel dramatized, among other things, the infantilization of the American girl of the earlier Genteel Era in order to put into historical perspective the failure of the emotional

---

7 Margaret Mead, "Sex and Achievement," *Forum,* 94 (November 1935), 301–303.
8 Nan Bauer Maglin, "Women in Three Sinclair Lewis Novels," *Massachusetts Review,* 14 (1973), 783–801.
9 See Dorothy Dunbar Bromley, "Feminist—New Style," *Harper's,* 155 (October 1927), 152–160.

development of the American woman. May Welland, the heroine, is victimized by a conception of female education, of the female role, so narrow that she has little room for action beyond that of domestic manager. With little or no education in books, ideas, art, politics, business, sex, or society (except as circumscribed and constituted by her family's small circle), May has few attractive graces capable of sustaining the attention of her husband.

The "innocence" of that era, according to Mrs. Wharton, was the innocence of men and women ignorant of the nature of passion and human sexuality. Her Old New York is intended to be representative of genteel urban middle-class American society, insofar as May, a typical girl, is expected to know nothing about sex before marriage, her husband Newland (theoretically) everything. "What could he and she really know of each other, since it was his duty, as a 'decent' fellow, to conceal his past from her, and hers, as a marriageable girl, to have no past to conceal." And yet overnight, on her honeymoon, May Welland, "the center of this elaborate system of mystifications," would be plunged "into what people evasively called 'the facts of life.'" Mrs. Wharton calls May's innocence "an artificial product," a "factitious purity," which had been "cunningly manufactured by a conspiracy of mothers and aunts and grandmothers and long-dead ancestresses, because it was supposed to be what [Newland] wanted, what he had a right to, in order that he might exercise his lordly pleasure in smashing it like an image made of snow." An American girl who suffers the "innocence that seals the mind against imagination and the heart against experience"[10] can hardly sustain a marriage, and May's husband inevitably drifts toward an extramarital grand passion, requiring her to use all of her sweet guile and cunning to keep the marriage intact. Both she and her husband, according to Mrs. Wharton, were victims of the double standard and of sexual inhibitions that crippled the emotional well-being of the whole Genteel Era.

Though the conclusion of Mrs. Wharton's novel forecasts the sexual liberation of both men and women in the twentieth century, Grundyism, the conspiracy of silence against sexual candor, and "the domestic enslavement of the American woman" continued to vex the imagination of our major writers throughout the twenties. And in varying degrees all of them denounced the crippling effects of the double standard and "respectability." In Dreiser's *Jennie Gerhardt*

---

10 Edith Wharton, *The Age of Innocence* (New York: D. Appleton, 1920), pp. 41–43, 145. For an exaggerated case for Mrs. Wharton's "feminism," see Josephine Jessup, *The Faith of Our Feminists* (New York: Richard R. Smith, 1950).

(1911), Wharton's *Summer* (1917), and Sherwood Anderson's *Winesburg, Ohio* (1919) and *Many Marriages* (1923), the psychosexual pressures of respectability, especially in the small town, victimize and warp men and women into grotesques. In *Winesburg, Ohio*, Kate Swift, Elizabeth Willard, and Alice Hindman, who craves love so desperately that she runs naked through the midnight streets, are all poignant victims of a sexually repressive society that thwarts the emotional development of women. Zona Gale's *Miss Lulu Bett* (1920) explores the pathos of a woman—not really the spinster she is thought to be—who can find no place for herself in a family and society that view female singleness as in itself an anomaly. Willa Cather's heroine in *My Ántonia* (1918) suffers social ostracism over her premarital adventures, and in *A Lost Lady* (1923) the plight of Cather's heroine, dislocated from the center of her existence after a sexual scandal, is also poignantly explored. If Cather's tough, practical heroines survive, they do so by linking themselves to some large guiding suprapersonal, suprasocial conception—to nature, particularly to the grandeur of the prairies.

Something of this same kind of salvation is also achieved by the protagonist of Elizabeth Madox Roberts's *The Time of Man* (1926). Ellen Chesser's happiness is achieved and her identity is finally shaped by her development of a metaphysic of time and place, particularly by her recognition of the place she occupies in the temporal cosmic drama, in the generations of humanity successively unfolding in and through the time of man. Ellen Glasgow's heroines are strengthened by their deep attachment to the soil of Virginia, which gives them a durable vein of iron. In these novels by women, men and marriage are not the solution but are part of the anguish of living. As Dorinda Oakley says at the end of Ellen Glasgow's *Barren Ground* (1925), at the suggestion that she might remarry, "Oh, I've finished with all that. . . . I am thankful to have finished with all that."[11] How time and particularized space temper these women to the hardness of their lot on remote farms or prairies indicates that theirs is as much the ordeal of life itself as the ordeal of being female. As embodiments of the pioneer spirit, they reflect an earlier time rather than the turbulent postwar period. In the period with which we are concerned, a new type of woman was emerging of much more moment to the male novelists.

This new social type, the flapper, was something of a scandal to the respectables. Bruce Bliven's "Flapper Jane," in a 1925 issue of *The*

---

11 Ellen Glasgow, *Barren Ground* (Garden City, N.Y.: Doubleday Doran, 1933), p. 526.

New Republic, expressed shock at her dress, her cosmetics, and her devil-may-care attitude toward life. Clad in short skirts, rolled hose, and bust-confiner; bedecked with rouge, lipstick, and with bobbed hair; with a cigarette in one hand and a cocktail in the other (despite the Volstead Act); freed by Freud, the Hollywood talkies, and the sex and confession magazines newly popular—the modern woman, the "whoopee mama," danced into the limelight. [12] Proclaiming the liberation of the new generation of flappers and sheiks, she announced: "We are at war and we may as well acknowledge it. We are just as different in language and customs as if we belonged to different nations instead of different ages. We are foreordained enemies, and we youngsters are not ready to appeal to a court of arbitration, even when justice is administered by so neutral a judge as you [oldsters] try to be." [13]

Conservatives were aghast at the New Woman's radical attitudes toward courtship and marriage, the education of children, beauty contests, and companionate marriages. As George E. Mowry has shown, she signaled for them "the downfall of society." [14] The New Woman's declaration of war against traditional values had a profound effect on the writers of the period between the wars. In the following pages I propose to look at the response to her (and to other kinds of women) by three of our major writers—Fitzgerald, Hemingway, and Faulkner. Their treatment of women in fiction is part of the social history of the era. But I should be remiss in my duty if I did not say that, although they admired certain aspects of her bid for freedom, they were fundamentally ambivalent about her. And at times they were even hostile to what they felt as the threat she posed to an older ideal of women to which they more and more desperately clung. Their response to the New Woman is highly personal, sometimes indirect, and ultimately limited in the sense that their fiction does not tell the full story of women between the wars. But even though imaginative literature is not an adequate mirror of social actuality, by examining what is deeply felt by great writers of imaginative power we may be able to perceive how the sexual tensions in our culture then—created by what the feminist Carrie Chapman Catt called "the world-wide revolt against all artificial barriers which laws and cus-

---

12 Bruce Bliven, "Flapper Jane," *The New Republic,* September 9, 1925, pp. 65–67. One of them, calling herself "Last Year's Débutante," wrote a farewell, "Good-Bye, Dear Mr. Grundy," in the *Atlantic Monthly* in 1920.
13 "Good-Bye, Dear Mr. Grundy," *Atlantic Monthly,* 126 (November 1920), 642–646.
14 George E. Mowry, ed., *The Twenties: Fords, Flappers & Fanatics* (Englewood Cliffs, N.J.: Prentice-Hall, 1963), p. 173.

toms interpose between women and human freedom"—came to be used for the purposes of art.[15]

II

Fitzgerald's *This Side of Paradise* (1920) described the rebellion of Flaming Youth against orthodox religion, capitalist politics, and the social organization of the classes. But these issues pale before the real revolution, which for Fitzgerald was a revolution against the sexual restraints enjoined on the middle-class American girl. Fitzgerald understood the rebellious young woman intuitively, described her, and popularized her—with the result that he was charged, wrongly, with engineering the rebellion almost single-handedly. The "terrible speed" who told Amory Blaine that she had kissed dozens of men and supposed she would kiss dozens more was no different from thousands of her contemporaries who engaged in what Fitzgerald called "that great current American phenomenon, the 'petting party.'" Among other things, the novel dramatized how *class* attitudes toward sexual freedom had given way to *generational* attitudes toward it. "None of the Victorian mothers—and most of the mothers were Victorian—had any idea how casually their daughters were accustomed to be kissed." For Victorian mothers, promiscuity was the mark of the lower class. "*Servant*-girls are that way," observes one mother: "They are kissed first and proposed to afterward." But as the novel makes clear, American sexual mores were undergoing a change marked by the steady decline of the Popular Daughter from the role of "belle" to "flirt" to "flapper" and "baby vamp." Fitzgerald's protagonist Amory Blaine "saw girls doing things that even in his memory would have been impossible: eating three-o'clock, after-dance suppers in impossible cafes, talking of every side of life with an air half of earnestness, half of mockery, yet with a furtive excitement that Amory considered stood for a real moral let-down. But he never realized how widespread it was until he saw the cities between New York and Chicago as one vast juvenile intrigue."[16]

Fitzgerald's revelation of the "desperate adventure" of petting in "the mobile privacy of the automobile," where "confidences were exchanged and the old commandment broke down," created a sensation among mothers, ministers, editors, and other defenders of public morality. Lionel Trilling has remarked "how innocent of mere

---

15 Quoted in Chafe, *The American Woman,* p. 20.
16 F. Scott Fitzgerald, *This Side of Paradise* (New York: Scribner's, 1920), pp. 64–65.

'sex,' how charged with sentiment is Fitzgerald's description of love in the Jazz Age," and J. W. Aldridge has observed that "It was an intrigue of manners, merely, conducted by glittering children who could hardly bear to be touched. . . ." But although, as Leslie Fiedler observes, there is "little consummated genital love in his novels," Fitzgerald's treatment of sexuality still had the effect of introducing to many young readers a liberated heroine, a girl emancipated from the sexual Grundyism to which she was still expected to conform.[17] In *F. Scott Fitzgerald: A Critical Portrait*, Henry Dan Piper has noted that "unlike her Western counterpart, who was a product of the more free-and-easy frontier, the Eastern girl was still subject to such old-fashioned European customs as the chaperon, an elaborately formal system of etiquette, and an educational philosophy which advocated the separation of the sexes and the incarceration of girls into prison-like boarding schools." Fitzgerald's Midwestern heroines, modeled on the girls he had known in St. Paul, were egotistical, spontaneous, flip, sensual, calculating, and candid—apparently attractive models of freedom to young Eastern girls chafing under conventional restraints. It is no wonder that Fitzgerald was "so puzzled by the Boston and Philadelphia ministers and editors who accused him of trying to corrupt their daughters," as Piper has observed, or that he was "puzzled by the daughters themselves who saw his novel as a clarion call to revolt."[18]

Although Fitzgerald's heroines reflect this liberated Midwestern social type, they also express a deep fantasy about beautiful, emotionally inaccessible, wealthy, and socially desirable women. His view of women is finally inseparable from his view of wealth. *This Side of Paradise, The Great Gatsby* (1925), and *Tender Is the Night* (1934) all reflect his disastrous loss of Ginevra King to Billy Mitchell and the near loss of Zelda Sayre because, as he put it in his notebook, "a poor boy shouldn't think of marrying a rich man's daughter."[19] Nevertheless, even though he was strongly attracted to her, Fitzgerald suffered deep anxiety over the rich girl who did not promise to fulfill the con-

17 F. Scott Fitzgerald, *The Crack-Up*, ed. Edmund Wilson (New York: New Directions, 1945), pp. 14–15; Lionel Trilling, "F. Scott Fitzgerald," in *F. Scott Fitzgerald: The Man and His Work*, ed. Alfred Kazin (New York: Collier Books, 1962), p. 198; J. W. Aldridge, "Fitzgerald: The Horror and the Vision of Paradise," in *F. Scott Fitzgerald: A Collection of Critical Essays*, ed. Arthur Mizener (Englewood Cliffs, N.J.: Prentice-Hall, 1963), p. 32; Leslie Fiedler, *Love and Death in the American Novel* (New York: Criterion Books, 1960), p. 304.

18 Henry Dan Piper, *F. Scott Fitzgerald: A Critical Portrait* (New York: Holt, Rinehart, and Winston, 1965), pp. 60–61.

19 Andrew Turnbull, *Scott Fitzgerald* (New York: Scribner's, 1962), p. 72; Arthur Mizener, "Scott Fitzgerald and the Top Girl," *Atlantic Monthly*, 207 (March 1961), 55–60.

ventional role of middle-class wife and mother. If writers of the Genteel Era tended to romanticize the American girl (Howells's Kitty and Lydia, James's Milly Theale, for example), Fitzgerald and other young postwar writers began to create versions of what might be called "the young American bitch" and to explore a new intense hostility between men and women never before seen in the American novel. Gloria Gilbert in *The Beautiful and Damned* (1922) rejects domesticity not out of any libertarian principle or career aspiration but out of sheer theatrical hedonism. "What grubworms women are to crawl on their bellies through colorless marriages!" Gloria records in her diary. "Marriage was created not to be a background but to need one. Mine is going to be outstanding. It can't shan't, be the setting—it's going to be the performance, the live, lovely, glamorous performance, and the world shall be the scenery. I refuse to dedicate my life to posterity. Surely one owes as much to the current generation as to one's unwanted children. What a fate—to grow rotund and unseemly, to lose my self-love, to think in terms of milk, oatmeal, nurse, diapers."[20] There is no question that Fitzgerald's inspiration, his muse, was an ideal of feminine beauty. But Ideal Beauty incarnated itself in the style of his time, as *The Beautiful and Damned* makes clear—as "a ragtime kid, a flapper, a jazz-baby, and a baby vamp" (*B&D*, 29). Small wonder the attraction-repulsion in his portraits of Rosalind, Isabelle, Gloria, Daisy Buchanan, and Nicole Diver. Attractive as she was, the New Woman could hardly fulfill Fitzgerald's high expectations or realize his dream. In the perception of this fact he found his theme, for he could not help recognizing in the New Woman what she so often recognized in herself—boredom, insincerity, triviality, and hedonistic irresponsibility. "I've got a streak of what you'd call cheapness" (*B&D*, 73), Gloria concedes; and this cheapness, desecrating Fitzgerald's ideal of love and beauty, manifests itself in the flapper's addiction to the speakeasy, the squiggling saxophone, and the seductive foxtrot. "I can't make my feet behave when I hear that tune. Oh, baby!" cries one of Fitzgerald's flappers. "God, I'm sophisticated," sighs another.

No wonder that for Fitzgerald, as for Amory Blaine in *This Side of Paradise,* "the problem of evil" solidified into "the problem of sex," and that beauty came to be "inseparably linked with evil"—touch "most of all with the beauty of women"—because, "after all, it had too many associations with license and indulgence."[21] This remarkable

20 F. Scott Fitzgerald, *The Beautiful and Damned* (New York: Scribner's, 1922), p. 147. Citations from this work will hereafter by given as *B&D*, in parentheses, in the text.
21 Fitzgerald, *This Side of Paradise,* p. 302.

association of womanly beauty with license and indulgence is most vividly presented in *The Great Gatsby*. Daisy Fay Buchanan symbolizes for the parvenu hero all the glamour of beauty and wealth in a desirable woman. She, like his own identity, is a creation of his imagination, with little relation to actuality. She is the fairy-tale princess in the king's tower whose voice is full of money—the epitome, in short, of the "golden girl" he has always desired. He cannot perceive "the basic insincerity," the "incurable dishonesty" of her character. And in the end, of course, he is murdered for the crime she commits. Fitzgerald's memorable heroes all suffer at the hands of rich, bored, sophisticated, insincere women who "smashed up things and creatures and then retreated back into their money or their vast carelessness, or whatever it was that kept them together, and let other people clean up the mess they had made." [22] (Though Fitzgerald's criticism here is principally directed at both Buchanans as representatives of an affluent economic class without ethical values, the moral character of the women of this class, especially Daisy, is the major object of his attention.) Gatsby is a representative of all the sad young men in Fitzgerald's fiction because his ideal of woman, his need for love, cannot find its proper incarnation in an age of vamps and flappers. And in the histories of these young men, entrapped by their own fantasies, we may observe Fitzgerald's anxiety over the emasculating power of the New Woman of the Jazz Age, to whom nevertheless he was powerfully attracted.

All of Fitzgerald's stories have a touch of disaster in them because he was clearly detached enough from his own aspirations to recognize that "living wasn't the reckless, careless business these people thought—this generation just younger than me," "the wildest of all generations, the generation which had been adolescent during the war." He accurately foresaw the moral letdown in store for them as "things were getting thinner and thinner as the eternal necessary human values tried to spread over all that expansion," and finally "the most expensive orgy in history" came to an "abrupt end" when "the utter confidence which was its essential prop" received an "enormous jolt" on Black Friday in 1929, and the whole "flimsy structure" came crashing down. "It was borrowed time anyhow," Fitzgerald later observed, "the whole upper tenth of a nation living with the insouciance of grand ducs and the casualness of chorus girls." [23]

By 1929 and the onset of the depression, as Elizabeth Stevenson

22 F. Scott Fitzgerald, *The Great Gatsby* (New York: Scribner's, 1925), pp. 180–181.
23 Fitzgerald, *The Crack-Up*, pp. 21–22.

has shown in *Babbitts and Bohemians,* the flapper as a type had disappeared—into harlotry, some said, or, as others said, into middle-class respectability. [24] Fitzgerald inclined toward the former view, for he was incapable of imagining that the liberated woman of the twenties, severed from her traditional role, could achieve a happiness and fulfillment he could admire. His essays on the Jazz Age, written in the 1930s, underline the moral implicit in his earlier stories. To his daughter Scottie he wrote in 1937: "For premature adventure one pays an atrocious price. As I told you once every boy I know who drank at eighteen or nineteen is now safe in his grave. The girls who were what we called 'speeds' (in our stone-age slang) at sixteen were reduced to anything they could get at the marrying time. It's in the logic of life that no young person ever 'gets away with anything.' They fool their parents but not their contemporaries. It was in the cards that Ginevra King should get fired from Westover—also that your mother should wear out young. I think that despite a tendency to self-indulgence you and I have some essential seriousness that will manage to preserve us." [25]

Fitzgerald's remark to his daughter is paternal, personal, and moralistic; but it also suggests the thirties view of the twenties experience. Fitzgerald's saving grace, what preserves him for us, was his sensitivity to the social transformations liberating young American women (and men), the accuracy with which he recorded their moral experience, and the aesthetic power with which he organized and expressed his ambivalent feelings—with the effect that we are as attracted to his heroines as he was, but in the end are equally disillusioned with the self-indulgent uses to which the American girl of the twenties, as he saw her, had put her freedom. "If I had anything to do with creating the manners of the contemporary American girl," Fitzgerald once lamented, "I certainly made a botch of the job." [26]

III

In his early career, Hemingway also portrayed the new young woman very much as Fitzgerald did—with fascination and distaste. Hemingway's heroines are not dizzy flappers foxtrotting in New

---

24 Stevenson, *Babbitts and Bohemians: The American 1920s* (New York: Macmillan, 1967), pp. 138–151. Compare Fitzgerald's remark in *The Crack-Up* that "the flapper never really disappeared in the twenties—she merely dropped her name, put on rubber heels and worked in the dark" (p. 210).

25 *Letters of F. Scott Fitzgerald,* ed. Andrew Turnbull (New York: Dell, 1966), pp. 27–28.

26 *Letters of F. Scott Fitzgerald,* p. 367.

York speakeasies, but many of them are comparably self-indulgent, hedonistic, and deracinated from older stable moral and social values. There is a measure of truth in the commonplace observation that Hemingway's *The Sun Also Rises* (1926) reflects the "lost generation." Brett Ashley is a desexed symbol of the effect of the "dirty war" on Hemingway's generation. Her bobbed hair and man's felt hat, her alcoholism and sexual promiscuity, her drunken consort with male homosexuals in Parisian bars are physical and sexual symbols—like Jake's genital wound—of the spiritual damage the generation had suffered.[27] For several decades of Hemingway criticism the representative character of this novel, as a reflection of our social history, has been accordingly emphasized.

But the characterization of Hemingway's women also suggests that he was profoundly disturbed about male and female sexuality. In particular one may observe that his deep (if masked) suspicion of women reflects a neurotic anxiety, like Fitzgerald's, over their emasculating power. Brett is portrayed with considerable sympathy, but we cannot ignore her incapacity for serious feeling, which wreaks Circean havoc on the men in her life—Mike, Robert Cohn, Romero, and Jake Barnes. Margot, in "The Short Happy Life of Francis Macomber," is presented as "simply enamelled in that American female cruelty"; and Wilson, the British safari guide, remarks of American women that they are "the hardest, the cruelest, the most predatory and the most attractive and their men have softened or gone to pieces nervously as they have hardened."[28]

This fictional view of emasculating American female cruelty and male insecurity and nervousness is doubtless a response to Hemingway's own experience with women. But it may have a more specific origin in his friendship with Zelda and Scott Fitzgerald. For in *A Moveable Feast* (1964) Zelda is portrayed as having virtually emasculated Scott by telling him that, genitally, he was insufficiently endowed. "But why would she say it?" Fitzgerald asked, after he and Hemingway had compared measurements in the men's room of a

---

27 Theodore Bardacke, "Hemingway's Women," in *Ernest Hemingway: The Man and His Work,* ed. John K. M. McCaffery (Cleveland and New York: World Publishing Co., 1950), p. 343.

28 "The Short Happy Life of Francis Macomber," in *The Short Stories of Ernest Hemingway* (New York: Scribner's, 1953), p. 8. For fuller treatments of Hemingway's view of women, see William Phillips, "Male-ism and Moralism: Hemingway and Steinbeck," *American Mercury,* 75 (1952), 93–98. See also Phyllis Bartlett, "Other Countries, Other Wenches," *Modern Fiction Studies* 3 (1957–1958), 345–349; Anne Greco, "Margot Macomber: 'Bitch Goddess,' Exonerated," *Fitzgerald-Hemingway Annual* 1972, pp. 273–280; and Bernice Kert, *The Hemingway Women: Those Who Loved Him—The Wives and Others* (1983).

bar. "To put you out of business," Hemingway replied. "That's the oldest way in the world of putting people out of business, Scott."[29] In "Mr. and Mrs. Elliott," Hemingway presents a husband effectively put out of business by an aggressive (possibly lesbian) American wife. And in "The Snows of Kilimanjaro" Hemingway explores the question of whether the "rich bitch" sapped her husband's writing talent by making life too comfortable for him, by "womanizing" him, with the effect that he failed to realize his literary gift. The rich wife is finally absolved of responsibility for her husband's failures. And we may take note that the hunter Wilson's view of American women is not that of his author. Yet the recurrence of bitchy women in Hemingway's fiction suggests a continuing deep aversion to the aggressive New Woman of his time. The character of the erogenous combat between Hemingway's couples suggests an incompatibility between the conflicting needs of men and women so deep that his men often find it easier to go it alone. Hemingway continually played variations on the theme of *Men Without Women* (1927) because the new female of the species was in fact, for him, deadlier than the male.

Nevertheless, Hemingway is the tender poet of heterosexual love during the period between the two world wars. And in *A Farewell to Arms* (1929) and *For Whom the Bell Tolls* (1940) he celebrated that love tragically, poignantly, and at times even sentimentally. We are asked to admire his heroines, Catherine Barkley and Maria, because they are not New Women, Circes, vampires, or bitches. They appealed to Hemingway's imagination because of their utter sexual willingness, submission, and passivity. Both are idealizations of the womanly woman stereotype. They are old-fashioned, self-sacrificing, and totally involved in and devoted to fulfilling the needs (sexual, physical, and emotional—but not intellectual) of the men in their lives, Frederic Henry and Robert Jordan. Catherine says, "There isn't any me. I'm you. Don't make up a separate me. . . . You're my religion. You're all I've got." And Robert Jordan assures Maria, "You are me now. . . . Surely thou must feel it, rabbit."[30] And for her, for both of them, the earth moves.

It is intentional, therefore, that Catherine has long blond hair and that Maria suffers deep shame at her head's having been shaved by the fascists. Long hair for Hemingway is the physical symbol of genuine femininity, and in these heroines he celebrates an ideal of womanhood which seemed to him to have largely vanished after

---

29 Ernest Hemingway, *A Moveable Feast* (New York: Bantam Books, 1965), p. 188.
30 Ernest Hemingway, *A Farewell to Arms* (New York: Scribner's, 1929), p. 120; and *For Whom the Bell Tolls* (New York: Scribner's, 1940), p. 463.

World War I, except perhaps in Europe. The mindless heroine with no will, ego, or identity of her own is rightly objectionable to many contemporary women. But Hemingway's sensibility required him to idealize that kind of woman, for he was not equal to the emotional skirmishing often present in normal heterosexual relationships. His distrust of aggressive women in marriage grew out of the traumas of his own parents' relationship, devastatingly portrayed in "The Doctor and the Doctor's Wife." "Once a man's married he's absolutely bitched," Bill tells Nick in "The Three-Day Blow." "Fall for them but don't let them ruin you."[31] Yes, Nick agrees, their emotional claims can be devastating. In "Cross-Country Snow," Nick has to give up skiing in Switzerland and settle down in the United States because his wife Helen is going to have a baby. The "domestic enslavement" of the wife, treated in works like Lewis's *Main Street,* here becomes the plight of the husband. But such "enslavement" is only one of the ways women ruin Hemingway's men, "bitch" their lives.[32]

In Hemingway's order of values, masculine independence had an extraordinary importance. Its source was his need for emotional self-protection, his fear of damage to the self. His feelings about women were inextricably involved with his perception of the meaninglessness of life—which is nasty, brutish, and short—and his fear of death. Given the valueless world, the problem (as Jake defines it in *The Sun Also Rises*) is "how to live in it,"[33] what kind of code to devise in order to protect the self from anxiety arising out of the fear of death. One solution is the "giant killer" of drink, ritually consumed in a clean, well-lighted place (a limited area of self-imposed order): drink blots out the consciousness of nihilism, the *nada* pervading all existence.[34]

---

31 *The Short Stories of Ernest Hemingway,* p. 122.
32 These remarks are not meant to suggest that Hemingway was a latent or overt homosexual, as is sometimes alleged. (Homosexuality and lesbianism were profound evils for Hemingway, true perversions of rightly directed human sexuality.) Nor are they meant to suggest that he was a misogynist, like Henry Miller. Kate Millett's *Sexual Politics* and Norman Mailer's *The Prisoner of Sex* take up the issue of Miller's view of women. I have no wish to rehearse their quarrel here. But to observe the degradation of women in, say, *Tropic of Cancer* (1934) is to realize that Hemingway was no misogynist. For Miller, women were mere receptacles of male lust. "O Tania," Miller rhapsodizes, "where now is that warm cunt of yours, those fat, heavy garters, those soft bulging thighs?" In Miller's fictionalized "genito-urinary" relationships, women are offered no real commitment, compassion, or affection. What is obscene in Miller's prose is not the diction, the graphic description of sexual or excremental acts (though these indubitably shocked Americans in the depression years and led to the banning of his work), but rather his manifest degradation of women as a sex and his embrace of the narcissism and "inhumanism" by which he justified that degradation.
33 Ernest Hemingway, *The Sun Also Rises* (New York: Scribner's, 1926), p. 148.
34 "A Clean, Well-Lighted Place," *The Short Stories of Ernest Hemingway,* pp. 379–383.

Another "giant killer" is of course sex, for the ecstasy of orgasm and the attendant emotions of uncomplicated, undemanding, and adoring heterosexual love may alleviate the solitude of existential dread. This is the wisdom of Pilar in steering Maria and Robert Jordan into the double sleeping bag: together, within it, they make an "erotic alliance" against "the things of the night."

But this union offers Hemingway's lovers only a momentary deliverance from the consciousness of *nada*, for even the supreme value of romantic love is shown to be ineffectual before the fact of death, seen by Pilar in the lines of Jordan's hand and symbolized by the rain that terrifies Catherine Barkley. Thus the question becomes, "how to live in it" if love is not enough. "A man must not marry," advises the Italian major in "In Another Country." "If he is to lose everything, he should not place himself in a position to lose that. He should not place himself in a position to lose. He should find things he cannot lose." [35] (This bitter feeling is the consequence of his young wife's having just died.)

One is interested here in how Hemingway's men cope with the emotional complication caused by relationships with women. In "Indian Camp," the brave slits his own throat because he cannot bear his wife's agony in childbirth. At Adrianople in *In Our Time*, childbirth, the fruit of love, is attended by the chaos of war and death in the steady rain. The speaker in "On the Quai at Smyrna" must resort to irony to cope with the horror of "the women with dead babies. You couldn't get the women to give up their dead babies." [36] And in *A Farewell to Arms* Frederic Henry is left alone at the end with his grief—Catherine's death being the price of his sleeping with her, of his giving himself so fully to a woman that he is absolutely vulnerable to the cruelty of fate. He might have known better. "There is no lonelier man in death, except the suicide," Hemingway once poignantly observed, "than that man who has lived many years with a good wife and then outlived her. If two people love each other there can be no happy end to it." [37]

The need for love, then, the complete gift of the self, dangerously exposes the Hemingway hero to his own emotional vulnerability. Woman is a party to an eventual assault on him by *nada* and death;

35 *The Short Stories of Ernest Hemingway*, p. 271.
36 *The Short Stories of Ernest Hemingway*, p. 87.
37 Compare Cleanth Brooks's speculation that Hemingway "might very well have taken his motto from the German romantic poet Novalis: "All passions end like a tragedy. Whatever is finite ends in death." *William Faulkner: The Yoknapatawpha County* (New Haven: Yale University Press, 1966), p. 207.

and the knowledge of this fact often makes him emotionally aloof from her. But even his own body betrays him—through emotions like fear or the need for love, by mental fatigue, physical frailty, and old age. How to live in it: Hemingway's stories suggest that only the disciplined will, resistant to the seductions of happiness and the illusion of its permanence, only the stoic power of endurance, hardened by the cruelties of fortune, can give his protagonists a means of triumphing over the meaninglessness of existence. Though momentarily "unmanned" by his grief, the major in "In Another Country" straightens himself and walks out of the hospital, his dignity recovered, intact. Nick, Jake, and Frederic Henry all seem "bitched" by the women with whom they become involved. Their histories evidence the author's deep fear—if not of women, at least of man's "weakness" in "succumbing" to his own emotional need for woman. Looking at Hemingway's strong men, the ones who survive, we take note of Santiago in *The Old Man and the Sea*, the major in "In Another Country," and the old man in "A Clean, Well-Lighted Place" as instances of the "undefeated," men redeemed by an inwardness of stoic strength in which, finally, women have no part—except as poignant memories of love the hero once momentarily had but lost.

IV

The power of endurance is also a major value in Faulkner's fiction. But he celebrates not the careful old men but the enduring spiritual strength of women. What Faulkner felt about women and how he characterized them have been so frequently misrepresented that the judicious reader of his novels may well be astonished. His New Women are without question unflatteringly portrayed in *Mosquitoes* (1927) and *Sanctuary* (1931). And Joanna Burden in *Light in August* (1932) and Drusilla Sartoris in *The Unvanquished* (1938) are neurotic, even perverted women. It is true that one of Faulkner's characters (Jason Compson) remarks, "Once a bitch always a bitch," and that another regards women as "articulated female genital organs with an aptitude for spending whatever money you may happen to possess."[38]

But it is by no means true, as Maxwell Geismar has argued in *Writers in Crisis*, that Faulkner has "a suspicion of women when it is

---

38 William Faulkner, *The Sound and the Fury and As I Lay Dying* (New York: Modern Library, 1929), p. 198. For recent treatments of Faulkner and women, see the 1985 Yoknapatawpha Conference on *Faulkner and Women*; Mimi R. Gladstein's *The Indestructible Woman in Faulkner, Hemingway, and Steinbeck* (1986); and Minrose Gwin's *The Feminine and Faulkner: Reading (Beyond) Sexual Difference* (1990).

not contempt and contempt when it is not hatred," or that Faulkner sees "the Female source of life itself as inherently vicious." Nor can one agree with Leslie Fiedler's claim in *Love and Death in the American Novel* that "In no other writer in the world do pejorative stereotypes of women appear with greater frequency and on more levels, from the most trivial to the most profound." It is likewise ridiculous to claim that if Faulkner "dared treat in such terms any racial minority, his books would have been banned in every enlightened school in the country."[39] Such remarks distort Faulkner's novels by identifying the author's viewpoint with the views of his characters. In fact, Faulkner's novels contain a large gallery of women, of all ages, several races, and many social and psychological types. Though he holds up a mirror to American (particularly to Southern) womanhood, his aim is to dramatize conflicts of the human heart at moments when conduct and feeling are at an extremity of crisis.

Like Fitzgerald, the young Faulkner was captivated by an ideal of woman—young, alluring, virginal, inaccessible—symbolized in his recurrent allusions to Keats's "still unravished bride of quietness." The glorification of this kind of feminine ideal used to be natural to romantic young men. But the Southern tradition of reverencing what a character in *Sanctuary* calls "the most sacred thing in life, womanhood,"[40] gave a special intensity to Faulkner's portraits of women. He did not believe in the Southern cult of womanhood, of course, but his imagination was captivated by its effect on sensitive young men twisted by their own sexual idealism. Horace Benbow in *Sartoris* (1929) is one such young man; Quentin Compson in *The Sound and the Fury* (1929) and *Absalom, Absalom!* (1936) is another. Neither of the sisters of these young men is equal to the purity expected of the Southern lady, for the need for love in women, as in men, is powerful; and sex is a drive in Faulkner's women that sometimes masters them. The idealistic young man's incapacity to deal with female sexuality (particularly that of his sister) is often, therefore, his doom as well as hers.

Actual women, as Faulkner well understood, cannot without violence be put to the service of abstract idealism. Despite the obsolete American myth that women are purer or more spiritual than

---

39 Maxwell Geismar, *Writers in Crisis* (Boston: Houghton Mifflin, 1942), p. 180; Fiedler, *Love and Death in the American Novel*, p. 309. For other treatments of this subject, see David M. Miller's "Faulkner's Women," *Modern Fiction Studies*, 13 (1967), 3–17; and Samuel Yorks's "Faulkner's Woman: The Peril of Mankind," *Arizona Quarterly*, 17 (1961), 119–129.

40 William Faulkner, *Sanctuary* (New York: Modern Library, 1931), p. 276.

men, Faulkner's novels reveal that sex is a great natural procreant urge that cannot be constrained by Calvinism. In "Hair" Ratliff observes: "There's not any such thing as a woman born bad, because they are all born bad, born with the badness in them. The thing is, to get them married before the badness comes to a natural head. But we try to make them conform to a system that says a woman can't be married until she reaches a certain age. And nature don't pay any attention to systems, let alone women paying any attention to them, or to anything."[41] The comedy of Faulkner's rhetoric undercuts the suggestion that sex is in itself evil. But it is clearly an irrepressible energy at the very center of woman's being. In the portrait of Eula Varner in *The Hamlet* (1940), this natural female sexuality is elevated to the myth of the Earth Mother at its highest, wildest, funniest pinnacle. Her brother Jody, her teacher Labove, and the other men of Frenchmen's Bend who have been shaped by "the harsh functioning of Protestant primary education" are powerless before Eula's sexuality, which communicates itself as "a moist blast of spring's liquorish corruption," the men's hysterical desire illustrating "a pagan triumphal prostration before the supreme primal uterus."[42]

The life-affirming, procreative character of female sexuality, irrepressible and hardly subject to theological or social constraint, is also comically presented in *Light in August*. The protagonist Joe Christmas is destroyed by a series of tragic adventures, often with women, who try to minister to his needs. (Feeding him is the giveaway sign of their nourishing function.) Joe cannot reconcile himself to the ambiguity of his racial identity or to the ministration of women, however, and is eventually destroyed. Lena Grove's story, which envelops Joe's, puts his tragedy into perspective by celebrating her as the embodiment of fulfilled female sexuality in harmony with the natural rhythms of existence. Despite Joe's importance to the novel, "that story began with Lena Grove," Faulkner once observed, "the idea of the young girl with nothing, pregnant, determined to find her sweetheart. It was—that was out of my admiration for women, for the courage and endurance of women."[43] Nature and the female seasons: throughout Faulkner's best work, the two are equivalents for the reproductive, nourishing, life-sustaining and affirming basis of existence—symbolized in *Sartoris,* for example, in Aunt Jenny's gardening in springtime. It is tempting to generalize the op-

41 "Hair," *Collected Stories of William Faulkner* (New York: Random House, 1943), p. 133.
42 William Faulkner, *The Hamlet* (New York: Random House, 1940), p. 114.
43 *Faulkner in the University: Class Conferences at the University of Virginia, 1957–1958,* eds. Frederick L. Gwynn and Joseph L. Blotner (New York: Random House, 1965), p. 74.

posing reckless, aggressive, and destructive energy in nature as the male principle. In *Absalom, Absalom!* Aunt Rosa Coldfield ("all polymath love's androgynous advocate")[44] gives it that name. But there are enough women in his novels devoted to Thanatos, and enough men devoted to Eros, to prevent easy generalizations about the male and female principles in Faulkner's work. The problem for both his men and women is to get into a creative, loving relationship with the life-giving force of existence, which is incarnate in nature (for example, in the wilderness in *Go Down, Moses* [1942]) as well as in human sexuality. What usually destroys Faulkner's men is their egotism, self-assertion, or their devotion to some concept of woman that has no relation to her actuality. Horace Benbow poeticizes his Ideal Woman and is blind to the reality of Narcissa and Belle Mitchell; Bayard Sartoris, in his quest for self-destruction, denies the woman who bears him a son; Joe Christmas throws the food offered by those who would mother him and vomits at this "woman's muck"; Thomas Sutpen callously exploits female sexuality to further his own grand design; and Popeye is impotent and sadistic before it—or before Temple's "playing at it."

The most poignant of Faulkner's self-destructive men who are severed from the affirming principle of life is Quentin Compson in *The Sound and the Fury*. Quentin is the son of an alcoholic father and a neurotic mother who has virtually abandoned her children; he and his brothers turn to their sister Caddie as a mother substitute. As Caddy grows into adolescent sexuality, however, Quentin's static inner world of order begins to disintegrate; he is driven to deny her sexuality and to fight with her boyfriends. But "the minute fragile membrane of her maidenhead" is unequal to sustaining the family's pride and honor, and Quentin eventually surrenders himself to the suicide he so desperately craves. The ideal of womanly purity thus wars vainly against the actuality of female need, so that, for the damaged idealist, woman sinks to the "delicate equilibrium of periodical filth between two moons balanced."[45]

The sources of Quentin's neurotic disorder are expressed in the terrible agony of his cry, *"if I'd just had a mother so I could say Mother*

---

44 William Faulkner, *Absalom, Absalom!* (New York: Random House, 1936), p. 146. For other views, see K. E. Zink, "Faulkner's Garden: Woman and the Immemorial Earth," *Modern Fiction Studies*, 2 (1956), 139–149; and Thomas M. Lorch, "Thomas Sutpen and the Female Principle," *Mississippi Quarterly*, 20 (1966–1967), 38–42.

45 Faulkner, *The Sound and the Fury*, p. 147. Compare John L. Longley, Jr., "'Who Never Had a Sister': A Reading of *The Sound and the Fury*," *Mosaic*, 7 (1973), 35–53; see also Charles D. Peavy's useful "'If I'd Just Had a Mother': Faulkner's Quentin Compson," *Literature and Psychology*, 23 (1973), 114–121.

Mother."[46] But Mrs. Compson is a hopeless hypochondriac, swollen in self-pity and egotism, and Caddy is growing into a woman with her own needs. Dilsey comes closest to fulfilling Quentin's profound need for maternal love, consolation, sustenance, and support. But neither he nor the others in the family who so desperately need and rely on Dilsey can recognize the precious gift of mothering she offers. Blacks may complain at Dilsey as an Aunt Jemima stereotype, and radical women may deplore her self-effacement and passivity. But Dilsey is the most important character, let alone woman, in all of Faulkner's fiction because she embodies the highest love Faulkner was capable of imagining. She incarnates the life-affirming principle of selfless love and devotion to those entrusted, by fate, to her care. As the true mothering presence in the disintegrating Compson household, she reflects an aspect of Caroline Barr (1840–1940), the black mammy who raised young Faulkner and to whom he dedicated *Go Down, Moses.* Born in slavery, Faulkner wrote, she "gave to my family a fidelity without stint or calculation of recompense and to my childhood an immeasurable devotion and love."[47]

Faulkner's best women are tough-minded pragmatists who have what Sally R. Page in *Faulkner's Women* has called "a greater commitment to the sustenance of life than do the men, a commitment which enables them to disregard traditional morality and rationality when the preservation of the well-being of life is at stake."[48] If we isolate some of Dilsey's characteristics, Faulkner may seem to be glorifying dependency, guileful submissiveness, and passive self-effacement—behavioral characteristics associated with social enslavement (whether racial or sexual) and moral inferiority. These are certainly not qualities likely to appeal to a militant black or to the modern liberated woman. Nevertheless, Faulkner valued the family as the cornerstone of society and as a repository of the wisdom of the race; and he celebrated those qualities which make for the stability and coherence of the family and the transmission, from generation to generation, of the "old verities of the heart"—pride, compassion, pity and honor, courage and endurance. Asked at Nagano about his view of women, Faulkner observed: "the opinion that women cause the trouble is not my own. . . . They have held families together and it's because of families that the race is continued, and I would be sorry to think that my work had given anyone the impression that I held

---

46 Faulkner, *The Sound and the Fury,* p. 190.
47 William Faulkner, *Go Down, Moses* (New York: Modern Library, 1952), n.p.
48 Sally R. Page, *Faulkner's Women: Characterization and Meaning* (Deland, Fla.: Everett/Edwards, 1972), p. 186.

women in morally a lower position than men, which I do not." As Chick Mallison remarks ironically in *Intruder in the Dust* (1948), "women couldn't really stand anything except tragedy and poverty and physical pain." This view of women as the power making for community is reflected again and again in the novels—in Granny Millard, Aunt Jenny, Lena Grove, and especially in Dilsey. Dilsey is the supreme example, in the words of Ms. Page, of how "through motherhood the Romantic ideals of creativity, self-transcendence, and union with the nature of existence can be achieved without evil or destructiveness."[49]

V

Faulkner's view of the supreme function of woman reflects what Betty Friedan once called the "feminine mystique." This view of the nature and function of woman, widely celebrated in the popular woman's magazines in Faulkner's time (*Ladies' Home Journal, The Pictorial Review, McCall's*), was, and is, endemic in our culture. Several decades of strenuous feminism have not eradicated it; and Aileen Kraditor's *Up from the Pedestal* has persuasively documented the extent to which the persistence of this view of woman's role prevented political and social action from having much real impact during the period between the wars.

Looking back over the major American novels of the period, one observes that for most of our writers the New Woman was unattractive, owing to her emotional insincerity, "misplaced" ambition, hedonism, and moral irresponsibility. In the end the best writers of the period—in my view Fitzgerald, Hemingway, and Faulkner—seem to have had greatest sympathy with the prevailing stereotype of the "womanly woman," the woman with an old-fashioned sense of her role as life-giving, nourishing, life-sustaining presence ministering to her husband or family. The power of this conception was endemic in the very way men and women had been reared and educated in America. And given the structure of the family and its distribution of male and female roles, that image powerfully affected the way novelists, male and female, created women characters.

Anaïs Nin once urged the contemporary woman writer "to sever herself from the myth man creates, from being created by him; she has to struggle with her own cycles, storms, terrors which man does

---

49 *Faulkner at Nagano*, ed. Robert A. Jelliffe (Tokyo: Kenkyusha, 1956), pp. 69–70; see also William Faulkner, *Intruder in the Dust* (New York: Modern Library, 1948), p. 208; and Sally R. Page, *Faulkner's Women*, p. 46.

not understand."[50] There is no doubt that Nin points here to emotional realities never grasped by the male novelists I have discussed. But Nin calls for what the major men and women novelists of the *l'entre deux guerres* period could not give. For what the major women novelists of this period celebrated—novelists like Cather, Wharton, Glasgow, Gale, and Roberts—does not notably differ from what their male counterparts praised and admired. Hence my reading of the fictive portraits of women can hardly constitute a revisionist literary history. Even in the lesbian Willa Cather's *My Ántonia,* for example, the final image of Ántonia Cuzak identifies her with the beneficence of natural sexual and biological processes, "the goodness of planting and tending, and harvesting." Cather's celebration of Ántonia as mother of a large and productive family may suggest to us an idealization of the common maternal stereotype. But Ántonia is meant to return us to what Cather called "immemorial human attitudes which we recognize by instinct as universal and true." Cather's narrator concludes: "It was no wonder [Ántonia's] sons stood tall and straight. She was a rich mine of life, like the founders of early races."[51] *Archetype* might therefore be a better word for her.

The social dislocation produced by the depression reinforced the feminine mystique and intensified literary idealizations of the woman as mother. John Steinbeck's *The Grapes of Wrath* (1939), written at the end of the depression, seems to me the ultimate celebration of the maternal ideal of the period, for Ma Joad holds the family together, nourishes and sustains it against adversity, and brings it through to California. In the final scene of that novel, her daughter Rose of Sharon (the baby stillborn) is encouraged by Ma Joad to give her milk-full breasts to the starving man in the barn so that his life may be saved. This scene has been called offensively coarse, degrading to women, possibly obscene. But the starkly physical character of the action is intended to present to us a graphic symbol of the highest function—according to some of the best American novelists of the period—that women may have. That the mother could be an emasculating destroyer is principally a post–World War II literary phenomenon, evident in the satire of writers like Philip Wylie, Bruce Jay Friedman, and Philip Roth.

---

50 *The Diary of Anaïs Nin,* ed. Gunther Stuhlman (New York: Swallow Press/Harcourt, Brace, and World, 1966), II, 234.
51 Willa Cather, *My Ántonia* (Boston: Houghton Mifflin, 1949), p. 229.

Tracking the
American Novel
into the Void

Writing in 1880 to his *Atlantic* editor, the novelist William Dean Howells, Henry James promised that his forthcoming novel, *Washington Square*, would be "a tale purely American." On a superficial level it is easy enough to see what James meant. His book would *lack* that bedrock of complex European social and cultural forms essential, he felt, to any novelist. What were these elements of a complex society, missing in America but available to any European novelist? James had notoriously listed them in his biography *Hawthorne* (1879):

> No State, in the European sense of the word, and indeed barely a specific national name. No sovereign, no court, no personal loyalty, no aristocracy, no church, no clergy, no army, no diplomatic service, no country gentlemen, no palaces, no castles, nor manors nor old country-houses, nor parsonages, nor thatched cottages nor ivied ruins; no cathedrals, nor abbeys, nor little Norman churches; no great Universities nor public schools—no Oxford, nor Eton, nor Harrow; no literature, no novels, no museums, no pictures, no political society, no sporting class—no Epsom nor Ascot! Some such list as that might be drawn up of the absent things in American life . . . the effect of which, upon an English or a French imagination, would probably as a general thing be appalling.

Hawthorne, James argued, finessed the problem of our cultural thinness by turning away from the novel of manners in favor of the romance of the single self. American social circumstances, James said, forced him to care for the "deeper psychology" of the individual —those ruminations on sin and guilt, say, in *The Scarlet Letter*. More interested in the dynamics of social relations than Hawthorne, James finessed the absence of cultural density by developing the international theme, as in *Roderick Hudson* and *The American*, where the contrast between the poverty of American culture and the density of the old European order, as they affect character, could be effectively thematized. *Washington Square,* he thought, would be harder to write. I think the tale of Catherine Sloper turns out all right, but James didn't reprint it in the New York Edition.

On a deeper level *Washington Square* raises a question about what a pure American novel may be; or, to put it in another way, what the *American* novel purely is. There are of course two parts to this definition. James was fairly sure of what the novel is: he called it that most elastic of literary forms, indeed, a form so flexible that every *a priori* attempt to define it or to constitute its characteristics was bound to meet with defeat. So much for generic precision.

As to the *American* novel, James is equally explicit: none, certainly of any merit, had yet been written by the time he took up his pen. His theoretical essay "The Art of Fiction" and his many reviews of would-be American novels are rather clear on that point: outside the *romances* of Hawthorne, America had produced little worthwhile book-length fiction, and no *novels* worth setting alongside the major productions of Balzac, Flaubert, Turgenev, and the other European masters. Thus arises the argument that the American novel is most characteristically itself when it is not a novel at all (which is, after all, a European mode concerned with social relations) but rather a romance, that is, a fiction preoccupied with the invention of the possible rather than representation of the actual. This is the popular position taken by Richard Chase in *The American Novel and Its Tradition*, who emphasized the differences in the way in which the two forms, novel and romance, "view reality." For Chase, the romance

feels freer to render reality in less volume and detail. It tends to prefer action to character, and action will be freer in a romance than in a novel, encountering, as it were, less resistance from reality. . . . The romance can flourish without providing much intricacy of relation. The characters, probably rather two-dimensional types, will not be complexly related to each other or to society or to the past. Human beings will on the whole be shown in ideal relation—that is, they will share emotions only after these have become abstract or symbolic. To be sure, characters may become profoundly involved in some way, as in Hawthorne or Melville, but it will be a deep and narrow, an obsessive involvement. In American romances it will not matter much what class people come from, and where the novelist would arouse our interest in a character by exploring his origin, the romancer will probably do so by enveloping it in mystery. Character itself becomes, then, somewhat abstract and ideal, so much so in some romances that it seems to be merely a function of plot. The plot we may expect to be highly colored. Astonishing events may occur, and these are likely to have a symbolic or ideological, rather than a realistic, plausibility. Being less committed to the immediate rendition of reality than the novel, the romance will more freely veer toward mythic, allegorical, and symbolic forms.

In short, the quintessentially American masterpieces are, for a critic like Chase, romances that turn away from representations of our ordinary life in society and emphasize Huck on the raft, Ahab sinking with the *Pequod*, and Leatherstocking striking out into the Indian territory. To ask the question of what is an *American* novel, or what is *the* American novel, is then to provoke issues of complex cultural significance, of comparative national definition, and of literary form—issues that touch upon our deepest sense of ourselves as a people. I propose to ask the question again here for the sake of formulating some positions about the American literary tradition and what is happening now in fiction.

II

I begin with the premise that, as to the poverty of our social experience, James was theoretically dead wrong, although in actual fact he was very nearly right. Sufficient richness and complexity, range and variety, and a density of American cultural experience *were there* in Hawthorne's time, adequate for the purposes of the novel, and have been ever since. The rich bibliography of American social history makes that evident. Even so, our most famous literary critics have already decided that the American social novel is beneath intellectual discussion, rather like the TV show *Dallas* or *Peyton Place*.

An instance of this prejudice was the view of Lionel Trilling that "American writers of genius have not turned their minds to society." This seemed to him the case because he accepted the definition of our social life as James described it. It is true that the American social order has never perhaps been quite so visible as the European, with its older crude division of classes, but we nevertheless do have social forms. And we have had a number of compelling American social novels of the kind now sometimes breezily dismissed in the academy: Catherine Maria Sedgwick's *Redwood*, James Fenimore Cooper's *Home as Found*, Howells's *The Rise of Silas Lapham* and *A Modern Instance*, Edith Wharton's *The House of Mirth* and *The Age of Innocence*, Sinclair Lewis's *Main Street* and *Babbitt*, Fitzgerald's *The Great Gatsby*, John O'Hara's *Appointment in Samarra* and *Ten North Frederick*, John P. Marquand's *The Late George Apley* and *Point of No Return*, James Gould Cozzens's *Guard of Honor* and *By Love Possessed*, and Louis Auchincloss's *Portrait in Brownstone* and *The House of Five Talents*—not to speak of James's *Washington Square, The Europeans,* and *An International Episode.*

How could it succeed here? For one thing, the American novel is not coterminous with the national experience. We had no novels for the first century and a half of American colonial existence. But the novel in this country *does* burst into existence about the time the nation throws off the colonial yoke and asserts its separate identity. That identity claimed to be exceptional—in its origin, its manifestation, and destiny. America was to be a city set on a hill, a shining light of liberty and freedom for all the nations, in art as well as in politics and religion. Jefferson's great Declaration and Emerson's "The American Scholar" intend nothing less than to launch the nation forward into a democratic future of political and artistic self-sufficiency.

There is no denying that the doctrine of American "exceptionalism"—our distinctiveness, originality, and manifest destiny, as enunciated in its various forms—vigorously animated the passions of most Americans before our time. At the heart of the doctrine of our exceptionalism is of course the claim of liberty as the prior condition of all politics, religion, and social organization. This doctrine is no less at the heart of American artistic endeavor, particularly in the novel. In one way or another, the fiction, poetry, and drama claiming to be most distinctively *American* begins with revolutionary pretensions to MAKE IT NEW, with a rejection of the traditional—not merely the traditional in European art but in past American "traditions" in art as well. American fiction is, among other things, a self-conscious enterprise intent on nothing less than appropriating the liberty claimed in the great political and social declarations so as to remake afresh the fictive forms of representation.

Literary "exceptionalism," a form of American nationalism that asserts that we have indeed produced a new literature adequate to our original revolutionary politics, may produce a wan smile on the face of the historian, the political scientist, and the sociologist. For there is plenty of evidence to show that our early immigrants transported here from Europe (or later borrowed from abroad) and domesticated in our own institutions a good deal of their Old World cultural baggage. What, among other things, they domesticated here was the romance form, which Trilling and Chase have claimed to be so distinctive to American fiction. Most great American romances—Charles Brockden Brown's *Wieland*, Cooper's *The Pathfinder*, Hawthorne's *The Marble Faun*, Melville's *Moby-Dick*, Norris's *The Octopus*, Faulkner's *Light in August*, Pynchon's *Gravity's Rainbow*, for instance—merely continue, in fact, fictive traditions derived from the Gothic or picaresque extravagance of such European practitioners of the romance as Cervantes, Fielding, Horace Walpole, Monk Lewis, Ann Radcliffe, Emile Zola, D. H. Lawrence, and others. Further, most of our romances are actually a mixed bag of elements, including the quintessentially novelistic or even *dramatic* modes of Shakespeare and Scott, Dickens and George Eliot, and others. Generic purity has rarely been a national trait.

In Melville's great epic, the original intention—to write a novel, featuring Ishmael, about the realistic conditions of the whale fishery, more or less along the lines of his own experience aboard the *Acushnet*—gets abandoned about a third of the way through in favor the romance mode: Captain Ahab, whose leg has been sheared off by Moby Dick, is given center stage, his revenge upon the white whale dominates the action, the narrative of the "fiery hunt" is allegorized by allusions to the rites of Zoroastrianism and Satanism, and the novel becomes, among other things, a metaphysical voyage on strange seas of thought. Deranged old Ahab wants, in killing Moby Dick, nothing less than to challenge the universe, to strike through the mask of appearances, to assault the God who has allowed him to be maimed, or at least to expose the nothingness that lies behind the mindless phenomena of the world. "Talk not to me of blasphemy, man! I'd strike the sun if it insulted me" is the Promethean, the Titanic style by which Ahab elevates subjective personality, the self, above both the divine and the natural order. It is no wonder that Melville told Hawthorne that the secret motto of the book was *Ego non baptizo te in nomine patris, sed in nomine diaboli.*

No less extreme, in its way, though more politely expressed, is Isabel Archer's claim, in *The Portrait of a Lady*, for the primacy of her freedom from all external social constraints. At the outset Isabel is described as the "independent niece": "I'm very fond of my liberty." Isabel's jealousy of her liberty receives its first test at the end of the seventh chapter, where Mrs. Touchett, Isabel, Lord Warburton, and Ralph are sitting up late in the evening. When Mrs. Touchett decides that it is time for bed, she urges Isabel to come with her. But Gardencourt conventions infringe upon Isabel's liberty, and she invokes subjective desire as the test of human and social obligation. When Mrs. Touchett explains to her that, at least in England, "Young girls — in decent houses — don't sit up alone with the gentlemen late at night," there follows an exchange about the proprieties that throws a great deal of light on Isabel's character and the disastrous choices she will later make in the novel. "You were right to tell me, then," said Isabel. "I don't understand it, but I'm very glad to know it." "I shall always tell you," her aunt answers, "whenever I see you taking what seems to me too much liberty." "Pray do," says Isabel; "but I don't say I shall always think your remonstrance just." "Very likely not," her aunt answers. "You're too fond of your own ways." "Yes, I think I'm very fond of them," Isabel replies. "But I always want to know the things one shouldn't do." "So as to do them?" asks her aunt. "So as to choose," Isabel insists.

This claim of freedom is quite attractive to readers, and there are those among my students who will hear little criticism of Titanic Ahab and the wonderfully self-reliant Isabel. But these characters' refusal of reasoned dissuasion—whether in the form of Starbuck's ineffectual argument that the white whale is just a dumb beast, or the several unheeded warnings that Isabel receives before she marries Gilbert Osmond—these refusals mark the style of personal self-assertion, carried to an extreme in the face of accumulated human and social wisdom, that makes for the catastrophic ending of both novels. Are we in the presence of a trait distinctively American, something expressive of our revolutionary origins, Emersonian self-reliance here transposed into aesthetic form?

Doubtless an argument might be made on this head, but I am inclined to think that the Faustian overreacher Ahab has likely origins in European literature, and that the figure of the headstrong girl has plenty of antecedents in Richardson, Fielding, Thackeray, and George Eliot. I hold out, that is, for the continuity of aesthetic traditions. In fact, *Moby-Dick* attains its transposition into a romance under the pressure of the *Dantean* elements in Hawthorne; and Melville's book explodes into its dramatic form only after the discovery of Shakespeare, whom Melville started to read for the first time as he composed the book. Describing Shakespeare's mind, Melville wrote:

But it is those deep, far-away things in him; those occasional flashings-forth of the intuitive Truth in him; those short, quick probings at the very axis of reality,—these are the things that make Shakespeare Shakespeare. Through the mouths of the dark characters . . . he craftily says, or sometimes insinuates the things which we feel to be so terrifically true that it were all but madness for any good man, in his own proper character, to utter, or even hint of them. Tormented into desperation, Lear, the frantic king, tears off the mask and speaks the same madness of vital truth.

Can anyone doubt that it is *King Lear*, the Bible, Icelandic sagas, British maritime literature, Greek tragedy, and a whole host of other European sources that serve in part to make *Moby-Dick* what it is?

III

Quite a few American novelists are taken by such extremes of passion and feeling as Lear and Captain Ahab exhibit; and almost all of our literary critics are. Things are not terrifically true, and conflict is not conflict, it would seem, unless characters are tormented into desperation and unless vital truth has not about it something of madness. Hence the critical esteem, amongst certain writers and professors (many of whom now are both), of novels featuring driven or grotesque characters living a nightmare existence, undergoing pointless or monomaniacal quests through bizarre worlds that never were on land or sea, meanwhile giving expression to paranoid conspiracy theories, as they are driven toward wild, often apocalyptic endings. A few instances of how the American imagination is driven to extremes, in the effort to make it new, will serve to illustrate what I mean.

Let's take character in the American novel first. The European tradition that survives into the American novels written by Howells, James, and other realists was committed to verisimilitude in the representation of character. Character in the novel is *composed* so as to reflect what we feel that we encounter in ourselves and others: a stable core of identity. Howells's Silas Lapham, James's Catherine Sloper, and Fitzgerald's Nick Carraway are susceptible of change, under the pressure of their novelistic conflicts. But the novel's representation of character-in-the-process-of-change essentially manifests the freedom of the individual will actualizing the potentialities of that core of stable identity. This notion of the self, at least as a fictive device, is continuously being subverted in American fiction, which has an appetite for extreme irrationalist psychologies that disintegrate stable character. Too normal seems to be too boring.

In *Wieland; or The Transformation*, Charles Brockden Brown offers us a madman who murders his wife and children at the command of imaginary voices (perhaps projected by the sinister ventriloquist Carwin) and who then, in a fit of remorse, undergoes *spontaneous combustion*! Nothing boring about that. Poe is an even more exemplary sensationalist because, as Allen Tate has rightly remarked, Poe "discovered our great subject, the disintegration of personality." Not only does Poe savor the fragmentation of character through a *doppelgänger* motif in "William Wilson," he disintegrates personality, fractures identity, through presentations of abnormal or altered states of consciousness ranging from inebriation ("The Black Cat"), hypnosis ("The Facts in the Case of M. Valdemar"), and nightmares and cataleptic trances ("The Fall of the House of Usher"), to drug-induced hallucinations ("Ligeia") and the free-associating madness of obsessional paranoia and schizophrenia ("The Cask of Amontillado" and "The Tell-Tale Heart"). So far as character is concerned, the preoccupation of Brown and Poe with abnormal states of consciousness may be said to lay the groundwork for the deranged protagonists of William Burroughs, the paranoid fruitcakes of Thomas Pynchon, Vladimir Nabokov's madmen, and the schizoid thought disorder we find in Donald Barthelme's stories. In fact, Nabokov's *Lolita* is so centrally influenced by Poe's *doppelgänger* in "William Wilson" that he is obliged to parody his own Humbert Humbert in order to render his indebtedness to Poe as a form of self-mockery intended to disarm professorial source hunters.

The instability of character in the American novel may have historical roots in the odd mixture of the romantic notion that one may create his identity *ex nihilo* and the impact of social fluidity in the life of Americans on the frontier. Fitzgerald's provincial James Gatz comes out of the West convinced that he can remake himself into the suave and mysterious Jay Gatsby, but it never works. He is merely one reflection of J. J. Hooper's confidence man Simon Suggs, who remarks, "It's good to be shifty in a new country." In fact, we have a long line of con men in our literature, moving in and out of isolated societies, whose identities are anything but stable. How American novelists like to play with the dramatic possibilities of this type.

The doubtful modern notion, advanced by social psychologists like Erving Goffman, that identity is merely a function of the several roles that one must play in the social drama, is anticipated by the duke and the king in Twain's *Adventures of Huckleberry Finn*. Twain's frauds appear successively as the Dauphin and the Duke of Bridgewater, the Wilks Brothers, the actors Edmund Kean and David Garrick, Hugh Capet (King of France), the phrenologist Dr. Armand de Montalban, and a Reformed Pirate turned preacher. To ask who they really are is as pointless as asking who Huck is, for Huck is merely a transparent satirical device who is variously himself as well as George Jaxon, Tom Sawyer, and even a girl, Sarah Mary Williams—suggesting Clemens's interest in gender metamorphosis. Why not? Doesn't real life give us Dr. Renée Richards? That Clemens was obsessed with the metamorphosis of identity is proved by his taking on the pen names of Thomas Jefferson Snodgrass, Quintus Curtius Snodgrass, W. Epamonidas Adrastus Blab, and John Snooks before finally settling on "Mark Twain," the pseudonymous double identity that, according to his biographer Justin Kaplan, Clemens in fact "became" in old age.

So frequent are these devious American con men, with protean identities, that they constitute a special subgenre of our literature. Melville's *The Confidence Man* anticipated readerly objections to character fragmentation in his own work by observing that "if the acutest sage be often at his wits' ends to understand a living character, shall those who are not sages expect to run and read character in those mere phantoms which flit along a page, like shadows along a wall?" Metamorphic character transformation and disintegrated personality, as a literary device, Melville claimed to ground on the actualities of life: "no writer has produced such inconsistent characters as nature herself." In real life, he observed, "a consistent character is a *rara avis.*"

If the destruction of anything like stable character is one feature of the American novel, produced by the revolutionary pressure to make it new, it has an analogue in the presentation of physical deformity, of which it is the symbol. For, after all, did not Emerson observe in "The Poet" that "the soul makes the body, as the wise Spenser teaches"? And don't our novelists seem verily to believe that, as Emerson put it in *Nature*, "Every spirit builds itself a house." If so, they likewise believe that man is "the dwarf of himself." The persistence of this phenomenon has led William Van O'Connor asyntactically to observe in "The Grotesque: An American Genre," that "our literature is filled with the grotesque, more probably than any other Western literature." In any case, we have quite a gallery of physical freaks in our fiction—including the hunchback Chillingworth in *The Scarlet Letter*, the lightning-scarred and one-legged crazy old Ahab, the pockmarked Eleanor and birthmarked Georgiana in Hawthorne's tales, Poe's exophthalmic Ligeia and Berenice with her *sentient* teeth,

Melville's stutterer Billy Budd, Holmes's Elsie Venner of the serpentine neck, Hawthorne's stonyhearted Ethan Brand and Donatello with his pointed and furry ears, Twain's and John Barth's extraordinary Siamese twins, Melville's "grotesque negro cripple" in *The Confidence Man* who, "owing to something wrong about his legs, was in effect cut down to the stature of a Newfoundland dog," *Miss Lonelyhearts'* girl with no nose and Robert Stone's man with two noses in *A Hall of Mirrors*, Howells's one-armed Lindau, John Hawkes's one-eyed tuba-playing schoolteacher in *The Cannibal,* Henry James's stump-fingered Spencer Brydon in "The Jolly Corner" and the cross-eyed Mrs. Wix, in *What Maisie Knew*, whose "obliquity of vision" requires optical "straighteners."

IV

These physical deformities in the American novel are sometimes a manifestation of the takeover of humanity by the devil himself, who in Hawthorne's "Young Goodman Brown" announces that "Evil is the nature of mankind," a point of view seemingly congenial to many recent American authors. The devil importantly appears not only in Hawthorne but in Twain's *The Mysterious Stranger* and *Letters from the Earth,* Ambrose Bierce's *The Devil's Dictionary,* Flannery O'Connor's *The Violent Bear It Away,* John Hawkes's *The Cannibal,* Updike's *The Witches of Eastwick,* Alexander Theroux's *Darconville's Cat* and William Gaddis's *The Recognitions.* Wolfgang Kayser has argued in *The Grotesque in Art and Literature* that the invocation of the devil was historically intended to "subdue the demonic aspects of the world." But this presupposes a belief in both God and the devil. In most of our literature, however, God would appear to be dead, and the devil exists largely as a metaphor for the evil men do. Flannery O'Connor and John Hawkes, in fact, corresponded animatedly about the devil figures in their fiction. O'Connor, a Christian novelist, wasn't kidding, and had to my mind the last word. She wanted to be "certain that the devil gets identified as the devil and not simply taken for this or that psychological tendency":

> My Devil has a name, a history and a definite plan. His name is Lucifer, he's a fallen angel, his sin is pride, and his aim is the destruction of the Divine plan. Now I judge that your Devil is co-equal to God, not his creature; that pride is his virtue, not his sin; and that his aim is not to destroy the Divine plan because there isn't any Divine plan to destroy. My Devil is objective and yours is subjective.

With the exception of O'Connor, and perhaps Theroux, Updike, and Gaddis, the devil in most American fiction is subjective, a mere symbol of immoral human tendencies. But I can't think of another national literature so preoccupied with identifying the devil with man himself.

Baffled humanity used to ask, along with Job, why God *allowed* Satan to afflict suffering humanity. Surely he could have done a better job with creation. This irritation with the world as created, and with human life as it is, we can see in John Barth's remark that the trouble with God, viewed as a novelist, is that he is a realist: the idea that the world will always be as it is (France shaped like a teapot, Italy like a boot) "can get to you after a while." Hence Barth has reconstructed creation in a series of antirealistic novels projecting a world more to his own liking. He has even rewritten the Bible, as the Revised New Syllabus, in *Giles Goat-Boy*. (It appears to have won few adherents.)

When, however, we look at the imaginary worlds created by authors dissatisfied with the God-given, that is, with reality as such, and when we study the invented landscapes most expressive of this disappointed American sensibility, the invented worlds are anything but Edenic. (One exception may be the feminist Charlotte Perkins Gilman, who perpetrates a lost utopia without men in *Herland*, where the women, thank heaven, reproduce parthenogenetically. It is a popular book with the members of NOW.) But the *Inferno* is the major American model—not the *Purgatorio*; and, as to the *Paradiso*, forget it. Twain is typical of this type of American malcontent in having created for himself—in *What Is Man?* and *The Mysterious Stranger*—a cosmos populated by the "damned human race." Such a population must have a God, so Twain concocts a God who is in fact Satan, for he creates human life only to destroy it (inadvertently or for his pleasure), rationalizing his brutality by saying that he can always create anew. In *Letters from the Earth*, Twain's Little Satan describes God as possessed of "a wild nightmare of vengefulness," for he has "bankrupted his native ingenuities in inventing pains and miseries and humiliations and heartbreaks wherewith to embitter the brief lives of Adam's descendants." Humanity is contemptible to Little Satan because man "equips the Creator with every trait that goes to the making of a fiend, and then arrives at the conclusion that a fiend and a father are the same thing."

Although Wallace Stevens posited "the ultimate elegance" as "the imagined land," it seems fairly clear that American novelists have been hell-bent on creating inelegant infernos and in even outmatching the Deity in inventing pains and miseries for their characters.

Scan the antiworlds of Poe's so-called "Toledo" in "The Pit and the Pendulum," Twain's Camelot in *A Connecticut Yankee*, the world of Jack London's *The Scarlet Plague,* Hawkes's wandering Caribbean island in *Second Skin*, Barthelme's land of red snow where sex involves such "technical refinements" as "impalement," "dimidiation," and "quartering" ("Paraguay"), Burroughs's hallucinated world of *The Cities of the Red Night*, Nabokov's Antiterra and Demonia in *Ada*, Vonnegut's horrors in sci-fi novels like *The Sirens of Titan*, the "Europe" of Pynchon's *Gravity's Rainbow*—scan these invented worlds and it is clear that the older utopian aspiration for a better world, has dissolved into a landscape of dystopian nightmares.

Many of our older American obviously "invented worlds" attacked current social and economic conditions, which were viewed as unjust, unfair, or otherwise destructive to human well-being—for instance, Howells's *A Traveller from Altruria*, which features a world without money where all are economically equal. Such novels assume the inevitability of "progress" or "melioration" if only, say, the Socialists or the women get the power. Such notions may be cockeyed, but they do assume the rationality of the world.

But rationality is too great a constraint on the inventive American imagination; it is an obstacle to really making it new. Under the pressure to be original, a good many American novelists have preferred to imagine that the world itself is governed by insanity. Hence the paranoid idea of some vast conspiracy to destroy the individual: it animates Poe's "The Imp of the Perverse," Hawthorne's "Young Goodman Brown," Melville's *Moby-Dick*, Heller's *Catch-22,* Ken Kesey's *One Flew over the Cuckoo's Nest*, Robert Coover's *The Public Burning*, William Burroughs's *Naked Lunch*, and Thomas Pynchon's *The Crying of Lot 49*. No doubt these works push to a *reductio ad absurdum* Emerson's peculiar view, in "Self-Reliance," that society itself is "in conspiracy against the manhood of every one of its members." In any case, institutions are evil. As Richard Hofstadter has remarked in *The Paranoid Style in American Politics and Other Essays,*

> The distinguishing thing about the paranoid style is not that its exponents see conspiracies or plots here and there in history, but that they regard a "vast" or "gigantic" conspiracy as *the motive force* in historical events. History *is* a conspiracy, set in motion by demonic forces of almost transcendent power. . . . The paranoid spokesman sees the fate of this conspiracy in apocalyptic terms—he traffics in the birth and death of whole worlds, whole political orders, whole systems of human values.

V

It is but a small step from the view that life is a nightmare of insane horrors, set in motion by demonic conspiratorial forces, to the view that the world deserves annihilation. So depressed was Poe by life's incapacity to realize his ethereal idealist longings that in *Eureka* he posited a big-bang theory according to which the universe is now at the maximum point of its diffusion and thankfully is beginning to contract back into the original unity of God's oneness: *"In the Original Unity of the First Thing lies the Secondary Cause of All Things, with the Germ of their Inevitable Annihilation."* Unwilling to await events, however, Poe obliterated the universe himself in a fiery holocaust in "The Colloquy of Monos and Una" and "The Conversation of Eiros and Charmion." No matter: in "The Power of Words" Poe ascribes to the poet the ability to call another physical world, a better star, into being through language alone. I can't think of another national literature so given to the writer's substituting himself for the God of Annihilating Wrath. (One exception is Alexander Theroux, who in "Theroux Metaphrastes" defends "the God/Artist equation" as the means by which "the writer concelebrates creation" or "re-extend[s] the script of creation.")

The notion of Armageddon and the Apocalypse are as American as apple pie, and—deeply rooted as they are in Christian millennial thought—descend to us from the Bible and from Puritan works like Michael Wigglesworth's *The Day of Doom* and Jonathan Edwards's "Notes on the Apocalypse." For Christians, however, this awesome consummation of human history is purposeful and redemptive, the longed-for hope of resurrection and transfiguration. On the whole, however, this faith has evaporated from our fiction. So American novelists have been driven to the extreme of picturing the Apocalypse out of mere rage at human folly. Melville's annihilation of the *Pequod* in *Moby-Dick* and Twain's Battle of the Sand Belt in *The Connecticut Yankee* are local apocalypses of a sort that, like the Deity's wrath in the time of Noah, obliterate recently created evils in order to reinstate a *status quo ante*. But such partial measures can hardly satisfy an American imagination intent on testing the limits. Brooks Adams's *The Law of Civilization and Decay* and Henry Adams's *The Education of Henry Adams* are of a piece with Max Nordau's *Degeneration* and Spengler's *The Decline of the West* in announcing the end of the world, whether by bang or whimper, or at least the end of Western civilization, a pessimism that finds its way into *The Waste Land* of T. S. Eliot. This kind of nihilism reaches its apogee in

Thomas Pynchon's *Gravity's Rainbow* and Kurt Vonnegut's *Cat's Cradle,* where the world is fictively annihilated, Pynchon's by a nuclear firestorm, Vonnegut's by ice.

VI

It is the condition of the romantic imagination, as Emerson observes in "The Transcendentalist," continually to call for the "transfer of the world into the consciousness." For Emerson, the subjectivization of actuality merely confirmed an objective truth—"a rule of one art, or a law of one organization," that essential unity underlying all forms of existence. For most of the romantic American extremists I have discussed here, however, the incorporation of the world into consciousness is a desperate effort to resolve a now unintelligible world into a unity seemingly provided only by the imagination. Poe's solipsistic sense of the fragmentation of the world and his imaginative effort to reunify it is conceptually akin to the pluralistic universe of William James and Henry Adams, where, as *The Education* puts it, "Chaos was the law of nature; Order was the dream of man." The view that world order is a delusion or at best a human invention leads directly to the aestheticist self-preoccupation of these fictive heterocosms. In *The Necessary Angel,* Wallace Stevens best formulated the skepticism that emerges out of the loss of a sense of religious order in our time.

> The paramount relation . . . between modern man and modern art is simply this: that in an age in which disbelief is so profoundly prevalent, or, if not disbelief, indifference to questions of belief, poetry and painting, and the arts in general, are, in their measure, a compensation for what has been lost. Men feel that the imagination is the next greatest power to faith: the reigning prince. Consequently their interest in the imagination and its work is to be regarded not as a phase of humanism but as a vital self-assertion in a world in which nothing but the self remains, if that remains. So regarded, the study of the imagination and the study of reality come to appear to be purified, aggrandized, fateful.

For a time in this century it seemed as if the religion of art might very well substitute for a lost religious faith, that belief in the imagination might really assert itself "in a world in which nothing but the self remains, if that remains." At least for older modernist writers, art was some kind of compensation for lost certitude. Something of that modernist aestheticism survives into the postmodern imagination. But the limits of that gratification have already been tested and found wanting. Following the line of deconstructionists like Jacques Derrida, Paul de Man, and Jacques Lacan, who deny the capacity of language to refer to any reality, the novelist William Gass, in *Habitations of the Word*, is reduced to calling the novel "an intense interior, formed like a flower from within, and opening out only into absence." Very poetic, but not very helpful. If language is merely a rhetorical construct, what is the American novelist to do? Increasingly, the situation of the writer, driven to make it new, is a desperate one. The novelist Ronald Sukenick has put the matter rather poignantly in complaining that the American novelist now has to start from scratch:

> Reality doesn't exist, time doesn't exist, personality doesn't exist. God was the omniscient author, but he died; now no one knows the plot, and since our reality lacks the sanction of a creator, there's no guarantee as to the authenticity of the received version. Time is reduced to presence, the content of a series of discontinuous moments. Time is no longer purposive, and so there is no density, only chance. Reality is, simply, our experience, and objectivity is, of course, an illusion. Personality, after passing through a stage of awkward self-consciousness, has become . . . a mere locus for our experience. In view of these annihilations, it should be no surprise that literature, also, does not exist—how could it? There is only reading and writing . . . ways of maintaining a considered boredom in the face of the abyss.

Even so, the American writer's ordeal of pushing the imagination to its limits has produced—in writers like Melville and Poe, Barth and Barthelme, Nabokov, Gass, Hawkes, and the others—some striking and original fiction. It may not tell me much about America, or the America I inhabit, but it *is* intensely American. My own inclination is to see them through the eyes of Valéry, who once observed, in connection with Poe, that "The glory of man, and something more than his glory, is to waste his powers on the void."

A NOTE ON
"TRACKING THE AMERICAN NOVEL INTO THE VOID"

When the editors of The World and I *commissioned the essay above,[1] they were interested in the question of what is American about the American novel. At the same time, they also commissioned responses to my essay from several literary critics and novelists. Those replying to me included Denis Donoghue, David Reynolds, Kenneth S. Lynn, Josephine Hendin, Audrey Foote, Chilton Williamson, Jr., and Virgil Nemoianu. Each composed an essay of his own; the total length of the responses forbids reprinting them all here.[2] But I was invited to reply to them and did so in the remarks that follow. My reply, however brief, may serve to indicate some of their perceptions of (and objections to) the issues I have raised.*

Leave it to David Reynolds to remind me of a glaring omission. He is quite right to point out that the American romance rises not only out of European models but out of the native American subterranean literary currents in which our authors were immersed. His massive new study, *Beneath the American Renaissance*, is a treasure trove of popular, subliterary, and subversive elements that were reworked by our classic authors into memorable high art. I, for one, am glad to know about these hidden sources of *The Scarlet Letter* and *Moby-Dick*—especially the whaling story in *Uncle Sam*. But until Kenneth Lynn shows me manuscript evidence to the contrary, I'll still hold to George Stewart's altogether plausible argument that Melville's intention, while writing *Moby-Dick*, changed as the dark elements of Hawthorne, Shakespeare, and Dante coalesced in his imagination. Lynn is quite right, however, that "facts [in *Moby-Dick*] do not disappear" as Melville grows more symbolic; I never meant to suggest that they did. In fact, Melville quite consciously packed the

---

1 See "Tracking the American Novel into the Void," *The World & I: A Chronicle of Our Changing Era*, May 1989, pp. 450–468; 520–528.

2 See Denis Donoghue, "The Real and the Romantic in Literary Imagination" (pp. 468–478); David Reynolds, "Literary Lights from the Void" (pp. 478–490); Kenneth S. Lynn, "Realism and the American Novel" (pp. 490–496); Josephine Hendin, "The Literature of Negation" (pp. 496–502); Audrey Foote, "The Social Tradition and the American Novel" (pp. 502–508); Chilton Williamson, Jr., "Reassessing the Abnormality of American Literature" (pp. 508–516); and Virgil Nemoianu, "The Literature of Place," in *The World and I*, May 1989.

book, even overloaded it, with cetological data—all for a purpose:

> So ignorant are most landsmen of some of the plainest and most
> palpable wonders of the world, that without some hints touching the
> plain facts, historical and otherwise, of the [whale] fishery, they
> might scout at Moby Dick as a monstrous fable, or still worse and
> more detestable, a hideous and intolerable allegory.

Equally intolerable to me is the idea that American social life exhibits a bland, classless sameness. Denis Donoghue has questioned, if
not the social complexity of the American scene, at least its force for
American writers. I concur that it did not have much force for Hawthorne, and James thought that Europe could offer class variations in
greater abundance. But I still hold that American society has always
had a complexity adequate for the purposes of social fiction—as we
see in the novels of manners I have listed. Certainly we do not have a
titled aristocracy of wealth, birth, and breeding, founded on the
hereditary possession of landed estates providing extensive revenues
in rents, and enjoying an ornamental, leisurely existence both in the
country and town. But that is not to say that America did not, or
does not, have distinctive social groups—with parvenus and the established, or ethnic and other groups and individuals, vying for
power and prestige. All this is available to the interested novelist.
What else animates the conflict of *The Rise of Silas Lapham, Main
Street, The Age of Innocence, Portrait in Brownstone,* and so many other
novels of manners? But frankly, we don't like to talk about class in
America. It is one of our dirty little secrets.

James himself reluctantly *conceded* the American class structure in
Hawthorne (1879)—a book written in the "English Men of Letters"
series for a British audience—but only to deny it. Knowing little
enough about Hawthorne's life in Salem, he got all of his facts from
A Study of Hawthorne (1876) by George Parsons Lathrop, Hawthorne's son-in-law. Quoting Lathrop, James acknowledged "that
there existed at Salem, during the early part of Hawthorne's life, 'a
strong circle of wealthy families,' which 'maintained rigorously the
distinctions of class,' and whose 'entertainments were splendid, their
manners magnificent.'" But James panders to the superciliousness of
his British audience in saying that Lathrop's description of Salem
society was only "a rather pictorial way of saying that there were a
number of people in the place—the commercial and professional
aristocracy, as it were—who lived in high comfort and respectability,
and who, in their small provincial way, doubtless had pretensions to
be exclusive." Look at what Jane Austen could do with such material!

James's snobbishness, in any case, tends to deny the reality of the very social distinctions to which Lathrop had attested and which we see in Howells, Wharton, James himself, Auchincloss, Lewis, Marquand, and others. He was more to the point in observing of Hawthorne that, "thoroughly American in all ways, he was in none more so than in the vagueness of his sense of social distinctions, and his readiness to forget them if a moral or intellectual sensation were to be gained by it." James was at times ready to forget them himself, in favor of the more vivid social variations to be found in Europe, but *Washington Square, The Bostonians, The Europeans,* and *An International Episode* make plain that he really could not.

Why couldn't he? Why did he transpose to America, asks Professor Lynn, the *donnée* of *Washington Square*? As I sit here, typing this response in old Federalist Era brownstone on Washington Square, just a few doors down from the site where Henry James's family lived, as I compose this response in a high-ceilinged room with windows overlooking the park, a room very much like that in which I imagine James's Catherine Sloper to become resigned to her needlework, I am moved by Lynn's remark that American literature might be "more distinguished by cherished recollections of the real world" than by "the hideousness of its invented infernos."

But as to why James transposed the *donnée* of the English tale to Washington Square, I have a theory. When the Englishman Laurence Oliphant published his satirical novel *The Tender Recollections of Irene Macgillicuddy* in *Blackwood's*, James complained in an 1878 *Nation* review about Oliphant's claim that the chief feature of New York fashion was "the eagerness and energy displayed by marriageable maidens in what is vulgarly called 'hooking' a member of the English aristocracy." Oliphant's English novel encouraged him to believe that "it is possible, after all, to write tales of 'American society.'" But why, he asked,

> should it be left to the cold and unsympathetic stranger to deal with these things? Why does not native talent take them up—anticipate the sneers of foreign irony, take the wind from its sails and show us, with the force of real familiarity, both the good and the evil that are to be found in Fifth Avenue and Murray Hill? Are we then so dependent upon foreign labor that it must be left to the English to write even our "society stories"?

I submit that Catherine's story, as well as *An International Episode, The Europeans, The Portrait of a Lady*, and *The Bostonians*, reflects James's attempt to write the American society novel, especially in relation to calculated upward social mobility in marriage. Nationalistic pride, however ambivalent, had been stung. Professor Lynn also complains that the gallery of sensationalist writers I have tracked into the void—Hawkes, Barthelme, Burroughs, Pynchon, Vonnegut, Heller, Coover, and Barth—are literary "pygmies." I think he's quite right: *that's what they are*, God save us all. But aren't these just the writers who get the front-page reviews, the book awards, the TV talk-show invitations, the Guggenheims, and even tenure? They now represent an unignorable cultural fact of appalling implication, and are therefore a phenomenon worth our attention.

If I didn't sufficiently explain the fashionableness of these pygmies, I'll do so now. Simply put, we live in a decadent age. It is athirst for degraded and degrading sensations, and it pays well those who supply them. Poe was ahead of his time in realizing that sensationalist antirealism would always have a mass following, and he justified his tales by citing the public's love of "the ludicrous heightened into the grotesque: the fearful coloured into the horrible: the witty exaggerated into the burlesque: the singular wrought out into the strange and mystical."

But Lynn is quite right that something more sinister than mere sensationalism is at work in the antirealism of some of the contemporary writers I've mentioned: namely, a detestation of America—her capitalist economic structure, troubled internal and international relations, her history, social patterns, and racial relations. Particularly culpable is America's indifference to *soi disant* intellectuals who want to make over the world and our conservative immovability in the presence of the latest utopian schemes. These celebrity-writers are the creation of admen, agents, media types, and the bored professoriate, and the writers repay us with just the kind of nihilistic symbolic assaults that Lynn has cited. I have no quarrel with his view of the permanent worth of these novelists, may flies in a short summer. In fact, I'll go a bit further than Lynn. What really disturbs one about their wild fictional deviations from a world like our own is captured in Gerald Graff's unimpeachable account of "The Politics of Anti-Realism."

> The imagination's independence from reality exemplifies the human spirit's break with political oppression and psychic repression, with all preestablished ideas of reality. As Frank Kermode writes, echoing [Roland] Barthes, "the whole movement towards 'secretarial realism'" represents "an anachronistic myth of common understanding and shared universes of meaning." By refusing to hold a mirror

up to nature and by exploding the very idea of a stable "nature," art undermines the psychological and epistemological basis of the ruling order. The revolt against realism and representation is closely tied to the revolt against a unitary psychology of the self. As Leo Bersani argues in *A Future of Astyanax*, "the literary myth of a rigidly ordered self," a myth perpetuated by realism, "contributes to a pervasive cultural ideology of the self which serves the established social order."

Of course the "political oppression" and "psychic repression" writers claim to feel is delusional. And Irving, Wilder, and Saul Bellow, as Virgil Nemoianu and Denis Donoghue suggest, may give us a kind of consolation in the present circumstance. But we must not, Donoghue implies, be too censorious. If the romance form "gives privilege to one's desires, fears, and visions," we ought to give the writer his *donnée*, even if it fails "to endorse the sense of reality we have acquired." I have no objection to this Jamesian principle, and will resist the state's censorship. But I reserve the citizen's right to be censorious, to speak my mind about the manifest virtues of the established social order in America and my doubts about the fiction writers who seem to have something worse (or nothing else) very clearly in mind. I carry the Jamesian principle forward against them, asking whether their novels were, after all, worth doing, and answering for myself, "Not really." In their freedom I recall them, that is, to a nobler purpose.

Louis Auchincloss:
The Image of Lost
Elegance and
Virtue

The simplest truths are the most consoling:
one of them is that New York will always have
a past, together with writers consumed with
nostalgia for lost days. Henry James and Mrs.
Wharton—even Washington Irving—looked
back at things that were gone, and we have become accustomed to look back at these writers
who are also gone, in this way obtaining a
doubled effect of remoteness, looking down a
corridor of mirrors endlessly reflecting the
image of lost elegance and virtue. The past,
however, need not be distant nor the authors
dead.
                              —Gouverneur Paulding

Louis Auchincloss resembles Henry James in the emphasis he
gives to the moral issues that grow out of the social lives of
the very rich in New York City. And because he once described himself as a "Jacobite," reviewers long ago concluded that it is enough to
describe him as an imitator of the Master. He most differs from
James, though, in the informed analysis he is able to give to the
complex problems of ethics in the legal profession—a command of

the world of Wall Street brokers and bankers which James himself sorely regretted not having. Auchincloss called himself a Jacobite because so much of his youthful reading was "over the shoulder of Henry James." To read the fiction of Proust, Trollope, Meredith, Thackeray, George Eliot, and Mrs. Wharton in the light of the criticism, fiction, and letters of James, Auchincloss observed, is to be exposed to the full range of possibility for the novel of manners," to be conducted through the literature of [James's] time, English, American, French and Russian, by a kindly guide of infinitely good manners, who is also infinitely discerning, tasteful and conscientious." James, for Auchincloss, has always been a "starting point," a "common denominator."[1] But, once started, Auchincloss has always gone his own way—often qualifying and contesting, as well as defining and enlarging, the social insights of the nineteenth-century novelist of manners.

Since a brief account of his long and distinguished career as writer, lawyer, and teacher may be helpful in the following analysis, these facts may be given. Louis Stanton Auchincloss was born in Lawrence, New York, in 1917 and was brought up in New York City. His family was wealthy and large—full of innumerable cousins, uncles, aunts, and in-laws. As a boy he spent his summers at Bar Harbor and on Long Island. Later he went to Groton and Yale, where he was Phi Beta Kappa and editor of the *Yale Literary Magazine*.

After three years in New Haven, he left Yale and entered the University of Virginia at Charlottesville, where he took a law degree in 1941. During World War II he spent four years at sea, where he had ample time to read the great novelists of manners and to serve his own apprenticeship as a writer. After the war he returned to New York City and practiced estate law until he retired from the Wall Street firm of Hawkins, Delafield, and Wood in 1986. Despite his devotion to his wife Adèle and their children, and despite the years devoted to client trusts and wills, as well as to city commissions, charities, and municipal offices (he was for some time president of the Museum of the City of New York), Auchincloss has nevertheless published (thus far) nearly forty volumes of fiction and nearly twenty volumes of literary criticism, history, biography, autobiography, and social history. Among his many novels are *The Indifferent Children* (1947), *Sybil* (1952), *A Law for the Lion* (1953), *The Great World and Timothy Colt* (1956), *Venus in Sparta* (1958), *The Pursuit of the Prodigal*

---

1 Louis Auchincloss, *Reflections of a Jacobite* (Boston: Houghton Mifflin, 1961), pp. vii–viii. Hereafter, quotations from this volume will be cited as *RJ*, in parentheses, in the text.

(1959), *The House of Five Talents* (1960), *Portrait in Brownstone* (1962), *The Rector of Justin* (1964), *The Embezzler* (1965), *The House of the Prophet* (1980), *The Golden Calves* (1988), *Fellow Passengers* (1989), and that beautifully dedicated novel *The Book Class* (1984).

He has also produced a great many volumes of short stories — *The Injustice Collectors* (1950), *Skinny Island* (1981), *Narcissa and Other Fables* (1983), *False Gods* (1992), *Tales of Yesteryear* (1994), and *The Atonement and Other Stories* (1997) among them — and a great many studies in literary criticism like *Reflections of a Jacobite* (1961), *Pioneers and Caretakers* (1965), and *Edith Wharton: A Woman in Her Time* (1971). As if a long career in writing and another career in the law were not enough, the indefatigable Auchincloss, after his retirement from Wall Street, commenced a third career. Between 1992 and 1996 he was a member of the faculty of New York University, where, to great acclaim and with consummate poise, he taught English and American literature to both graduates and undergraduates. Quite naturally, he lectured on the great historians of manners — James, Proust, Wharton, and Adams; but his program also included Shakespeare and the Jacobean playwrights.[2]

It may seem mechanical merely to have listed above so many of Louis Auchincloss's novel and short-story titles. But although I have not listed them all, this sampling is justified, I think, as a way of suggesting the remarkable imaginative reach of this accomplished writer. In fact, he is, as Susan Cheever has recently observed, "one of the best writers alive."[3] And that being the case, it behooves anyone interested in the literary art in America to get to know some of the books he has produced.

The world brought to life in the novels of Louis Auchincloss is the nineteenth- and twentieth-century life of the metropolitan rich in New York City, particularly the lives of the lawyers, bankers, trust officers, corporation executives, and their wives and daughters. As a lawyer, Auchincloss knows them in their Park Avenue apartments and in their Wall Street offices. He sees the glitter and glamour of their world, its arrogant materialism and its unexpected generosities. He knows the rigidity of its conventions — just how far they can be bent, at what point they break, just when convention may break a

---

2 For a remarkable introduction to Auchincloss's early life and literary apprenticeship, see his autobiography, *A Writer's Capital* (Minneapolis: University of Minnesota Press, 1974); Carol W. Gelderman's biography *Louis Auchincloss: A Writer's Life* (New York: Crown, 1993), extends coverage of the writer's life into the early 1990s.

3 Susan Cheever, "The Most Underrated Writer in America," *Vanity Fair* (October 1985), p. 105.

character. He understands what happens to the idealistic men and the unfulfilled women of this world. And he is able to tell their stories with unusual sympathy. Rarely has Auchincloss ventured from this small but exclusive world, because it is the world he knows best. For this "narrowness" he has been criticized. But if he does not write panoramic novels of the U.S.A., great fluid puddings encompassing the whole of the American scene, it is because he has learned from Henry James the lesson James tried to teach Mrs. Wharton: that she *must* be "tethered in native pastures, even if it reduces her to a back-yard in New York."[4] The New York *haut monde* is, as it were, Louis Auchincloss's backyard.

II

Not all of his novels are novels of manners—he is fascinated by the unexhausted possibilities of the novel of character—but most of them hinge upon the imperatives of private morality in a world where so-cial morality no longer, apparently, exists. In many of these books Auchincloss explores the ambiguities of selfhood, affirming, finally, the freedom and autonomy of the human personality. Most novelists of manners, profoundly influenced by the behaviorism of the natur-alistic sciences (Wharton, Wells, Bennett, O'Hara, Marquand, for ex-ample), tend to believe that the personality is thoroughly condi-tioned by the material environment. They create character, as Vir-ginia Woolf objected, in very close correlation to, and through descriptions of, houses, clothes, furniture, and the like. Auchincloss rejects this approach to characterization. For him, "character" or per-sonality exists independent of the web of the material environment that surrounds it. As Ida Trask Hartley observes in *Portrait in Brownstone,* in describing the narrow grey limestone façade of Mr. Robbins's house—with its "grinning lions' heads and balconies for flowerpots supported by squatting ladies, and topped with a giant dormer studded with bull's-eye windows": "Nobody passing it today would believe that it had not been built by the most pushing par-venu. Yet I know how little the houses of that era sometimes ex-pressed the souls of their occupants."[5]

In *A Law for the Lion* Eloise Dilworth wants to find out whether there is any real "identity" beneath the various roles she has played during her lifetime—the childish niece to her aunt and uncle, the

---

4 *The Letters of Henry James,* ed. Percy Lubbock (New York: Scribner's, 1920), I, 396.
5 Louis Auchincloss, *Portrait in Brownstone* (Boston: Houghton Mifflin, 1962), p. 76. Hereafter, citations from this book will be given as *PB,* in parentheses, in the text.

submissive wife to her indifferent husband, the taken-for-granted mother to her children. Her search for an answer leads her to reject the arbitrary manners and conventions of the social world she has been brought up in. But her losses are more than compensated for by her discovery that there is a real "self" beneath the functions imposed on her by her social existence. This kind of "Who am I?" theme is also developed in *Sybil, Portrait in Brownstone*, and *The House of Five Talents*. A variation on it is the "Who is he?" theme developed in *The Rector of Justin*. In this novel Frank Prescott, recently deceased headmaster of a preparatory school, is recreated through the differing recollections and impressions of several characters—the priggish young admirer, the irreverent daughter, the wife, the friends, the students and alumni. What the novel suggests is that we can never know what Prescott was really like because none of the narrators knew the real Prescott—he presented a different side to each of them. It might well be asked whether there was any "real" Prescott behind his various masks. The answer is yes, but we can never know him except as a composite of the limited points of view of his various biographers. Auchincloss's dramatic technique in this "conventional novel of character" creates a built-in ambiguity comparable to that of James's *The Awkward Age* or, for that matter, to Faulkner's *Absalom, Absalom!*

Auchincloss's preoccupation with identity in fiction is based, I believe, on the question of the relation of objects and institutions in the material world to the soul, the inner spirit of the individual, or to consciousness itself. These matters find a definitive formulation in the question posed by James, in a conversation between Isabel Archer and Madame Merle in *The Portrait of a Lady*, about the "shell of circumstances" and the irreducible self. "What shall we call our 'self?'" Madame Merle asks Isabel.

> Where does it begin? Where does it end? It overflows into everything that belongs to us—and then it flows back again. I know a large part of myself is in the clothes I choose to wear. I've a great respect for *things!* One's self—for other people—is one's expression of one's self; and one's house, one's furniture, one's garments, the books one reads, the company one keeps—these things are all expressive.[6]

Isabel denies the importance of things, the shell, but James's pain-

---

6 Henry James, *The Portrait of a Lady*, ed. Leon Edel (Boston: Houghton Mifflin, 1963), pp. 172–173.

terly technique, as Isabel's portrait takes form before us, suggests that Madame Merle's is the sounder view. Isabel's naïve New England transcendental sense of the self as standing apart from circumstances leads her only to anguish and unhappiness. Auchincloss seems to reject the behaviorism of Madame Merle; nor, apparently, does he agree with Mrs. Wharton, who observed that the bounds of personality are not reproducible by a sharp black line, but that each of us flows imperceptibly into adjacent people and things." [7] The personality of the Rector of Justin is never adequately expressed by the impressions of others, just as the irreducible "I" of Eloise Dilworth is never fully expressed by her furniture or the sum of her functions.

But to make this point is to oversimplify what is in fact a complex problem for Auchincloss as a creator of character. For in some of his novels he is at great pains to show that the world (with its misimpressions) and time (with its alteration of phenomena) do impinge on the self which, *for other people,* expresses itself through its various roles. For Eloise, for Timothy Colt, for Sybil Hilliard, Ida Hartley, and Augusta Millinder, the triumph of the personality over the roles imposed by the external world makes for a kind of limited victory of the self. But Auchincloss's world has its darker depths, and his novels by no means always end in moral triumphs. For Geraldine Brevoort in *Portrait in Brownstone,* for Michael Farrish in *Venus in Sparta,* and for Guy Prime in *The Embezzler,* the world is an arena of ever more burdensome responsibilities arising out of the illusory importance of caste and class. For each, society offers only one role, complete with props—a role he cannot play.

Michael Farrish, for example, is brought up to satisfy the social expectations of his mother. A Farrish leads a certain kind of life. So Michael is sent off to Averhill prep school, then to Harvard; he is taken into the Hudson River Trust Company; eventually he becomes a partner. He is slated to become director and chairman—all of this because it is expected of him: he is, after all, a Farrish. But Michael Farrish is emotionally unequipped for the role society has fashioned for him. He has no psychological armor against the arrows of the bitch goddess success and the socially created myth of what constitutes manhood. And when a crisis occurs in his professional life and his marriage goes on the rocks, he tries to escape his social role by running away to Mexico.

The figure of the child fearing and expecting punishment for some failure to live up to the expectations of the adult world is a

---

7 Edith Wharton, *The Writing of Fiction* (New York: Scribner's, 1925), pp. 6–7.

recurrent image in Auchincloss's fiction. Frequently he welcomes punishment as a relief—such is the burden of his guilt at not success-fully playing his role. And if punishment does not come, he often seeks the relief of guilt through some suicidal or self-destructive act. Timothy Colt punishes himself, for abandoning his idealism, by courting his own professional destruction: he openly confesses a misprision that could never have been proved against him. Guy Prime invites the governmental inquiry into the stock exchange which leads to his own imprisonment. Geraldine Brevoort jumps from an eighth-story hotel-room window. And Michael Farrish ends by drowning himself in the ocean. Such is the toll exacted, for lost virtue, of some of the characters of Auchincloss's fiction. It is not a tragic cost. None of his characters is of tragic importance. In fact, Auchincloss himself has conceded that "pathos has a bigger place than tragedy in the study of manners" (*RJ*, 144). But it is a poignant cost to which, in the subtlety and insight of Auchincloss's character-ization, this summary does inadequate justice.

III

The House of Five Talents (1960) and *Portrait in Brownstone* (1962), two of Auchincloss's best early novels of manners, are set in New York City. Both deal with rich and aristocratic families during a period of several generations. Both portray the emergence of a woman as matriarch of the tribe (although one is an old maid). And both offer a bittersweet portrait of the image of lost elegance and virtue. Opening at the death of Queen Victoria, *Portrait* focuses on the Denisons of Fifty-third Street from the turn of the century into the 1950s. Full of rich and illuminating flashbacks, the novel is a social history of the brownstone era told from the point of view of Ida Trask Hartley, a passive and obedient child who matures into the leader of a large and refractory family. Auchincloss's narration of how she comes to manipulate, in her passive way, the children and grandchildren, the cousins and uncles and aunts of the tribe, is a truly impressive achievement—based, very probably, on the character of Martha Little in Edith Wharton's "Duration" (published in *The World Over* [1936]). Ida's emergence as the dominant force for unity, in a family disin-tegrating from external and internal pressures, is accompanied by a perceptive study of the changing manners and morals of the American aristocracy in New York City. All shades of changing sexual behavior, for example, are reflected in the lives of Ida and her family. Ida has her first chaste kiss (the seal of her engagement) in the Egyptian Room of the Metropolitan Museum in 1911. One of the few meeting places for unchaperoned couples in her youth, this museum setting serves a symbolic function comparable to the setting for Newland Archer and Ellen Olenska's last interview in Wharton's *The Age of Innocence*—the room of Cesnola archaeological antiquities. That the manners and mores of Ida's youth have become antiquated archaeological curiosities by the 1950s is indicated by Ida's advising her daughter to try going to bed with her boyfriend before she decides whether or not to marry him. Dorcas, of course, takes her mother's advice. Such is the transition between the age of Victoria and the age of Dr. Kinsey. Auchincloss's sense of the effect of time on the conventions and attitudes that affect people's behavior has been shaped, I believe, by Mrs. Wharton's studies of Old New York. He knows, as she and Proust knew, that any society "will apply all known standards together or individually, or in any combination needed to include a maverick who happens to please or to exclude an otherwise acceptable person who happens not to." And he knows that society people are not the least conscious of their inconsistency and that arbitrariness is the mark of their values. He also knows that society is "not aware of changing its standards, for it has no memory except for its own acts of condemnation, and for these only so far as the individual condemned is concerned" (*RJ*, 107–108, 110).

One of embezzler Guy Prime's greatest resentments is that it would do him no good to return to New York, after paying his debt to society, because its mind is made up: "The late Mrs. Edith Wharton, who was a childhood friend of my mother's," Guy Prime tells us, "wrote a very apt little story on this subject called 'Autres Temps.' It deals with a wife who is cast out of New York society for eloping with her lover and who comes back, a generation later, to find that the doors of her erstwhile friends, who have accepted the same conduct in her own daughter, are still closed to her. The world," Prime concludes, "is too busy to revise old judgments."[8] Granville Hicks once suggested that Auchincloss writes as if Proust had never written.[9] But this irrationality in society—that the world is too busy to revise old judgments—is one of Proust's major themes. Auchincloss has, in fact, learned a great deal from Proust as well as from Mrs.

---

8 Louis Auchincloss, *The Embezzler* (Boston: Houghton Mifflin, 1965), p. 6. Hereafter, quotations from this work will be cited as *E*, in parentheses, in the text. It is worth pointing out that Mrs. Wharton's *The Mother's Recompense* also treats this irrational "autres temps" attitude of old New York society.

9 Granville Hicks, "A Bad Legend in His Lifetime," *Saturday Review*, 49 (February 5, 1966), 6.

Wharton: Prime goes off to Panama when he gets out of jail.

Portrait in Brownstone is also an *ubi sunt* lament for a New York image of lost elegance and virtue, for an older New York now accessible only in King's *Notable New Yorkers,* in old letters rescued from Newport attics, and in the memories of those who knew the face of New York before it began to change so rapidly. But it is not a New York that anyone, particularly Auchincloss, wishes to bring back. In a passage that might have come from Mrs. Wharton's *A Backward Glance,* Ida reflects:

> As for the past where Derrick had first proposed to her, that quiet brownstone past, with its fussiness and its quibbling and its love, how was it possible to bring *that* back? And why, really, should she want to? Was it not better to forget it altogether with its emotional tangle of stultifying family duties. Had it not forgotten itself? Where were the Denisons of Fifty-third Street, she wondered as she came out to the sunlight through Aunt Dagmar's heavy grilled doors. Uncle Philip's house at the corner was gone. A jewelry store occupied its site. Uncle Willie's had made way for a parking lot, and her father's was a nightclub, or perhaps worse. Everything in New York reminded one of the prevalent dust to which, almost immediately, it seemed, one was condemned to return. If one didn't seize the day, a contractor would (*PB,* 243).

Such are the ravages of time on these old New York families that, at the end of *The Embezzler,* the Prime house is torn down to make room for a commuter parkway.

IV

The House of Five Talents recounts the rise of an American middle-class family from parvenu origin to aristocratic status during the period 1875–1948. It is the story of the five Millinder children, who descend from one of the most ruthless robber barons of the age of Grant, a tale of their fortune, and of what became of it. In chronicling the story of the Millinder money, Auchincloss addresses himself to what he believes are some prevalent misconceptions about the relationship between wealth and American society. In the first place, although social mobility nowadays is "a clanging escalator," Auchincloss does not hold with the old chestnut that it takes only three generations from shirtsleeves to shirtsleeves. At the end of the novel, the twelve living grandchildren of old Julius Millinder have all multiplied their talents. All are rich. As Oswald, the family Communist, complains: "Why, they're spread all over the globe! I figure that it takes no less than a thousand human souls to wait on the old pirate's progeny!"[10] Another myth Auchincloss deflates is the belief that the rich really *are* different from you and me. Fitzgerald, O'Hara, and Marquand all wrote stories with that thesis. But for Auchincloss, as for Hemingway, this is a middle-class illusion: quantity of money does not, for him, qualitatively affect our essential humanity. For Auchincloss, men are pretty much the same, however much money they may have. A fortune may permit a choice of masks to don before the world, but little else. "There has always been the theory, embraced alike by Tory and Red," Augusta Millinder reflects, "that there is something actually different about the rich. But I wonder if this theory still exists." Her opinion is that the Millinders had about as much talent and beauty and capacity for life among them as most families. But none of them as individuals particularly excelled at anything: "None of us would really have stood out from the crowd without the money" (*HFT,* 10–11).

Told from Augusta's point of view, *The House of Five Talents* is a series of episodes illustrating the poignant effect of the money on the members of the family. Gussie believes that money is intended to help people over their difficulties. And she summons her own huge fortune to rescue many of her relatives. But most often her good intentions end in disaster, the novel illustrating the triumph of money over love, compassion, affection, and honor. The failure of Gussie's engagement to Lancey Bell, the murderous rivalry between her mother Eliza and Aunt Daisy in the Victorian social game, Lucius Hoyt's ruthless victory in business over his equally ruthless but incompetent father, the human failures of Ione and Lydig, the defalcation of Collier Haven, and Oswald's retreat into communism—all of these episodes illustrate the triumph of the power of money over a group of people who, Gussie insists, were at all times "simple, ordinary people, pursuing simple, ordinary tasks, who stood out from the crowd only in the imagination of those observers who fancied from reading the evening papers that tiaras and opera boxes made an organic difference. Perhaps that is my ultimate discovery of what the money meant," she concludes, "that it meant nothing at all, or, at any rate, very little" (*HFT,* 368).

At the same time, *The House of Five Talents* is the comedy of an old maid who never married because she feared that her one suitor

---

10 Louis Auchincloss, *The House of Five Talents* (Boston: Houghton Mifflin, 1960), p. 133. Quotations from this work will hereafter be cited as *HFT*, in parentheses, in the text.

wanted only her money. A silly girl who grows up reading Ouida and Marie Corelli (hidden behind the wrappers of Henry James novels), Gussie Millinder thinks of life largely in terms of the romantic fiction she has read. When Lancey Bell begins to court her sister Cora, Gussie reflects: "It was a traditional part of the picture that the beau should treat the gawky young sister with an affectation of gallantry and that she should fall in love with him, and Lancey and I were faithful to our roles" (*HFT,* 48). Later, when her sister Cora marries a foreign aristocrat and Lancey proposes to *her,* Gussie assumes that he is the fortune hunter of romantic fiction, and she foolishly rejects him. But Gussie matures as she grows older. One of her enlarging perceptions is that people react to others largely in terms of stereotypes and that these stereotypes can be not merely lived with but even exploited. In her thirties she resents the fact that she is becoming an old maid because she dislikes the dry implications of the stereotype—implications brilliantly studied, incidentally, in Edith Wharton's *Old New York: The Old Maid (The 'Fifties)* (1924). But Lucius Hoyt urges Gussie not to be afraid of labels and stereotypes, not to fear to be an old maid. Ione also urges Gussie to give up her fear that people are interested in her only for her money: "We're all bits and pieces of our background, our tastes, our inheritances, even our clothes," she says in a passage reminiscent of Madame Merle's theory. "It's only natural for people to be curious because you're a Millinder and live in a big house. It's up to you to turn that curiosity into something better!" Ione teaches her that

> the role of an old maid could be a far bigger one than I had ever imagined, that an old maid could reach the young because she was neutral in the conflict between generations and because she was the priestess at the shrine of tradition. An old maid, at least a rich one, could wear big jewelry and drive around in an antique town car and wear fussy clothes out of fashion and weep at the opera and threaten naughty street urchins with her stick; she could join the boards of clubs and charities and be as officious and bossy as she liked; she could insist on giving the family party on Christmas Eve; she could even, in her new, shrewd, noisy way, become the head of the remnants of the Millinders.

In other words, she could become, for the whole extended family, the wonderful person she yearned to be. She could accept her situation and turn it to theatrical effect and secure the love she sought. "Be a great old maid!" Lucius Hoyt urges her. "Be a magnificent old maid! It was the simplest idea in the world," Gussie concedes, "yet it changed my life" (*HFT,* 216–217, 141).

In becoming an indomitable old maid, Gussie discovers that people are only too happy to treat her with the respect that such a conception of herself requires. "Civilized life is a fancy-dress party," she reflects, "and everyone is encouraged to don a costume. It makes for color to have queens and cardinals about, and for enough color nobody minds doffing a hat. The illusion is created as much by him who performs the reverence as to whom it is made. Both, after all, are members of the same cast" (*HFT,* 267). Gussie's props are the pearl choker, the antiquated car, the faithful servants, the opera box, the rigid punctuality, and the respectful visits of submissive relatives. She *stages* a dramatic performance.

Old Aunt Daisy, a genuine relic from Newport days, really thinks it is still possible to live Augusta Millinder's role. Daisy will not talk on the telephone, go into a department store, attend the movies or tolerate smoking, drinking, Democrats, short skirts, traffic, or taxes. She believes herself to be the incarnation of social standards formed in the days of *the* Mrs. Astor, and she is not about to abandon them because of the changing times. In fact, she intends to defend them against the modernist assault. Thus on opening night at the opera, when Gussie wishes to avoid publicity and suggests going in by a side door, Aunt Daisy refuses and insists on going in through the front foyer; it is what society expects of her:

> "Thank God, I can still do my duty!" was her indignant rejoinder as she and I descended from the tall old green Rolls-Royce, like two big dolled up, gaudy bugs, and made our slow way through the crowd of cameramen, our evening bags held resolutely up to cover our faces. The men shouted familiar but friendly greetings to Aunt Daisy like "Go it, old girl!" and I was sure that behind her pursed lips and forward-looking stare her heart was beating with a fierce pride at so fitting a Nunc Dimittis (*HFT,* 214).

What saves Augusta Millinder from ridicule is that she is conscious of the wonderful comedy inherent in living (as Aunt Daisy does) or playing (as she does) such arbitrary roles. Gussie never lets herself forget that hers is a role performed largely to satisfy other people's need for illusions. It is also an act by which she softens the hard reality of her own life—the fact, for example, that she had only one proposal, never married, and was never loved by a man, as she believed, wholly for herself. But she has the wisdom to recognize that happiness may consist in electing the role other people have cast her in. In accepting the obligation to dramatize the role, Augusta becomes, indeed, a magnificent human being.

Auchincloss has always maintained that "the paralyzing effect of a class-conscious background is largely illusory." Nowadays people are "not as preoccupied with their exact social niche as writers like [John] O'Hara, for example, suggest." Consequently, the novelist of manners may invest his form with a new dimension of psychology by showing that the function of a character's background "may be only his misconception of it. . ." (*RJ*, 147–148). Certainly this is the case with the twentieth-century Auchincloss protagonist. The real cause of his hang-up is likely to be psychological, not social, pressure. The conventions of aristocratic caste are entirely a thing of the past, as Auchincloss understands them, but if a man's self-image obliges him to behave as if the obligations of caste are changeless and inflexible, he can do no other. This, according to Angelica, is Guy Prime's problem: he still believes in the old myth of the splendor of the Prime family. "Guy saw his family as the readers of tabloids saw them, in tiaras and opera boxes. Like many people in the social world he preferred the account of a party in a gossip column to his own recollection of it" (*E*, 228). According to Angelica, the Primes were not a distinguished family. But such is Guy's enslavement to this obsolete myth of their caste importance that his conduct is almost wholly determined by it. Thus the twentieth-century novel of manners may shift its center from the objective to the subjective, from society to psychology: manners become the gestures by which characters, believing in the reality of their own theatrical self-presentation, frustrate and finally destroy themselves. One of the delights of Augusta Millinder is that she has no illusions about herself or about the supposed "authority" of her class or the "obligations" imposed upon her by it. Her sanity is reflected in a recognition that her role is both a charade *and* an anachronism; she caps her act, this old fossil, by bequeathing her fortune to an archaeological institute.

V

In cultural criticism with a political slant there used to be objections to the kind of people Auchincloss writes about. It was sometimes said, for example, that the world of New York society people is somehow not as interesting as that of sharecroppers, boxers, or big-game hunters. Granville Hicks once confessed this bias in remarking that "to many people, myself included, an Italian boy who robs a poor Jew is a more challenging subject than an upper-class New Yorker who misappropriates funds, and a bewildered intellectual in search of wholeness of spirit belongs more truly to our times than the aged headmaster of a fashionable preparatory school."[11]

But there is no necessary reason why this should be true. Are *The Assistant* and *Herzog* better novels than *The Embezzler* and *The Rector of Justin*? If we suppose they are, that can have nothing to do with the subject matter or the transient "relevance" of these books to momentary ethnic or multicultural interests. If they are superior, that can only be a reflection of superior fictional art. In justifying the attention Auchincloss gives to people like Guy Prime, Augusta Millinder, Ida Trask, and Frank Prescott, I find it instructive to remember what he has to say about the universality of Tolstoy's art: "What he understands is that if a human being is described completely, his class makes little difference. He becomes a human being on the printed page, and other humans, of whatever class, can recognize themselves in his portrait. The lesson of Tolstoy is precisely how little of life, not how much, the artist needs" (*RJ*, 163).

His view of Proust also casts light on Auchincloss's choice of subject. In arguing that "there has never been so brilliant or so comprehensive a study of the social world" as that found in Proust, Auchincloss observes:

> To him the differences between class and class are superficial. Snobbishness reigns on all levels, so why does it matter which level one selects to study? Why not, indeed, pick the highest level, particularly if one's own snobbishness is thus gratified? Society in Proust parades before us, having to represent not a segment of mankind, but something closer to mankind itself. It is the very boldness of Proust's assumption that his universe is *the* universe . . . that gives to his distorted picture a certain universal validity. It is his faith that a sufficiently careful study of each part will reveal the whole, that the analysis of a dinner party can be as illuminating as the analysis of a war. It is his glory that he very nearly convinces us (*RJ*, 111).

Without drawing the parallel too closely, I submit that Auchincloss too sees that the differences between these so-called "classes" really are superficial and that there is therefore no adequate reason why one should not deal with headmasters and lawyers, bankers and brokers, if they permit the kind of social analysis that illuminates our essential human predicament. The problem implicit in his choice is that of making us believe that this universe is—if not *the* universe—at least a *believable* universe, and describing his characters so fully and convinc-

---

11 Hicks, pp. 35–36.

ingly that we do not care about the class they belong to. It is Auchincloss's difficulty that, as vivid as some of his novels are, he does not always so convince us. But that is a matter of imaginative recreation, not of fictive material.

It is, in fact, a mistake to think about Auchincloss's characters as belonging to a distinct "class." He does not believe that the United States is a classless society. But he does recognize that it is not possible for the contemporary American novelist of manners to write the kind of social fiction produced by Howells, Wharton, and James. The increasing democratization of the United States, he argues in *Reflections of a Jacobite,* has resulted in a rearrangement of social attitudes, so that today "snobbishness is more between groups than classes, more between cliques than between rich and poor. Surely there is a difference," he remarks, between the feelings of the man who has not been asked to dinner and those of the man who has been thrown down the front stairs" (*RJ,* 148–149).

Most of these groups, however (labor-capital, East-West, North-South, young-old, workers-intelligentsia), do not provide much social conflict for the would-be novelist of manners. "It is my simple thesis," Auchincloss has argued,

> that the failure more generally to produce this kind of novel is not attributable to the decadence or escapism of mid-twentieth century writers, but rather to the increasingly classless nature of our society which does not lend itself to this kind of delineation. I do not mean that we are any duller than the Victorians, but simply that the most exciting and significant aspects of our civilization are no longer to be found in the distance and hostility between the social strata (*RJ,* 142).

And surely if we take the long view, and look at the midcentury radical critics once so dismissive of Auchincloss's fiction, we see that they have much more in common with him than one would have supposed thirty years ago. (I refer to the spectacle of the old-time leftists [the Alfred Kazins and Irving Howes] who, after rising in the socioeconomic scale and in celebrity, thereafter lunched with him at the Century Club, traveled abroad with Auchincloss on State Department junkets, and appeared with him on television talk shows.) In any case, Auchincloss has increasingly turned away from society as such toward the inward world of his characters in order to explore why, in this classless society, people hang onto their snobbishness in the ways they do.

The divided career of Louis Auchincloss as lawyer-novelist and his indifference to sociological explanations of evil have led other critics to attack his social and moral criticism as fakery and to claim that he is captivated by the very social prejudices that are his subject. Robert M. Adams, for example, has ridiculed Auchincloss for writing, like a latter-day Trollope, "a pseudo-critique of commercialism which collapses docilely as soon as one perceives it is being launched from a platform provided by commercialism itself." [12] And Brooke Allen, for another, has remarked that "Auchincloss is a little in love with his own milieu. He is not a traitor to his class, as some have claimed; he is an astute and observant member of it. The fact that it is dying only deepens his affection, and his warmth toward his subject has an unfortunate tendency to turn to sentiment." [13]

These assumptions require interrogation. First, all writers write from a platform provided by some kind and degree of economic security. If their economic security is not derived from inherited wealth, it comes from a commercialism of some kind—from a job, from book royalties, honoraria, speaking fees, or commissions. It is folly to think that writers on the left are somehow free of commerce or acquisitiveness and therefore morally pure because of their politics. The Communist writer Mike Gold was as much a free-lance entrepreneur as any venture capitalist. The Christian critique of commercialism, moreover, was launched well before Marx was ever heard of.

Second, the "class" of wealthy and powerful families that Auchincloss has written about is not dying. It still controls great wealth, preserves its status in schools like Groton, Harvard, and Yale; it manages powerful institutions in commerce, government, and the arts; and it discloses itself through distinctive styles in speech, dress, and deportment. Since this "class" is not monolithic, some of the children may wind up at Princeton or Dartmouth or may marry attractive or wealthy *arrivistes*. But such have always been its processes of renewal. To those whose ideas are formed by the television show "Hard Copy" or "Lives of the Rich and Famous," this group will hardly be visible, but that is because it shuns the kind of attention courted by *nouveaux*. Moreover, although Auchincloss himself may be eighty, as of this writing, and although the past that he and his parents once knew may be dissolving into a representation charged with bittersweet pathos, the group is continuously renewing itself, not disappearing. Ask his sons, and their children. Who knows, some of them may turn out to be novelists of that world.

---

12 Adams, "Saturday Night and Sunday Morning," *New York Review of Books*, 11 (July 9, 1964), 15.
13 Brooke Allen, "Stingless WASP," *The New Criterion*, 13 (December 1994), 70.

Furthermore, Adams's idea that the novelist must stand outside the society he wants to criticize before his criticism can be authentic is of course arrant nonsense. Auchincloss may not pander to the left radicals at the *New York Review of Books*, but this indifference to radical politics does not invalidate an insider critique of the limitations—moral and social—of the world he describes. There is certainly adequate rational, theological, and moral justification for the claim that evil arises from selfish, snobbish, and dissipated people—more so, in fact, than for the claim that it arises from poverty as such. This latter view—common in leftist sociology—is in fact a slander upon the poor.

No politician, Auchincloss takes society, for literature, more or less as he finds it. Despite Ms. Allen's claim, I do not believe that he is guilty of what Edith Wharton called the tendency not infrequent in novelists of manners—Balzac and Thackeray among them—to be "dazzled by contact with the very society they satirize."[14] Auchincloss is fascinated by the world he portrays: he loves the details of an estate settlement as much as Thackeray loved the stylish little supper parties of Mrs. Rawdon Crawley; he is as fascinated by the complexities of a corporation merger as Proust was by the intricacies of precedence; and he is as delighted by the eccentricities of the rich as Balzac was by the spectacle of miserly greed. But if Auchincloss loves his world, he is not taken in by it. Conscious of the moral and social incongruities between his world and the world, say, of Malamud, he is as disturbed as any reader of the *New York Review of Books* that "no matter how painstakingly Proust underlines the dullness, the selfishness, and the fatuity of the Guermantes set, they remain to the end still invested with much of the glamour in which his imagination clothed them" (*RJ*, 104–105).

But Auchincloss has no wish to glamorize this "aristocracy," or to claim for it an elegance or virtue inconsistent with the known facts of New York City social history. Nor is he hankering after any "good old days." He has asked whether anyone would wish to return to a New York where "servants slept in unheated cubicles on the top of drafty brownstones, with an evening off every second week . . ." (*RJ*, 139–140). His love for the elegance and virtue of this affluent world is the love of an artist for his material, which is quite another thing from his feeling for it as a man. Every writer, he has observed, has two points of view about the society in which he lives:

that of a citizen and that of an artist. The latter is concerned only

---

14 Edith Wharton, *A Backward Glance* (New York: Scribner's, 1934), p. 325.

with the suitability of society as material for his art. Just as a liberal journalist may secretly rejoice at the rise of a Senator McCarthy because of the opportunity which it affords him to write brilliant and scathing denunciations of demagogues, so will the eye of the novelist of manners light up at the first glimpse of social injustice. For his books must depend for their life blood on contrast and are bound to lose both significance and popularity in a classless society (*RJ*, 140).

Our awareness of this distinction between society as experienced and society as transformed in fiction ought to discourage us from condemning, as reactionary, a splendid novelist who insists on exploring inequities and ambiguities from the inside of the social mechanism.[15] Auchincloss's virtue is that he brings alive the New York City life of Henry James and Mrs. Wharton by showing us that, however elegant or virtuous it may seem, it is neither very distant nor dead.

---

15 It is my impression, from conversations on a variety of subjects, that, at least on New York issues, Auchincloss the citizen can be accounted sympathetic to the policies of the liberal democrats. He was, for instance, though I am at a loss to explain why, a great supporter of the former governor Mario Cuomo.

Acknowledgments

Some of the essays in *A Fine Silver Thread* have previously appeared elsewhere. But while most of them have been rewritten or revised, sometimes extensively, I still want to thank the several editors and publishers of the entries below for granting permission to reprint the following: "The New England Character in Cooper's Social Novels," *Bulletin of the New York Public Library*, 70 (May 1966), 305–317. "The Trials of Edgar Allan Poe," *The New Criterion*, 6 (November 1987), 17–26. "Howells and the Manners of the Good Heart," *Modern Fiction Studies*, 16 (Autumn 1970), 271–287. "Henry James and the Venice of Dreams," in *Henry James e Venezia*, ed. Sergio Perosa (Firenze: Leo S. Olschki, 1987), pp. 37–52. "Finessing the Five of Hearts," *The New Criterion*, 8 (June 1990), 72–78. "American Literary Radicalism in the Twenties," *The New Criterion*, 3 (March 1985), 16–30; reprinted in *The New Criterion Reader*, ed. Hilton Kramer (New York: The Free Press, 1988), pp. 187–201. "*The Fruit of the Tree*: Justine and the Perils of Abstract Idealism," in *The Cambridge Companion to Edith Wharton*, ed. Millicent Bell (Cambridge: Cambridge University Press, 1995), pp. 157–168; reprinted with the permission of Cambridge University Press. "Seeing Slightly Red: Fitzgerald's 'May Day,'" in *The Short Stories of F. Scott Fitzgerald*, ed. Jackson R. Bryer (Madison: University of Wisconsin Press, 1982), pp. 179–195; reprinted by permission of The University of Wisconsin Press. "Dos Passos's America," *The Weekly Standard*, 2:8 (November 4, 1996), 37–39. "Introduction," *Selected Short Stories of Sinclair Lewis* (Chicago: Ivan R. Dee, 1990), pp. ix–xxiii. "Aiken's 'Mr. Arcularis': Psychic Regression and the Death Instinct," *The American Imago*, 20 (Winter 1963), 295–314. "Combat in the Erogenous Zone: Women in the American Novel Between the Two World Wars," in *What Manner of Woman? Essays on English and American Life and Literature*, ed.

Marlene Springer (New York: New York University Press, 1977), pp. 271–296. "Tracking the American Novel into the Void," *The World & I: A Chronicle of Our Changing Era*, May 1989, pp. 450–468, 520–525. "Louis Auchincloss: The Image of Lost Elegance and Virtue," *American Literature*, 43 (January 1972), 616–632. Finally, I should like to thank Mr. Christopher Carduff, now Senior Editor at Houghton Mifflin Company, whose advice and counsel on the form and style of my work, over the years, has always been incisive and invaluable to me.

Index

James W. Tuttleton is professor of English at New York University. Born in St. Louis, he studied at Harding University and the University of North Carolina. He has written on a wide range of American literature in such periodicals as *The American Scholar*, *The New Criterion*, *The Times Literary Supplement*, and *The Yale Review*. He is also the author of *The Novel of Manners in America*, *Thomas Wentworth Higginson*, and *Vital Signs: Essays on American Literature and Criticism*, and the editor of, among other books, *The Works of Washington Irving: History, Tales and Sketches* for the Library of America. He lives in New York City.